Praise for *On the*

"A record of extraordinary fascination. . . . Literally at times the reader holds his breath." —William McFee, *New York Herald Tribune*

"A narrative more thrilling than any imaginative adventure in the dark depths of the sea. The reader is caught in the struggle so closely that he sweats and grumbles and cheers like any member of the crew."
—*San Francisco Chronicle*

"Breathtaking, unexpected events." —*New York World*

"Crammed with incident, tingling with the thrill of danger."
—*New York Sun*

"Most completely exciting volume we have read this year."
—*New York Evening Post*

"A drama which needs no embellishment." —*New York Telegram*

"Marvelous . . . the reader lives with the writer to the very end."
—*New York American*

"Completely fascinating . . . for sustained adventure this book is unique."
—*Philadelphia Public Ledger*

Commander Edward Ellsberg

ON THE BOTTOM

Commander Edward Ellsberg

Introduction by Captain Edward L. Beach, U.S. Navy (Retired)

New American Library

New American Library
Published by New American Library, a division of
Penguin Group (USA) Inc., 375 Hudson Street,
New York, New York 10014, U.S.A.
Penguin Books Ltd, 80 Strand,
London WC2R 0RL, England
Penguin Books Australia Ltd, 250 Camberwell Road,
Camberwell, Victoria 3124, Australia
Penguin Books Canada Ltd, 10 Alcorn Avenue,
Toronto, Ontario, Canada M4V 3B2
Penguin Books (N.Z.) Ltd, Cnr Rosedale and Airborne Roads,
Albany, Auckland 1310, New Zealand

Penguin Books Ltd, Registered Offices: 80 Strand, London WC2R 0RL, England

Published by New American Library, a division of Penguin Group (USA) Inc.
This is an authorized reprint of a hardcover edition published by Flat
Hammock Press. For information address Flat Hammock Press,
5 Church Street, Mystic, CT 06355.

First New American Library Printing, April 2004
10   9   8   7   6   5   4   3   2   1

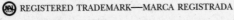
A collector's edition (with CD and DVD) of On the Bottom, *as well as other Edward
Ellsberg books, is available at www.flathammockpress.com. Additional information on
Edward Ellsberg can be found at www.EdwardEllsberg.com.*

to

THE MEN OF THE U.S. NAVY

BOOKS BY
EDWARD ELLSBERG
1891-1983

On the Bottom, 1929

Thirty Fathoms Deep, 1930

Pigboats, 1931

S-54, 1932

Ocean Gold, 1935

Spanish Ingots, 1936

Hell on Ice, 1938

Men Under the Sea, 1939

Treasure Below, 1940

Captain Paul, 1941

"I Have Just Begun to Fight," 1942

Under the Red Sea Sun, 1946

Cruise of the Jeannette, 1949

No Banners, No Bugles, 1949

Passport for Jennifer, 1952

Mid Watch, 1954

The Far Shore, 1960

CONTENTS

PUBLISHER'S PREFACE

The sinking of the U.S. Navy submarine *S-51* was familiar to readers of newspaper headlines in the fall of 1925. The public found the loss of thirty-three sleeping sailors in less than one minute during routine sea exercises appalling. It was the young submarine service's worst accident to date, and a third strike in a sequence of catastrophic events for the U.S. Navy. Scrutiny heightened as the tragedy became the subject of a musical ballad performed by one of the most popular singers of the day.

For months newspapers around the country reported the efforts being made by the Navy to raise the sunken submarine. Newsreel footage of the salvage operation was rushed to theaters throughout the nation. As time passed, however, people gradually lost interest.

When finally the submarine broke the surface of the ocean in July 1926, so too did it rise to the headlines once more. People read the papers and knew something extraordinary had taken place, but almost nobody knew enough about it to know how extraordinary it really was.

The incident again sunk below the level of memory and rested on the bottom, until the release of Commander Edward Ellsberg's *On the Bottom* in May 1929.

On the Bottom was a blow-by-blow account of the raising of the *S-51* with its cargo of dead sailors, from its collision with the steamship *City of Rome* to the removal of bodies in drydock at the Brooklyn Navy Yard.

It was the classic tale of man's struggle against the obstinate forces of nature, all set 132 feet below on the ocean floor. But unlike a treasure lifted from the depths, *On the Bottom* had no riches, and the victims of the accident had long been dead. What captured readers and reviewers alike was the adventure, dogged determination, courage, and loyalty of ordinary men—and every word of it was true!

The book excited a nation. Not since Charles Lindbergh's account of his historic New York to Paris flight had one story so fired the imagination and aroused the pride of all Americans. It was chosen as a

Literary Guild of America Selection and its first printing exceeded 85,000 copies. It was serialized in the *Saturday Evening Post*, topped bestseller lists for weeks, and was broadcast nationally on the Ever-Ready Radio Hour. Every major newspaper carried a glowing review. There were author lectures, signings, and honorary degrees. Even the divers and engineers named in the book enjoyed unaccustomed celebrity status.

Ellsberg became the U.S. Navy's most illustrious officer of the times. He was the first to receive his service's Distinguished Service Medal in peacetime, and through a rare special act of Congress he was promoted ten years ahead of his U.S. Naval Academy classmates. Reporters began including the name Edward Ellsberg in the same sentence with such naval heroes as John Paul Jones, Stephen Decatur, David Farragut, and George Dewey—a comparison Ellsberg did not welcome. Nonetheless, not since the Battle of Manila Bay, more than thirty years prior, had the nation cause to celebrate a single naval officer.

Aside from a national hero, Ellsberg was now an acclaimed author. Critics christened him a gifted and skillful writer and praised his confidence and firsthand descriptions. He would go on to write many more books on naval history, diving, and salvage operations, and he drew extensively from his *S-51* experience for his 1931 novel *Pigboats*, which was adapted for the MGM film *Hell Below*, starring Walter Huston, Robert Montgomery, and Jimmy Durante.

Ellsberg would have a rich and interesting career in and out of the Navy, and would come to be regarded as the world's foremost expert in ship salvage work. His contributions to the Allied forces in World War II were legendary as he played instrumental roles in Ethiopia, North Africa, and the Invasion of Europe. Ellsberg retired from naval service after the war with the rank of rear admiral.

In the seventy plus years since its release, *On the Bottom*—and Edward Ellsberg, for that matter—have rested below the surface. It is perhaps most fitting, then, that Flat Hammock Press, a publisher devoted to salvaging the maritime classics of the past, should pick this work for its initial offering. This expanded edition of *On the Bottom* includes additional photographs and information to expound upon certain aspects of Commander Ellsberg's original text. To provide as complete a picture of the tragedy and the author as possible, we have printed a collector's edition that includes a CD recording of the 1925 hit "Sinking of Submarine *S-51*" by Al Craver, followed by an oral interview with Edward Ellsberg; and a DVD of the silent Hearst International newsreel clips which was filmed during the salvage effort. The newsreel was narrated by Ellsberg in 1979, four years before his passing.

As for a fresh introduction to this expanded edition, there is no one more qualified than Captain Edward L. Beach to place the incident and Edward Ellsberg in context with the times. Captain Beach, as most readers of this book will know, was a renowned skipper who commanded submarines from World War II until the nuclear age. He was captain of the USS *Triton* when in 1960 it completed the first submerged, nonstop circumnavigation. Captain Beach is the author of many books on naval history as well as the bestseller *Run Silent, Run Deep*, the most acclaimed submarine novel ever written and the subject of a successful film.

It is most appropriate at this time to acknowledge the fine cooperation of Edward "Ted" Ellsberg Pollard, Edward Ellsberg's grandson, who has provided invaluable assistance and access to the Ellsberg Historical Archives. Among the thousands of pages of correspondence and clippings Ted has catalogued is a statement by Ellsberg as to why he wrote *On the Bottom*. The realizations expressed are as relevant today as then, and it is a fitting epigraph for the story that follows.

"It is, I think, a plain statement of fact to say that while I started out to salvage the sunken submarine *S-51* with a firm faith in the efficacy of engineering skill and the remarkable tools which modern science has placed in our hands, I came back from the task realizing that success was due not to engineering skill, not to modern machinery, but to the courage and to the unfaltering determination of common men. Pitted against the perils of the ocean depths and the fury of the ocean waves, I had firmly driven home the lesson that it is not machinery, but men that fight. During the nine months that our struggle with the sea went on, my wonder and my admiration grew day by day for the men who, on deck and on the bottom, battled the sea.

"And so *On the Bottom* finally came to life—not the recital of an engineering feat, not a tale of scientific marvels, but the stark battle of a band of men in desperate combat with the overwhelming forces of the sea."

INTRODUCTION

I must have been about seven or eight years old when I discovered Dad's personal library, and less respectful of it than I should have been. I literally destroyed his Navy novels, reading them on my stomach on our living room floor. After Dad's books came the several naval histories he had, and at some point I found out about the unfortunate *S-51*, rammed and sunk off Block Island by a merchant ship. At my very youthful age, the story mesmerized me, and it has ever since. Somewhere during that period I came upon *On the Bottom*, written by a man named Ellsberg who seemed to know a lot about the accident and how the Navy finally raised the wrecked boat and got it into a drydock. For some time, as I went on to read more about the Navy, the two things that stayed in my mind were *S-51* and Edward Ellsberg. His book fascinated me when I first read it, and now that I am a submarine professional and have read it several more times, it fascinates me yet. Somehow it combines the practicality and difficulties of deep-water salvage with concise description of the type of man the Navy needs to do it.

The second book by Ellsberg that struck my youthful mind, so many years ago, was a relatively short novel, written for young readers, that described the sinking of a submarine because she was proceeding on the surface with a deck hatch open. How could they have been that foolish, I remember wondering (already I was learning something)— but I wasn't yet a submariner, and lost sight of that problem in light of the unfolding narrative. The sea rose suddenly, and before anyone on watch thought of shutting the open hatch, water poured down the huge opening, and down she went. Fortunately, this took place in relatively shallow water and watertight doors were closed inside the stricken boat. I can still clearly remember details of the emergency measures the crew took to pump out the water against excessive sea pressure. Just how they were able to close the errant hatch that had caused the problem in the first place, I cannot recall, or even if they did. Calculations were described showing that if they could get rid of all the remaining water in all the tanks and bilges—everywhere they could reach it, in other words—they might be able to lift the stern to the surface and escape through the after torpedo tube. They used all their high-pressure air-blowing tanks, and finally the big problem was how to get power to the only pump available, and how to keep it running against the terrible sea-pressure overload to pump out the remaining water. In doing this there was drama aplenty, and I learned a lot more.

The theater of this still sticks in my mind. It was Ellsberg at his best, at least for the impressionable kid reading the story. To him, and there-fore to me, the big romance was with the sea; the internal combat was not against bad people or opposing forces, but against the persistent, ever-present insistence of the sea (nature, in other words) on doing what it always does, predictably and surely. The sea was not malevolent, but what it would do was absolutely foretold by its characteristics. These were fully known; its action was certain, and one did not break its laws. The sea always waited, just outside the submarine, for the opportunity to claim it if the people trying to work the boat failed in their percep-tion of how the sea functions. But if they knew their business, the sea was every bit as ready to help them as to kill them. Contrary to less profes-sional ideas, the sea was not an enemy. It had no mind of its own, no evil intent. But one did have to understand it—and into my then immature mind there seeped the awareness that Edward Ellsberg did, indeed, understand it, and knew well how to use it.

Further, he wrote about it exceptionally well. It was obvious to the boy reading his books—for after this initial experience, I sought out others—that not only did Ellsberg thoroughly know what he was writing about, he also could present it so that I, at age ten or eleven, under-stood, and wanted more.

Accidentally or not, though probably because that was the direction my young mind was already going, everything I read in those formative years was about the Navy. Nicholas Biddle, John Paul Jones, the War of 1812, the short war with Spain were meat and drink to my childish soul. Recall is less clear about the Civil War, perhaps because it was so much more complicated, but I made up for this in later years. Then I arrived at the Naval Academy and a few years later entered our Submarine School at New London, and once again Commander Ellsberg dawned upon me. I read everything I could find by him and about him. This, it turned out, was considerable.

One of the first things I discovered was that Ellsberg was, by a wide margin, number one man in his Naval Academy class of 1914. He walked off with nearly all the prizes awarded upon graduation, served an obligatory two years in the "line," then sought transfer to the Construction Corps, the staff corps responsible for design, construction, and repair of U.S. naval ships. In those days it was almost routine for the highest ranking midshipmen in each class to go to the Construction Corps, in spite of the resulting prohibition ever to attain ship command (this was true even in my day, a full quarter of a century later). Newly assigned Constructors were ordinarily sent to MIT (the Massachusetts Institute of Technology) for a year's study in the special intricacies of how to properly build ships. Ellsberg reported there in 1916, but our entry into World War I (April 1917) cut the course short, and in less than a year he found himself at the New York Navy Yard working on formerly interned German and Austrian ocean liners, now seized for conversion to troop transports. And so began the formative period of his life.

Ellsberg had two prominent characteristics: first, an all-consuming interest in how things worked; not superficial knowledge, but the intimate understanding of the inventor, or the repairer, of structure, especially the structure of ships, and the machinery that made them what they were. In addition, he proved himself adept at getting directly at the heart of whatever job fell to him—not surprising, certainly, for a man with an extraordinary memory and a bent for instinctive analysis. His second characteristic was perhaps less obvious. He was an exceptionally clear writer. His Naval Academy career was studded with literary accomplishment; he won prize after prize for essays on naval subjects, some of them more abstruse than one might ordinarily expect from a college (or naval academy) undergraduate. Obviously, his penchant for getting to the basics of the problem extended not only to the machinery involved, but to the written explanation as well. One would have thought that these combined characteristics would assure him success in the Naval Construction Corps and early recognition of his particular capabilities, but not so.

Edward Ellsberg was Jewish. His family had fled Russia in the late 1800s during one of the periods of repression in that country. In our Navy there are many instances in which Jewish naval officers achieved great, even outstanding, success. Many of them became very popular with their contemporaries. But there were others whose efforts were almost always somehow diminished by blatant prejudice. Ned Ellsberg was one of these. Although he invariably turned in superior—even outstanding—performance, his seniors often showed unusual reserve in their sometimes obligatory commendatory reports. One is forced to the conclusion that there must have been something in his personality that somehow "put them off." He was undoubtedly ambitious for praise and promotion (who, in truth, is not?) but perhaps he showed this too much. Being a Jew in a society not yet free from prejudice could only have emphasized any resulting antipathy. As a midshipman he lived alone. Roommates were the norm, but he had none, and the lone hours produced more writing and more study, with the usual rewards: more prizes than anyone else, higher grades, and the inevitable jealousy. Officially and unofficially, he was a marked man when he graduated from Annapolis ("officially" because of class standing and prizes won, "unofficially" because of jealousy and the lonely course he consequently set for himself). One can almost visualize his internal determination: "I'll show 'em!"

The trouble was that he did "show" them, and he developed the habit of injecting himself unasked into situations when he thought he had something to contribute. This procedure did not lend itself to popularity, unless, of course, it resulted in salvaging an otherwise failing effort, and even then, human nature being as it is, it took an extremely generous and objectively minded superior, especially if in the direct chain of command, to recognize it and praise it. Ellsberg frequently found his best efforts accepted and implemented, the wanted results achieved, but officially taken as a matter of course, ignored when it came to assigning credit. Since, in many cases, except when there was great press interest, no one else would officially recognize what he had accomplished, he himself sometimes wrote the story, feeling that doing so was good for the Navy, and also fairly and properly gave credit where it was truly due. His writings, in all such cases, are notable for specific praise lavished on the "ordinary" men of the Navy: the enlisted men who actually did the work. To them he seemed almost a heroic demi-god. He got them publicity, medals, promotions, and more pay. They loved him for his readiness to tell their stories and sing their praises and, as time went on, he found a ready market for the same, particularly if the fundamental theme was salvage and rescue. In a way, it was the first combination of science and storytelling. Today, one might compare his writings to something like early *Star Wars*, with the stipulation, however, that instead of imaginative fancy, everything described was the truth.

He received payment for his writings, beginning, it might be noted, with a twenty-five-dollar fee from the U.S. Naval Institute for an essay he wrote as a midshipman. Nor did he attempt to disguise his identity with a nom de plume. He wrote about the Navy, and he signed himself with name and rank, as many other officers, and some enlisted men as well, including myself and my father, have done. Father and I stand behind what we have written, and so did Ellsberg. So, for that matter, did Sims, Mahan, Dudley Knox, Bradley A. Fiske, Holloway H. Frost (who died much too soon), and numerous others. Unfortunately, somewhere there seems to have developed an idea that naval officers ought not write about their profession until they become admirals, regardless of the obvious fact that such writing, conscientiously accomplished, cannot but benefit it. There ought not be any cabal to the contrary, for such will only turn the interested national audience over to writers who do not know the subject.

As for Edward Ellsberg, there came the time when he branched into fiction, as Father and I have done, sometimes combining fact and fiction, though always hewing to the physical facts that legitimately must always control the fictional tale. We have also found ourselves receiving grateful payments from publishers, and from here may stem some of the jealousy Dad and I have occasionally felt. For Ellsberg, there must have been much more of this, for he wrote a lot more. All the same, as a writer about naval salvage matters in particular, he was extremely able, knowing not only his subject thoroughly, but also, as already noted, how to express it on paper so that others could fully savor it as well. In this he made a significant contribution to naval lore, and the results of his efforts are with us yet.

Were one able to reconstitute Ellsberg's life and career—do it over, as it were—perhaps it might be possible to correct the career mistakes he must have made. Perhaps he might have avoided antagonizing the powerful higher officers who kept from him the success he deserved. Yet it must also be noted that Admiral Ernest J. King, himself no easy patsy and known for his terrible temper, was one of his strong supporters. Frustrated at nearly every turn, however, and demoted twice over technical matters concerning precedence between the line and staff corps of the Navy, Ellsberg finally achieved what must have been one of his abiding ambitions: the rank of rear admiral in the Naval Reserve, based on the many decorations he received for service during World War II. He was photographed proudly wearing that uniform, shiny new admiral's stripes and all. Nonetheless, there must have been less than the full satisfaction he should have been able to feel in that august rank, for the Navy did not give it to him willingly, but in the Reserve, and in the "tombstone" category at that. He never served on active duty as an admiral.

And yet the credit he brought to the U.S. Navy, the successes he achieved for it, not only in the terribly difficult salvage of *S-51* but in all the functions of our Construction Corps, from the salvage of sabotaged German liners in World War I to meticulous construction of a new battleship (the *Tennessee*, which was severely damaged at Pearl Harbor many years later), to salvage of scuttled Italian ships in the Red Sea and finally to deep involvement in emergency fixes to the complicated Mulberry harbors designed to be towed to France for the invasion of Normandy, were worthy of far greater recognition than was given. Rear Admiral Ellsberg, to give him his final and correct title, did far more for the U.S. Navy than it did for him, and not the least of his contributions were the many fine articles and books, some of them fiction, he wrote about it.

Every one of his writings, like this one, *On the Bottom*, meticulously and accurately described the Navy during his day, and how it worked its wonders in the sea.

The United States Navy owes a very great deal to Commander, later Rear Admiral, Edward (Ned) Ellsberg.

— *Edward L. Beach, Captain, U.S. Navy (Retired)*

I

COLLISION

On a dark September night, with a cold breeze whipping up a choppy sea about fifteen miles to the eastward of Block Island, the steamship *City of Rome* plowed northward towards Boston. Four bells struck. The new lookout took his post in the bow, sheltering himself from the wind by crouching low behind the bulwark.

"Light on the starboard bow!"

The mate on the bridge acknowledged the report, and sent word to the captain in his cabin. The *City of Rome* kept on her course. The helmsman went below for an inspection, leaving the mate, who relieved him at the wheel, alone on the bridge.

The lookout watched the light, a single white point perhaps five miles off. Gradually it grew brighter as they overhauled it, but its bearing remained constant, broad on the starboard bow. Twenty minutes went by. The light grew very bright. The lookout gazed inquiringly at his own bridge. The other ship, whatever it was, had the right of way, but the *City of Rome* made no move to pass astern.

They were very close now. The strange light was almost under their bow when a red side light flashed into view close to the white one. Simultaneously the mate started to swing the ship to port and blew his whistle frantically.

Hearing the noise, the captain rushed to the bridge, took a hasty glimpse at the lights on his starboard bow, and then, disregarding their proximity, ordered his ship swung to starboard towards the lights, trying to pass astern of them.

For one brief second the lookout, peering over the side, saw the dim outline of a submarine as they swung towards her, then came the crash.

1

The submarine, struck just forward of its conning tower, rolled drunkenly to starboard, then fell away as the *City of Rome* slipped by. The captain of the submarine appeared on her bridge. The startled passengers on the steamer, looking over the side, caught a brief glimpse of his face looking up, heard one agonized cry from below:

"For God's sake, throw us a line!"

The *City of Rome*, speed unchecked, rushed on by.

II

ON THE S-51

Inside the *S-51*, except for the few men on watch, the crew were turned in, closely packed in their bunks in the battery room. On the little bridge, two officers and two seamen, heavily clothed, conned the ship;—course northwest, speed eleven and a half knots.

A cold spray broke over the low-lying hull. All hatches were secured, except the single one leading from the bridge down through the conning tower to the control room. The Diesel engines were drawing air from an intake valve just under the bridge.

Lieutenant Dobson, commanding the *S-51*, dropped into the control room to study the charts. He was closing on Block Island; in another hour he would head out to sea again to continue his twenty-four-hour reliability run.

Shortly after 10 P.M., the lights of a steamer were sighted on their port quarter. They gradually drew closer. The watch on the *S-51*'s bridge examined her. They had the right of way; under the "International Rules of the Road at Sea" the *S-51* was required to maintain its course and speed. As their own stern light was plainly visible to the other ship, they felt no alarm. The steamer would shortly change course and pass astern of them.

They watched as the *City of Rome* drew closer and closer, but saw no change in her bearing. A few more minutes and the steamer was looming over their port quarter, very close now. She was evidently going to run them down in spite of the rules. They must look out for themselves.

"Hard right!" The submarine's rudder went over and she started to swing to starboard. With relief her officers noted that the steamer, almost on top of them, was starting to turn to port, away from them, as she commenced blowing her whistle. Then to their horror they saw the steamer change her direction, and swing to starboard right for their side. The next instant, there was a terrific crash as the stem of the *City of Rome* struck the battery compartment.

The *S-51* was thrown violently to starboard. Through a huge hole in her port side, water started to rush into the room, filled with sleeping men.

Dewey Kyle, machinist's mate, flung by the shock from an upper bunk into the narrow starboard passage, found himself in water up to his waist when he hit the deck. Running aft through the battery room, the water followed as he stepped through the door into the control room. A few seamen, clothed as he was, only in their underwear, were climbing the ladder to the conning tower. The men on watch in the room stood by their controls; a chief petty officer there, who might easily have left, helped Kyle up the ladder but himself stayed below at his station.

Kyle scrambled up through the little conning tower and out the hatch to the bridge; as he did so he found himself swimming. The submarine had disappeared beneath his feet. He was the last man out.

A dark hull, looking mountain high, was disappearing in the darkness. The water was cold, the choppy sea made swimming difficult. Kyle thanked his luck he was not loaded down by clothing. Nearby he could see eight other swimmers,—his captain, the lieutenants who had been on watch on the bridge, the helmsman, the quartermaster, a few others. They were struggling desperately to rid themselves of their heavy clothes so they could swim.

One by one they vanished in the dark water, till only two beside Kyle remained afloat. Like him, Geier and Lyra had been catapulted from their bunks by the collision; being nearer to the control room they had escaped before him; now only these three unclothed swimmers of the crew of thirty-six remained on the surface.

Desperately they swam on in the wake of the steamer; after nearly an hour in the water, a small boat picked them up, and brought them aboard the *City of Rome.* In a few minutes, ship and survivors were on their way to Boston.

Some hours later, when nearing the entrance to the Cape Cod Canal, the *City of Rome* reported the accident by radio.

III

RESCUE EFFORTS

"**C**OMMANDER CONTROL FORCE TO COMMANDING OFFICER U.S.S. *Falcon*:

"*S-51* reported in collision latitude 41° 12' N., longitude 71° 15' W. *Falcon* proceed to scene immediately prepared for rescue work."

I handed the radio message back to Lieutenant Hartley. Already he was casting off his lines to the pier, and in a few minutes the *Falcon* was standing out of the New York Navy Yard and heading up the East River towards Long Island Sound.

The delayed report from the *City of Rome* had been picked up in Boston, and telephoned to the Submarine Base at New London. The *Camden*, flagship of the Control Force, had passed the word to us at New York.

The *Falcon* made her best speed, but it was one hundred and fifty miles to the position given in the orders. We could not arrive until after dark.

Meanwhile, Lieutenant Hartley, commanding officer of the rescue ship, plotted the position of the accident on the chart while I watched. His dividers pricked a point in the open sea, fourteen miles east of Block Island, fifteen miles southeast of Brenton Reef Lightship off Point Judith. We looked at the sounding printed there. Twenty-two fathoms,— one hundred and thirty-two feet deep. It was a bad position. Exposed to gales from every quarter. Nothing to break up the swells rolling in from the Atlantic when the winds subsided. And Point Judith was notorious as being the meeting place of all the winds that blew.

We steamed on through Long Island Sound, past New Haven, past New London, through The Race as the afternoon wore on. A message informed us that the diving launch from the Torpedo School at Newport, twenty-five miles away, had arrived on the scene at noon. Several destroyers searching had located the wreck by a stream of oil and air bubbles making a slick about two miles from the spot reported by the *City of Rome.*

Hartley broke out his diving gear and cleared the side for working. We had only two divers,—Chief Torpedoman Frazer of the *Falcon*, and Shipwright Anderson, whom I had brought from the Navy Yard. Two men in deep water could do little, but there would be a few others there from Newport.

As night fell we cleared the northern end of Block Island and stood out to sea in the darkness. The *Falcon* started to pitch as we met the waves. Far ahead we could see clusters of faint lights, and steered for these. By 10 P.M. we had arrived.

A weird scene. In the blue glare of searchlights from the mother ship *Camden*, a submarine stood sharply out against the background of black water, a stream of bubbles and oil frothing up against her side. From her conning tower two hoses led over the rail and disappeared in the sea. One hundred and thirty-two feet below they were attached to the *S-51.* The *S-50* was pumping air continuously to her stricken sister.

A piercing note coming through the water vibrated against the *Falcon*'s hull,—the *S-50*'s oscillator was sounding the lost submarine's call continuously. We listened on our microphones. No answer came from below.

In the darkness we could make out several destroyers, another submarine, some smaller boats.

Blinker lights flashed from the *Camden*'s yardarm. Our quartermaster spelled out the order:

"*Falcon*, anchor clear of *S-50*. Prepare for diving in morning."

Slowly we steamed to a spot about five hundred yards astern of the illuminated submarine. On the forecastle, Chief Boatswain Burnett tripped the locking gear, our anchor chain roared out through the hawsepipe, we came to rest.

Quietness reigned except for that haunting call vibrating steadily through the water. Nothing showed through the darkness except the gray sides of the *S-50*, shining ghostlike in the searchlight beams.

Soon the coughing of a motorboat broke the silence. A launch came alongside, heaving up and down against the low bulwarks on the *Falcon*. A petty officer was helped over our rail. Only one brief word from his shipmates,—"Bends." He passed into our recompression chamber, the heavy door swung to, compressed air started to whistle in as the needle on the gauge moved up. The first diver on the *S-51* was being treated in "the iron doctor" for the disease that makes the ocean depths so dangerous to penetrate.

About midnight, he came out, much relieved. A slight figure was Chief Torpedoman Ingram, diver on the Torpedo Testing Range at Newport. Briefly he told me his story.

"I went down the stream of air bubbles. The sub is lying way over on her port side with a big hole in her battery room. I walked her deck from bow to stern and I hammered on every hatch. Not a sound inside. They're all dead down there!"

Ingram gave us a few more details. Bubbles of air were leaking from around all the hatches. It was very hard to walk on the deck because of the heavy port list. He was the first man down, going over from the side of the little diving launch. They had no time to rig a telephone in his helmet, consequently he could not report what he saw while on the bottom. When he finally gave the signal on his line to come up, four jerks, those on the surface, anxious for the report, had hauled him up with only a short decompression.

A case of "bends" was the result, with no means of treatment till the *Falcon* arrived with her recompression tank.

Another diver, following Ingram, had attached air hoses to the salvage connections in the side of the *S-51*; the *S-50* was pumping air below in the hope that she might help any possible survivors.

I looked toward the *S-50*; the air was coming up in masses of bubbles as fast as she was sending it down.

When morning came, I was ordered to report aboard the *Camden*. I learned that the admiral there had hired a wrecking company for the rescue work; two of their largest derricks were already on the way from New York.

It was assumed that the survivors, if any, would be in the stern. If so, the after end of the ship would not be flooded, and the two derricks might be able to lift the stern to the surface.

There was nothing there for me to do. I left the squadron and returned to New York.

Meanwhile, the wrecking company's divers passed heavy wire slings under the stern of the submarine and held them at the surface with a small derrick. Two large derricks, the Monarch of one hundred and fifty tons and the Century of one hundred tons capacity, arrived and anchored behind the breakwater at Point Judith, fifteen miles away.

Two days had gone by since the sinking of the *S-51*. If men were alive inside the boat, their case was desperate. But in spite of that, three more days went by. The wreckers dared not tow their derricks out to sea except in calm weather. At the wreck, conditions were good enough for diving, but they were not good enough to permit the lumbering derricks to leave the shelter of the Harbor of Refuge. Twice the sea looked calm and they started, but a few miles out they struck the swells and with their heavy top-hamper swinging dangerously, their owners turned the derricks about and towed them back to Point Judith lest they capsize among the waves.

At last, after five days, came a very smooth sea, the derricks were finally towed to the wreck, hooked to the slings, and heaved down till they were taking their maximum lift. Nothing budged. The *S-51* was evidently flooded. Hastily the derricks were cast loose and hurried back to harbor before another breeze should spring up and catch them in the open sea.

There was no longer the slightest doubt. All hands inside the *S-51* were dead.

The rescue efforts were discontinued, the wrecking company was discharged, and the Navy Department turned to a consideration of salvage possibilities.

IV

VACILLATION

The Navy Department was in a quandary.

Early in September, Commander John Rodgers, attempting in a Navy plane the first nonstop flight to Hawaii, had disappeared from sight for nine days. A burst of criticism was leveled at the Navy Department. While Rodgers was still missing, the *Shenandoah*, flying over Ohio, was caught in a storm and destroyed with the loss of Commander Lansdowne and a large part of his crew.

Led by Colonel Mitchell, of the Army Air Service, a storm of criticism now burst around the Secretary of the Navy, who was charged with demoralizing the Naval Air Service.

Hardly two weeks later and the *S-51* was sunk with all but three of her company. The criticism now rose to the proportions of a flood and poured in on Washington in a demand that the *S-51* be raised and the bodies of her crew recovered.

The situation was difficult. No large submarine had ever been raised in deep water in the open sea. Raising the *S-51* did not look feasible, but at least an attempt must be made.

Neither in the Navy nor in private wrecking companies were there any means for the job, any reliable method of procedure.

The wreckers originally engaged on the work offered to undertake the job, provided the Navy furnished all needed equipment and divers, the diving ship *Falcon*, a sister submarine, and technical officers to assist,— everything in fact except one tug, a wreckmaster, and four divers, which the wreckers would furnish. The government, in addition to furnishing practically everything, was to pay a considerable sum whether the job was a success or not, and a bonus in addition if the *S-51* was raised.

This contract, which normally would not have been entertained for a moment, nevertheless looked good to the harassed Department. It was on the point of being signed in Washington, when I went to Admiral Plunkett, Commandant of the Navy Yard at New York, with a method for the Navy to raise the ship itself. The admiral, enthusiastic over the idea, seized the telephone and over the long-distance wire to Washington presented the scheme, only to learn that the Department was not interested. They were about to sign a contract with outsiders to do the work.

Admiral Plunkett was furious. "This is a Navy job! If we can't take care of our own ships, we ought to get out and let someone run the Navy who can!" And in that deep voice and in language which all those who ever served with him will easily remember, he burned up the wires till those at the other end agreed to delay the signing till our method could at least be explained.

The admiral dropped the phone, and looked at his watch. His aide went scurrying for a timetable.

"Here, Ellsberg, you've got twenty minutes to catch the next train. You explain it to them!"

I dashed from his office to the admiral's car; his two-starred flag on the running board took us through the traffic and in a few minutes I was leaving the Pennsylvania Station on my way to Washington.

It took most of that night to convince some of the officers from the Bureau of Construction and Repair that we had a feasible plan, but even so it was impossible next day to get a favorable decision. It seemed as if the Department felt that the raising was doomed to failure, and in the existing state of mind of the press and the public, they did not care to risk another failure by the Navy. Expensive though it might be, it appeared preferable to hire a commercial company so that the burden of failure, when it came, could be assumed by them, not by the Navy itself.

In this atmosphere, little was possible, and I felt that I had achieved a considerable measure of success when I finally obtained a postponement of any decision then and had the discussion transferred to New York.

Back at the Navy Yard next day, reinforced by Admiral Plunkett and several of the officers who had taken part in the early rescue work, we made the proposal to let the job go outside the Navy look so ridiculous that the Navy Department representatives capitulated and agreed to let us proceed. Even the wreckmaster of the salvage company, in view of his company's lack of equipment and submarine experience, was forced to admit the wisdom of that course.

As he left the conference, the wreckmaster turned and delivered his parting shot:

"I don't know who is going to do this job, but whoever he is, he'll wish before he gets through that he had been born a girl baby!"

Admiral Plunkett lost no time. Inside of ten minutes, orders had gone to the shops, and the construction of the pontoons for the salvage job started.

V

THE SALVAGE
PROBLEM

T he *S-51* was a vessel of one thousand tons surface displacement. Our task was to lift this weight one hundred and thirty-two feet to the surface, meanwhile working in the open sea, and then tow the ship one hundred and fifty miles to New York, the nearest harbor with a suitable drydock.

Ordinary lifting methods were ruled out, first because no derricks existed capable of lifting so much weight, and second because of the impossibility of working them at sea even if the derricks were obtainable.

We felt that we could seal up the undamaged after half of the boat and, by expelling the water, restore about four hundred tons of buoyancy, but that seemed to be the maximum that could be realized from the boat herself. The remainder of the buoyancy would have to be provided elsewhere.

In conference with the Navy Department, it was agreed to use submersible pontoons, which the divers were to attach to the hull, and the Navy Yard immediately started to build six such pontoons, each with a lifting capacity of eighty tons. The Navy owned two more, which had been used eleven years before to lift a small submarine from forty feet of water. These old pontoons were too weak to work in deep water, but we reinforced them while we built the new ones. That was to give us eight pontoons with a total lifting force of six hundred and forty tons, but it would take about four weeks to build the six new pontoons.

For a diving ship, the U.S.S. *Falcon*, Lieutenant Henry Hartley commanding, was assigned. The *Falcon*, an oceangoing tugboat, had been built as a minesweeper during the war, and afterwards converted to a rescue ship. She was small, only one hundred and eighty feet long, but well suited for the job. She carried special air compressors for diving and salvage work, extra wrecking pumps, a recompression chamber, and special winches and bitts for handling lines.

Obviously the *Falcon* was too small to berth all the divers, tenders, and officers required, and there was no room on her for shop machinery, extra boats, or stores. To provide room for these, Admiral Plunkett asked for the repair ship *Vestal*, Captain Tomb commanding, a large vessel fitted out as a floating machine shop for the fleet. The *Vestal* had a foundry, blacksmith shop, machine shop, carpenter shop, and large storerooms. She was well provided with small boats, and had ample room for the extra men we required.

As a rehearsal vessel, a sister ship of the *S-51* was assigned,—the *S-50*, commanded by Lieutenant Commander Lenney.

To help the *Falcon* in mooring, for handling pontoons, and for general service, two seagoing tugboats, the *Iuka*, Chief Boatswain Augustine, and the *Sagamore*, Chief Boatswain Cregan, were attached to our squadron. A smaller tug, the *Penobscot*, Chief Boatswain's Mate Ashland, was detailed as a despatch boat, to make daily trips to New London, fifty miles away, which was our shore base, and bring out stores, provisions, and mail.

The salvage squadron then consisted of six ships,—*Falcon*, *Vestal*, *S-50*, *Iuka*, *Sagamore*, and *Penobscot*. The whole squadron was placed under the charge of the Commandant of the Submarine Base, New London, Captain Ernest King, who in addition to his duties at New London was designated Officer in Charge, Salvage Squadron. Captain King was unfortunately compelled to divide his time between his duties at New London and these added ones, but he managed to spend half the time with us off Block Island.

Admiral Plunkett designated me as Salvage Officer. I was attached to no particular ship, but worked during the day on the *Falcon*, had a stateroom and an office on the *Vestal*, and occasionally slept on the *Sagamore* or *Iuka*.

As my assistants, I had Lieutenants Lemler and Kelly; and as a technical aide, Draftsman John Niedermair of the New York Navy Yard.

VI

DIVING

Nothing that the ingenuity of man has permitted him to do is more unnatural than working as a diver in deep water. As a result of this, if a vessel sinks a few hundred feet beneath the surface of the sea, she becomes as inaccessible as if transported to a distant star.

Still, many vessels laden with fabulous cargoes of gold have sunk in water less than a hundred feet deep. The lure of recovering this treasure developed the art of diving, but the divers of generations gone found that the sunken gold was purchased from the sea only at the price of life or health. Those who stayed down long enough to recover anything would shortly after their return to the surface be seized by terrible convulsions resulting, when quick death did not ensue, in paralysis for life. Many a diver working on the hulks of the Spanish Armada, around the coasts of England, or treasure ships off the Azores, learned this to his sorrow.

Because of the contortions of the sufferers, the early divers gave to the disease the name of "the bends." Its cause was long unknown, but its results were beyond question. No diver, in spite of fortune's lure, dared go deep nor remain over a few minutes.

Years ago, on one sunken galleon, access to the treasure room was easy; daily a Spanish diver entered, seized two bars of gold and hurriedly came up. It was slow work. At last the daily glimpse of pigs of gold piled high proved too much; cupidity overcame fear; the diver labored nearly an hour sending up a fortune in bullion. Finally the diver himself emerged, but the treasure was not for him; "bends" ending in paralysis of the spine ensued; he lived, but only to curse daily the gold which had tempted him to linger on the ocean floor.

The growth of medical skill and in other lines finally solved the mystery of "the bends" and in a measure provided a way to minimize the effects.

The usual diving dress consists of a copper helmet and breastplate secured watertight to a flexible canvas-covered rubber suit. The helmet is necessary to permit breathing; the suit may be dispensed with in warm shallow water, but is necessary in cold water or in deep water and is always necessary if the diver is to do any work requiring him to bend over or lie down.

Water is heavy; as the diver descends he is compressed by the weight of the column of water over him. Over the surface of his body, for each foot he descends, an added load of almost half a ton presses on him. At one hundred and thirty feet, the total load is nearly sixty tons. To prevent the diver from being crushed into a jelly by this weight, it is necessary for him to breathe air under pressure slightly exceeding that of the water; this internal air pressure is transmitted by his lungs to his blood, and enables him to balance the external water pressure. The diver is then in a condition similar to that of a pneumatic tire on a heavy automobile; the tire stays rounded out in spite of the weight of the car on it because it is inflated with air under sufficient pressure to balance the load. If, however, the inner tube is ruptured and the air escapes, down comes the weight of the car and flattens out the tire. In the same way, the diver inflated with compressed air, stands the weight of the sea pressing on him; but if through any accident, he loses the air pressure in his helmet, like a trip hammer down comes the weight of the sea and crushes him as flat as any blown-out tire.

As he goes deeper, a diver must increase the air pressure in his suit to correspond; it is therefore most dangerous for him if working on the deck of a ship to fall off suddenly into deeper water and be thereby subjected to greater pressure. If, under such circumstances, he cannot simultaneously raise his air pressure, he is crushed by the water into his helmet, and many men have died from such a "squeeze"; the latest instance occurring to a civilian diver in shallow water in the East River while we were working off Block Island.

It is directly due to this pressure that "the bends" arise. To exist underwater the diver must breathe air under heavy pressure. For the depth at which the *S-51* lay, the air had to be compressed to five times its normal pressure. With each breath the diver had to inhale five times his ordinary quantity of air. The large excess of oxygen consumes the tissues much more rapidly than is normal and produces a dangerous state of exhilaration somewhat akin to that caused by breathing pure oxygen; overlong exposure will cause "oxygen poisoning."

But it is the inert component of the air, nitrogen, which is the cause of "the bends." Nitrogen, which forms four-fifths of our atmosphere, is ordinarily breathed in and out, having no effect except to dilute the oxygen. However, when the air is much compressed, conditions change. Under heavy pressure, the nitrogen entering the lungs, instead of being all exhaled again, dissolves in the blood, and the heavier the pressure and the longer the period of exposure, the greater the quantity of nitrogen dissolved.

While the diver remains under pressure, that is, stays on the bottom, he notices nothing. The nitrogen goes into solution, the blood remains a clear liquid. But when the pressure is decreased as the diver rises to the surface, trouble starts.

A bottle of ginger ale is a good illustration of what happens. There is a gas, carbon dioxide, dissolved under pressure in the ginger ale. As long as the cap remains on the bottle, there is no evidence of the gas, the liquid inside is clear. But when the cap is removed, the pressure is released with a "pop," the gas bubbles out of solution, and the bottle froths over.

In the same way, when the pressure is released on the diver by his coming to the surface, the nitrogen dissolved in his blood bubbles out and forms a froth in his blood. These bubbles clog the arteries, impeding circulation, and causing convulsions or "the bends." In many cases, the bubbles gather in the spinal column, where they affect the nerves, causing paralysis. In less aggravated cases, a favorite place for bubbles is in the joints, resulting in great pain.

When the cause of "the bends" was finally discovered, the remedy was indicated. It lies in bringing the diver to the surface in a series of short rises, with a pause at each stage; lifting him enough each time so that under the decreased pressure some nitrogen will come out, but not decreasing the pressure so much at each step as to allow bubbles of any size to form. The "decompression time," that is, the length of time at each stage and the number of stages, depends on the amount of nitrogen originally absorbed, which in turn depends on the depth to which the diver has gone and the duration of his stay there. Consequently, for every depth, there is a limit to the time the diver can stay down (which period decreases rapidly as the depth increases), and the length of time the diver must spend in "decompressing" increases rapidly the deeper he goes and the longer he stays down.

When the causes of "the bends" had been laid bare, and proper tables of decompression worked out by experiment, diving in deep water became practical enough to permit work to be done after a fashion, though at great expense and considerable hazard.

But aside from his troubles from disease, the diver has many physical handicaps to struggle against. His diving suit, with helmet, lead belt, and lead shoes, weighs about two hundred pounds, and is both heavy and cumbersome. When fully dressed, the diver is quite bulky, and much impeded in action by his suit. Movements underwater are slow; if he stoops over or lies down, a different adjustment of his air valves must be made; a fog gathers on the face plate of his helmet and makes vision through it difficult; communication with the surface is always trying, even with a telephone, because of the roar of the compressed air through the helmet which makes it hard for the diver to hear. On the other hand, it is difficult for those on the surface to understand the diver, for when he passes below ninety feet depth, the air pressure causes his voice to lose its distinctive quality, his words sound all "mushed" up and become exceedingly difficult to understand. As an illustration of this, under such air pressure, a diver can no longer whistle. The "thick" air changes everything.

Everything that the diver sees is magnified by the water, but he rarely sees much. In northern seas, the water is nearly opaque, and objects ten feet away are often invisible. It resembles looking through a ground glass window; light comes through, but nothing is seen. Conditions are often even worse than this; if the bottom is muddy, fine silt rises up in the water in clouds and objects even a foot away are invisible.

Under such conditions, even powerful lights cannot pierce the water, and a diver a few feet from a boat has no idea where to look for it.

VII

THE DIVERS

Our most immediate need was to get sufficient divers. We estimated that thirty were required. There being only a few qualified commercial divers on the Atlantic Coast, it seemed necessary to depend on what the Navy could supply. We combed the navy yards and the fleet for deep-sea divers, particularly for those who had worked on wrecking jobs before. From northern waters we obtained Chief Torpedomen Frazer of the *Falcon*, Michels from the Submarine Base, Ingram from the Torpedo Station, Smith, Eiben, and Wilson from the Experimental Station. From Newport came Chief Gunner's Mate Eadie, then in the Naval Reserve Force, and Gunner's Mate Bailey; from the New York Navy Yard, Frank Anderson and his son George, one a shipwright, the other a rigger; from the Light Cruiser Squadron came Boatswain's Mate Carr; from a destroyer Chief Torpedoman Kelley. These men we knew about; they had worked on wrecks and in deep water; they were proved divers. But they were not half enough. To complete the crew, we asked for and had transferred to the *Falcon* every bluejacket whose record showed any qualifications as a diver.

The divers were of various types. Frazer and Michels were six-footers, powerful and broad. Eadie, Anderson, Carr, Eiben, and Wilson were of medium build. Smith, Ingram, and Kelley were slight in size, while Bailey was actually small. Most of them were quiet men, unexcitable, of more than usual intelligence. There was in their makeup no spirit of bravado, no sign of daredevil dispositions. They had all proved themselves good divers, but they were of such varied types physically, it was impossible to tell from them what a diver should look like. Every one had had long service in the Navy; nearly all were married.

VIII

OFF BLOCK ISLAND

On October 14, 1925, the *Falcon* sailed for Block Island, followed shortly by the *Vestal* and the other ships. At the wreck, bubbles and oil no longer marked the spot, but a buoy secured to the submarine located it immediately.

Lieutenant Hartley's first step was to prepare the site for long-continued diving operations. It is of the first importance to the diver that the vessel from which he is receiving his air supply shall remain steady in position while he is at the bottom. The few hundred feet of hose from him to the ship constitute literally his thread of life. If a heavy sea or a sudden squall should swing the diving ship away, especially while he is inside the wreck below, his airhose will be snapped off and he will be left to die.

Anchoring the diving ship is not enough. She will swing to her anchor all the time; if the wind or sea change, she will be swept far out of position. The diving ship must be firmly held over the submarine in spite of wind or sea so long as a man is on the bottom.

To accomplish this, Hartley planted six anchors in a circle about the *S-51*, the diameter of the circle being about six hundred feet. To each anchor was attached a short length of chain, and to that a double wire hawser which led to the surface where it was secured to a can buoy we borrowed from the Lighthouse Service. We then had floating in the sea a ring of buoys,—one ahead, one astern, and two on each side of the *S-51*. Before diving commenced, the *Falcon* was to steam into the circle, heading into the sea to the windward buoy, and secure a seven-inch manila hawser to it. Dropping back a little to leeward, a small boat was to run lines in succession to the other buoys, and secure them to rings there by pelican hooks in the ends of the hawsers. With the lines all secured, the *Falcon* could center herself over the wreck by hauling in or paying out on the various hawsers; when in position the hawsers radiated from her like the spokes of a wheel and served, in spite of changes in the direction of wind or sea, to hold her over the *S-51*. To make safety for the divers doubly sure, we made each diving hose six hundred feet long, of which only about two hundred and fifty feet was ordinarily paid out. The other three hundred and fifty feet hung in a coil on deck as a reserve for running out to the diver in case a hawser should part on us and let the *Falcon* swing away.

It took two days with the improvised gear Hartley had on the *Falcon* to plant the heavy anchors; at the end of that time all the ships had arrived and we were ready to begin. The *Falcon* steamed in, moored herself, and the salvage work was under way.

The first job was to clear the top of the submarine of radio antennae and other rigging in order to prevent the men from getting their air lines tangled up there.

The *S-51* sank with her radio mast up. From this point over the conning tower, the antenna extended to bow and stem; in addition, two heavy wire ropes ran from a ring in the stem up to a heavy A-frame over the bridge and then to another ring near the stern. These were the "clearing lines," intended to form a guide so the submarine could slide through a net without catching her gun or conning tower in the meshes. To one of these clearing lines was secured a thickly insulated "loop antenna" for underwater radio communication.

We removed these obstructions by cutting them with a special V-shaped knife attached to a line. Divers went down, hooked the V-bladed knife around the wires to be cut, lashed marline over the open side of the V to prevent the knife from slipping off, and then signaled us on the *Falcon* to heave on the line. A sharp pull on the *Falcon*'s winch, and the wire below, jammed into the notch of the V, was quickly severed. It took nearly an hour to secure the knife for each cut, and nearly two days to clear away all the rigging, but there was then no better way. About ten dives on this job and there were no more wires over the submarine's deck. The divers secured a four-inch manila line to the rail aft and another one to the gun forward as guides or "descending lines." These, brought aboard the *Falcon* at the surface, were to guide the divers down to the *S-51*. All was clear.

IX

In the Engine Room

The first effort towards raising the *S-51* was to seal up the undamaged compartments, and we decided to start on the engine room. Chief Torpedomen Frazer and Smith were selected for this job. I went with them aboard the *S-50*, where Lieutenant Commander Lenney, her captain, carefully explained to us what valves must be closed in that room to make it watertight. There were nearly thirty valves on voice tubes, oil lines, water lines, engine exhausts, and air inlets that had to be shut, many of them difficult to reach.

Frazer rehearsed the work carefully on the *S-50*, starting at the after end of the engine room and closing the valves in succession as he came forward between the engines. The valves were of various kinds, from small one-half-inch drain valves to the huge twenty-four-inch air inlet valve which admitted air to the two Diesel engines. Several times Frazer went over the room, noting in detail the location of each valve, for on the *S-51* he would have to find most of them by feeling around in the black water. At last he was letter perfect, he could locate all the valves in succession blindfolded. We returned to the *Falcon*; Smith and Frazer were dressed by the tenders.

With a man on each side to assist, Frazer dragged his heavily weighted figure to the rail, where he stepped on the stage, grasping the steel bails to hold himself erect.

"Up stage!" The winchman threw in his clutch, the stage rose till it cleared the rail. The boom swung over, the stage swung outboard, over the sea.

"Down stage!" Slowly the stage dropped into the water, the sea rose over Frazer's body, his helmet disappeared. A stream of bubbles broke the surface.

"Hold stage!" Several feet below the surface we could see Frazer adjusting his air valves. I took his telephone receiver, adjusted it over my head.

"All right, Jim?"

"All right. Take me to the descending line."

Frazer stepped off the stage. Nothing below him now. We hoisted in the stage. The tenders dragged him, dangling by his airhose, about twenty feet along the *Falcon*'s side to where the after descending line went below. Frazer seized it, wrapped his legs about it, sang out:

"Lower away!"

His tender rapidly paid out the lifeline. Frazer disappeared. Swiftly the line went out. Fifty feet, a hundred feet, he must be nearly there. The airhose stopped running through the tender's hands. I listened. A flat, strange voice came to me over the telephone:

"On the bottom!"

Frazer had landed on the submarine. We took Smith to the stage and hoisted him overboard also. Down he went, two streams of bubbles broke the surface of the sea. The line stopped running out. Once again came the report:

"On the bottom!"

On the deck of the submarine, Smith stood by the hatch to tend the lifelines while Frazer dropped through the opening into the engine room. He carried a powerful submarine lamp, but in the murky water inside the submarine it cast only a dim glow. While Smith paid out carefully on his lines, Frazer started slowly aft through the narrow passage between the engines. He passed between the first cylinders of the starboard and port Diesels, turned sideways to avoid catching his lines on the cams. Another step, some obstruction hit his helmet and blocked his passage. Swinging his light upward for a close look, Frazer saw it was the engineer officer of the *S-51* clinging to the throttle of the port engine, his half-dressed body jammed between the hull and the overhead valve gear, his legs hanging down into the passageway and closing it. Frazer set his lamp on the engine, seized the body by both legs, and pulled vigorously but without success. The man had been jammed in hard by the rushing water. Frazer could waste no more time. Picking up his lamp, he pushed the legs to one side, ducked low to pass under, and continued his way aft till he came to the door leading into the motor room. Here he set his lamp down on the floor plates, and feeling on the bulkhead, found the voice tube valve there. He screwed down hard on the handwheel to make sure it was tightly closed, then moved forward to the valves in the engine exhaust pipes. The exhaust clapper valves were closed,—evidently in that last desperate minute the engineers had tried to secure the boat for submerging. Frazer closed the globe valves on the inside of the clappers, then moved on to the multitude of smaller valves. All went well, a steady stream of air bubbles from his helmet trickled through the hatch at Smith's feet; Smith carefully took up the slack in Frazer's air line as he worked forward, to avoid having any loose hose to catch inside; on the *Falcon* we tended carefully both Frazer's lines and Smith's and kept them properly taut. The minutes went by, no word came from either diver, but we refrained from bothering them by questioning. Frazer's hour was nearly gone; in a few minutes we would signal him to start up.

Inside the boat, Frazer came once more to the dead engineer, pushed aside his legs, crawled under him, and made another attempt to pull him free. He was stuck too hard. Frazer left him and stepped forward to the last valve on his list. This was the largest one, the twenty-four-inch main air induction to the two Diesel engines, located overhead just forward of the number one cylinders, where it admitted air to the engines, somewhat after the manner of a huge carburetor. The valve was operated by a lever through a set of links and bell cranks. The operating lever was far over to starboard, with its locking ratchet in the "Full Open" notch on the guide arc. Frazer released the ratchet, grasped the handle, and pushed it to port. The handle swung over the guide arc evenly, the valve moved downward towards its seat, and finally it stopped with a metallic ring. Frazer swung his lamp close to the arc to make sure the valve was closed. It was not. The handle had stopped at "$1\!/\!4$ Open." There were still three inches on the arc to go to the "Closed" notch. Frazer pushed again, but the handle moved only a fraction of an inch further.

On the *Falcon*, the timekeeper moved over to the rail where I stood with the receiver from Frazer's telephone over one ear.

"Fifty minutes for Frazer and Smith."

Their time was up. I motioned to the tenders leaning over the rail. Four long jerks on Smith's airhose; the tender waited; in a moment he felt four answering jerks from below. Smith had acknowledged the signal to get clear and stand by to come up. In turn Smith gave four jerks on Frazer's line.

Frazer acknowledged the same way. It was time to leave, but the last and most important valve was still open. Seizing the handle with both hands, Frazer pulled the valve wide open to get a good swing, then shoved the handle to port with all his might. Over his telephone I heard a sharp metallic ring. Frazer looked at the handle, it was still "$\frac{1}{4}$ Open." I heard Frazer swear, then in the flat faraway tones of a man under pressure, he spoke for the first time since he went down.

"Mr. Ellsberg, the main air induction valve won't close!"

I could hear Frazer turn off his air while he listened for instructions. They were brief, but each word was spoken slowly and distinctly.

"Never mind. Time up. Come out."

And to make sure, once again we gave Smith the signal to stand by to come up.

Frazer came up the machinery hatch, assisted by Smith. He signaled us to take up the lamp, which we hauled quickly to the surface, and carefully turned off before taking it out of the water.

Then four jerks on each man's airhose, a moment's wait for the four answering jerks from each that showed they were clear of all obstructions and at the descending line ready to rise. We swung the stage over the side and lowered it, shackled to the descending line, to ninety feet. Two tenders seized Frazer's lines, and hand over hand, his lines came in over the rail as they hauled him up. At ninety feet, they paused, while Frazer let go the descending line and climbed on the steel stage.

"On the stage," shouted Frazer into his phone. I got it clearly.

"Frazer on the stage! Start Smith up!"

The tenders hauled on Smith, pulling him off the submarine and up, till he too sighted the stage, swung on to it, and reported.

"On the stage!" sang out the man at Smith's telephone.

"Frazer," I said, "unshackle the descending line." Frazer acknowledged, leaned over on the stage, and cast loose the shackle that held the side of the stage to the descending line. Freed, the stage swung away from the descending line, which disappeared from his view.

"All clear!" reported Frazer. Everything was clear for the next divers to descend. Smith and Frazer started their slow rise to decompress.

X

THE FIRST SNAG

About two hours later, we hoisted the stage over the rail. The two divers clung tightly to the bails, as we swung them, dripping, in on deck. A group of dressers gathered round, loosed belts, shoes, removed helmets. The divers' faces, a little pale, looked grotesque sticking above the heavy copper breastplates. Frazer leaned far over and a bucket of water ran out of his suit.

"Exhaust valve leaked," he explained.

The dressers pulled off their diving suits. In heavy blue underwear, they rose and stretched, relieved of the crushing weight of their equipment. Smith, looking thin and slight by contrast with the huge frame of his companion, asked for a cigarette. Frazer, wet to the skin, did not linger. The doctor gave him a drink, half hot coffee, half whiskey, and he ran below.

I found Frazer in his bunk, wrapped in blankets.

"I got 'em all, Mr. Ellsberg, except the main air induction. Maybe I got that too, but it isn't in the 'Closed' notch yet. I tried three or four times. It won't go any further."

Then he described his efforts to pull the engineer free, and his difficulties in working inside. The room was pitch dark, the water very dirty, he got only a dim glow from his lamp penetrating no more than a foot or two. It was very hard to walk inside because of the heavy list to port the submarine had; besides some of the steel floor plates had fallen into the bilges and it was necessary to hang on to the engines to get aft.

I pondered the question of the open valve. Possibly the links were set differently and the valve might actually be seated even as it was. But we had to be sure. We could never blow the water out of the boat if that valve was not tightly closed.

On the *Vestal*, I had Kyle, Lyra, and Geier, the three survivors of the *S-51*. Kyle was a machinist's mate, Lyra a fireman, Geier an electrician. Kyle's station was in the engine room. He should be acquainted with that valve.

On the *Falcon*'s bridge semaphore flags started to wave, spelled out: "*Vestal*. Send survivors *S-51* to *Falcon*."

The answering pennant rose to the *Vestal*'s yard arm. In a few minutes a motor launch, bouncing over the waves, made the run from *Vestal* to *Falcon*. The three survivors climbed over our rail.

Kyle, stocky and heavily built, came first; Lyra, a tall, loose-jointed youth, next; and Geier, a small, thin man, last. Kyle and Geier had not got over the shock of their experience; Lyra did not seem so much affected.

Kyle knew most about the valve. He had often operated it, the last time the very day the *S-51* was sunk. They had made a dive that morning. It was his duty to secure the engines when diving, then close the engine main air induction valve. The valve had always worked perfectly, he had had no trouble in swinging the lever to the "Closed" notch the last time he tried it.

To make doubly sure, I sent a radio to a former captain of the *S-51*, then in the Pacific Fleet. He confirmed Kyle's statements about the closed position of the handle.

Nothing but air had ever gone through the outer ventilation main to the engines before. The main intake in the conning tower fairwater was always closed before the ship submerged to keep water out of the main leading to the various compartments. The *S-51*, running in her surface condition, had sunk with that valve open; water rushing through the open main had evidently jammed something under the engine air induction. We would have to clear it.

The valve on the *S-50* was carefully inspected. There was no hope of getting into it from the inside of the submarine. And to reach it from the outside meant ripping up the deck to get at the valve bonnet, and then removing forty bolts to allow lifting the three-hundred-pound cover off the valve body. It would be a tough job. We could not afford to start it unless absolutely necessary. Perhaps in spite of all reports, the valve was closed. We must be sure before undertaking all that work.

On the bottom of the engine air induction valve was a small one-inch drain cock. I unscrewed this on the *S-50*, and made a feeler, three feet long, of heavy wire, bent to go through the hole left by the drain cock, reach up to the valve seat where the end of the wire, bent over at right angles, could feel between the valve disk and its seat. Frazer practiced with it on the *S-50*; the next day, Frazer and Smith made their second dive to the engine room. Frazer entered through the hatch, the feeler and a Stillson wrench tied to his belt. He found the drain cock, unscrewed it, carefully inserted his feeler rod and pushed it upward till it struck the disk, then moved it outward, to the edge. The hooked end passed between disk and seat; Frazer found three-fourths-inch clearance between them. Moving his feeler around the circumference of the disk, on one side it struck something between disk and seat. Frazer worked the valve handle and pushed with the feeler, but he could not dislodge the object. The valve would not close. Frazer and Smith came up.

We prepared to remove the superstructure deck over the engine room. With special long-handled socket wrenches to unbolt part of the portable wood sections, Frank Anderson and Applegate prepared to dive. Anderson was the Navy Yard diver, the oldest man we had, a veteran of long years' work in the water. He was about forty-five, I thought, really too old for deep water diving, but he had pleaded hard to come; I acquiesced, feeling his experience might compensate for his lack of youth. Applegate was about thirty; he had done many odd jobs in shallow water, and a little work at one hundred feet.

They were dressed, hoisted over the side, Anderson first. "On the bottom!" from Anderson; "On the bottom!" from Applegate. Hartley tied the long socket wrenches to a shackle, slipped the shackle around the descending line, and lowered away carefully on a small manila line, led forward to keep it clear of the descending line. The wrenches reached the submarine. Anderson unscrewed his diving knife from its sheath, cut the lashing holding the wrenches, gave Hartley four jerks on the manila lowering line. Hartley hauled it up.

Anderson took the wrenches, started aft along the sloping deck. Applegate attempted to follow him. A strong current swept over the ocean floor, making it hard to stand up. Applegate slipped to the low side, caught the rail, hung on. The heavy pressure started to affect him; he developed "oxygen-intoxication," an exhilaration very similar to the alcoholic type, but caused by the excessive oxygen he was breathing. He staggered drunkenly, trying to follow Anderson; he fouled Anderson's lifelines. Anderson dropped the wrenches, untangled his airhose from his companion, tried to recover the wrenches and go to work. He found himself in trouble, breathing with difficulty, fighting the sweep of the tide, trying to hold his feet on the slimy incline of the deck down which the current was pushing him. Applegate fell against the rail, started to topple overboard. Anderson seized him, pulled him erect again. It was all he could do to hold on himself, he had little to spare for his shipmate.

Anderson looked around. The wrenches lay at his feet against the hazy outline of the deck. Nothing seemed to stir, yet he felt the water pressing him overboard. He leaned over as if facing a heavy windstorm. His heart pounded violently as he breathed.

He made another attempt to get to work. Reaching low, Anderson recovered a socket wrench, found a corner bolt holding down a section of the deck, slipped the socket over the bolt head, and twisted hard on the T handle of his wrench. The bolt failed to start. He motioned Applegate to help him, but Applegate, clinging drunkenly to the rail, was in no state to do anything. The wrench slipped off the bolt.

Anderson felt himself weakening. He gave us the signal to come up. But first he cleared Applegate of all entanglements and saw him start ahead before he himself was hauled up the descending line. Hardly were his feet off the deck, before the vague outlines of the submarine faded from his sight.

Once aboard the *Falcon*, Anderson came to me much upset:

"I guess I'm too old to dive in deep water any more," he confessed. "I thought I could do it, but I can't stand the pressure the way I used to when I was young. I guess I'll have to go home. My son George will stay and do everything he can. You didn't know it, but I'm fifty-eight years old."

Fifty-eight! That settled it. Thirty-five is considered the age limit for deep work.

We kept Frank Anderson a week to make certain a cold he developed did not turn to pneumonia; then with regret we saw him board the *Penobscot* and sail for home via New London. A brave old man, trying to conceal his age for another chance to fight the sea. And so we lost the first of our small group of experienced divers.

Going down in pairs, other divers attacked the deck bolts with wrenches but the work was slow. We switched to crowbars, and with them managed to rip away about eight feet of the deck in way of the valve bonnet, leaving only the steel deck beams underneath. As we had no means of burning steel successfully then, it was decided to tear these deck beams out of the ship.

We shackled a large hook into the end of a six-inch manila line; Smith and Frazer dived to undertake the work of tearing out. Once on the bottom, they hooked the first beam near its starboard end; moused the hook with marline to prevent its slipping off; then stood clear and signaled us to heave on the line.

On the quarterdeck of the *Falcon*, the boatswain's mate took four turns of the manila line around the capstan; the winchman opened the throttle and started it revolving. Lieutenant Hartley at the rail gave the signal to heave. The line tautened and stalled the capstan. The boatswain threw on a few more turns of the line and hauled hard; the winchman opened his throttle wider and the capstan groaned as it slowly started to revolve again. The line stretched under the strain; suddenly it came free and the capstan started to race.

"All gone below!" I heard Frazer telephone. "Take her up."

Hartley heaved in slowly and soon brought over our rail a steel angle bar, broken at both ends where it had torn clear of the *S-51*. The boatswain's mate freed the hook and sent it down again on the descending line. Frazer secured it to a beam as before; another heave on the capstan and up came the second deck beam. Only three more required. Down went the hook, in a few minutes another signal from Frazer to heave in. The divers were making quick work of securing the hook. We heaved, broke out another beam, started to hoist it to the surface.

The two divers, standing on the slippery deck of the submarine just abaft the conning tower, looked out through the glass ports in their helmets and watched the manila straighten and stretch as the strain came, saw the deck beam bend where the hook gripped it, suddenly tear out of the ship, and start slowly for the surface. Then to his amazement, Smith saw Frazer rise gently from the deck and start upward at the same time. Smith grabbed Frazer's lead shoes and tried to hold him down. No use,—he felt himself being pulled from the submarine. He let go and dropped back to the deck. Frazer faded from his sight.

Smith shouted through his telephone; the man on deck could not understand. The boatswain's mate hoisted steadily on the capstan.

As he was jerked off the *S-51*, Frazer looked up and saw his lifelines had been caught in the hook. He felt the futile tug as Smith clung to his feet, then found himself rising steadily to the surface, without decompression. He tried to signal on his lifeline, but no jerk traveled past the point where he could see his lines, none too securely caught, fouled in the point of the hook. His ears were ringing from the effects of the rapid decrease in pressure. He shouted in his telephone, "Stop heaving! Stop heaving!"

On deck, Frazer's telephone man caught the tone, not the words. But the tender on Frazer's lifelines, feeling them coming slack over the rail, sensed something wrong and called out "Avast heaving!" Hartley motioned the capstan to stop. The hook was halfway to the surface.

We got Smith clearer now.

"Stop heaving! Frazer is foul of the hook!"

On deck, we looked at each other in consternation. Whatever we did, Frazer was in a tight place, either from "bends" or from a "squeeze." We started instantly to lower very gently.

Meanwhile, Frazer, dangling from the hook ten feet above his head, felt himself stop. He was seventy feet from the bottom. He could see the slack in his lifeline hanging in a loop on the other side of the hook, which, much magnified as he saw it through the water, was not quite overhead. He streamed away from it a trifle, carried over by the current. If his lines came off the hook, he would have a free fall to the bottom.

Frazer had been diving many years; visions of divers who had been "squeezed" before shot across his mind; the victims always had to be dug out of their helmets,— jelly.

Frazer felt himself start slowly down, then to his horror, his lifeline slipped free of the hook. No longer supported, his lines now all slack, weighted down with two hundred pounds of lead and copper, he started a swift plunge into the abyss. His suit clung to his body; he felt as if encased in a formfitting mold which was quickly shrinking on him; his ribs started to collapse. A little more pressure as he shot lower and it would be the end.

In this extremity, beyond all help from others, Frazer thought swiftly. One thing alone could save him,—compressed air. Plunging through the depths, death but a few seconds away, Frazer swung one hand to the control valve over his left breast. He gripped the valve handle, turned it wide open. Under high pressure a stream of air rushed through his helmet, ballooned out his suit. In spite of lead shoes and heavy diving rig, his distended suit was now buoyant. He stopped sinking, hung suspended in the water, then released a little air and floated gently down to the bottom of the sea. He landed in the midst of a school of fish, which swam around him excitedly. His head was dizzy, his chest felt weak, his ear drums ached, nearly burst from the rapid variations in pressure they had undergone.

Frazer looked around. Several feet away the hull of the *S-51* loomed up, half buried in the ocean bottom. A few steps across the hard sand, and he leaned against her bilges while he pulled himself together.

A frayed line was hanging down the side near him. Lightening up a little, he dragged himself on board. Nearby was Smith, half crazed with anxiety about his fate. In relief, Smith hugged his shipmate. The startled fish eyed them curiously.

Possibly a minute had elapsed since Frazer was first torn from his companion's side.

Kelley, Carr, Eadie, Michels, working in succession, completed the removal of the deck beams, tore away all other obstructions, exposed the valve bonnet.

The next day, Frazer and Smith, armed with short socket wrenches, attacked the bolts holding down the cover. It took three days on their part to remove the forty bolts, and break the joint on the cover by driving wedges under it. On the fourth day, the divers pried the cover loose; held by screw clamps we hoisted it to the *Falcon*.

With the bonnet gone, the next diver down, Ingram, reaching into the huge valve body, felt a pipe jammed between the valve disk and its seat. Eadie, his mate, dropped inside the engine room, and swung the valve wide open. Ingram pulled the obstruction out, a rusty piece of one-inch iron pipe, some three feet long, evidently left inside the ventilation main by some careless workman when the submarine was built. With the pipe removed, Eadie swung the valve handle over; it went home easily, latched itself in the "Closed" notch. The valve was closed.

It had taken five days and twenty dives to close a valve that should have closed in five seconds.

XI

THE CONTROL ROOM

There were three of the five main compartments on the *S-51* which were undamaged. These three,—the control room, the engine room, and the motor room,—we hoped to seal up and free of water.

We had managed to close the necessary valves in the engine room,— we now turned attention to sealing up the control room. This was the central compartment of the ship, from which its operation was directed. Overhead was the conning tower; on the port side were the bow and stern diving rudder wheels, the drainage manifolds, the myriad valves required for blowing ballasts, venting tanks, flooding for submerging.

Amidships, the three periscopes, in their housed positions, looked like columns supporting the framing overhead. Abaft the periscopes was the mast housing well.

On the starboard side, the main switchboard covered the whole area, with its controls for the numerous electrical appliances, from the huge switches for the main motors for submerged propulsion, to the tiny ammeters showing the current taken by the gyro compass. Abaft the switchboard was a small soundproofed room for the radio operator; just across from this was a cubbyhole with an electric range for the ship's galley.

The room was jammed full of apparatus; a narrow passage on the port side in front of the manifolds and a small space in front of the switchboard constituted the whole clear area. Valve wheels and control levers stuck out in every direction,—from both sides and ends of the control room, from the floor below, from the deck overhead.

Being in surface condition when sunk, the hatches from the control room up through the conning tower were open, but unfortunately these hatches were so small that it did not appear possible for a diver in his bulky suit to get through them. The other means of access were through the door from aft leading to the engine room; through the forward door leading to the battery room; or through a special escape trunk just forward of the conning tower, called the gun access trunk.

We specially desired to close the door in the bulkhead between control room and battery room,—this was to form the dividing wall between the damaged and the undamaged parts of the ship. But to get to this door from forward meant entering the battery room, which was the crew's sleeping quarters, and worming aft twenty feet through a narrow passage jammed with bunks, floating mattresses, and corpses. It looked hazardous.

To get to the door from aft meant passing through the narrow engine room door, which was difficult, and then working forward the whole length of the control room, which was dangerous.

The gun access trunk, however, was almost vertically over the door we wished to reach, and the most important manifolds were close under it. If a diver could get through there, he would be directly at his work. We determined to enter that way.

John Kelley and George Anderson, both small-sized divers, were chosen for the job. Kelley was a chief torpedoman, with a long experience in diving, including, together with Frazer, the long but unsuccessful attempt to raise the *S-5* five years before. George Anderson was much younger. He had been raised a diver by his father but had always worked before in the relatively shallow water around the New York Navy Yard.

Kelley, Anderson, Hartley, and I went to the *S-50* to study the job. The gun access trunk was a small vertical cylinder about six feet high and four feet in diameter, located over the forward end of the control room, just in front of the conning tower and just abaft the gun. The top of the trunk stood perhaps four feet above the superstructure deck. There were two hatches in the trunk, one top and one bottom, both of which opened upward. The top hatch had a coiled spring on its hinge pins, which caused it to fly open when the catch inside was released. The lower hatch had four dogs to jam it watertight on its seat when closed. There were several small glass eyeports in the side of the trunk.

The gun access trunk had a twofold purpose. Primarily it was intended as a means of quick entrance to the inside of the boat for the gun crew in case of need. If the submarine were chasing and shelling a merchantman, with the gun crew on deck serving their gun, the captain of the submarine could keep the Kingston valves to his ballast tanks open and ride on his air vents, ready for a "crash dive." Should the answering fire from the merchantman come uncomfortably close, or a hostile man-of-war suddenly appear and open fire, the skipper could promptly submerge by opening his vent valves and rapidly flooding his tanks, without delaying to wait for his gun crew to get inside through the conning tower. As the boat went under, the gun crew could jump into the gun access trunk just behind them, close the outer hatch, then at their leisure open the lower hatch and enter the boat. During the late war, some German boats, not equipped with such trunks, were forced to dive so fast by approaching Allied destroyers that the gun crew could not get into the conning tower before the boat submerged and were left swimming for the enemy to pick up.

The secondary function of the gun access trunk was to act as an escape lock for the crew of the submarine, in case they were trapped at the bottom, unable to rise for any reason. For this purpose, a compressed-air line from the ship's air banks led to the trunk. A small wire line was shackled to the underside of the upper hatch, led downward near the floor around a small pulley, and then the wire turned upward to where it ended in an eye secured to a hook on the inside of the trunk. The pulley was secured to a sliding vertical rod which passed down through a watertight stuffing box in the deck, into the control room, where the rod terminated in a handle with a tightening screw for pulling it down.

In case the boat were sunk with the crew or part of it still alive and able to get to the control room, escape was theoretically possible through the gun access trunk. The first man to try escape opened the lower hatch, entered the escape trunk, closed the lower hatch. His shipmates in the control room released the tightening gear on the pulley rod, allowing this rod to slide up and slack the wire attached to the upper hatch. The man in the trunk then turned on compressed air, building up the pressure inside the trunk as rapidly as possible till it equaled the weight of the water outside pressing down on the top hatch. When the pressures were equalized, he tripped the latch holding the top hatch closed, and the spring caused the hatch cover to fly open. The air inside rushed out in a large bubble; the man escaping was supposed to duck out through the open hatch in this bubble and float or swim to the surface.

The men remaining in the control room below then hauled down on the pulley rod, tightening the wire to the upper hatch and pulling it shut. When this was done, they opened a drain valve in the bottom of the escape trunk, allowing all the water in it to drain into the control room below. The lower hatch to the trunk could then be opened and another man could enter the trunk. The process of escape was thus continued one by one by each member of the crew.

This is the theory of operation of the air lock or escape trunk on a submarine; in deep water it has never been done; in shallow water (fifty feet down) it was tried by two officers endeavoring to escape from the sunken British submarine *K-13*; one rose to the surface, the other was killed in the attempt.

I examined the gun access trunk on the *S-50* carefully. The outer hatch to the trunk on the *S-51* was closed. How to open it from the outside was a problem. Finally I decided it was possible to do it by smashing the glass port on the starboard side and tripping the lock under the hatch cover with a steel rod pushed through the broken port. It required a rod four feet long, with some seven different twists and bends in it to go through the eyeport at the side, clear obstructions inside, and reach up and forward in the trunk to hook around the handle of the latch. We removed an eyeport on the *S-50*, bent a rod to suit, and Kelley practiced reaching in and releasing the catch. It required a knack in holding the rod just right outside while fishing with the hook in the trunk, but at last Kelley became so proficient he could trip the latch nine tries out of ten.

The tightening wire remained as an added obstacle against the hatch opening. To take care of this, the port we selected for Kelley to smash was the one closest to the wire. The blacksmith on the *Vestal* made us a hook-shaped knife, small enough to go through the port. A stout line was secured to the knife. Kelley was to reach inside the trunk with the knife, hook the wire, and we would cut it for him by heaving on the line from the *Falcon*.

When all the tools were ready, and Kelley and Anderson were well drilled in their parts, they held one last rehearsal and then hurried aboard the *Falcon*. The divers were dressed, hoisted over the side, Kelley first with the tools. He disappeared off the stage in a swirl of bubbles. The tender ran out his lifelines. "On the bottom!" sang out the telephone man perched in the superstructure. We assisted Anderson to the stage, hoisted him overboard, watched him step off the stage and sink below. It was George Anderson's first dive in deep water. His father had had a tough time on the *S-51*; I wondered how his son George would handle himself.

His lines ran out steadily,—no pause in his descent. "On the bottom!" repeated Anderson's telephone talker. George Anderson was standing by Kelley's side, just abaft the gun on the *S-51*.

While Anderson was going down, it flashed across my mind that the divers might find an obstruction in the trunk that I had not provided for in fashioning the tools. However, the men were gone. No use trying to instruct them over the telephone. It was up to them.

Kelley moved to the high side of the submarine and came abreast the trunk. The starboard eyeport was about even with his belt. Kelley stooped over, looked through the glass. It was utterly black inside. He drew back, hit the glass sharply with the hook, and drove the fragments of the eyeport into the trunk.

Kelley took the rod from Anderson. Carefully, he entered it through the opening, pushed it home, lined up the handle outside truly athwartship to the trunk, and then hooked forward with the inner end. It caught the latch on his first attempt. A vigorous push aft and the latch released, but, as Kelley expected, the hatch cover stayed closed. The wire was still holding it.

He removed the rod, exchanged it with Anderson for the hooked knife. Kelley shoved his forearm through the hole and felt around inside the trunk for the wire. He groped in vain until reaching a little forward, his fingers came in contact with it, stretched taut. He shoved in his knife, hooked the wire, telephoned up:

"Heave on the line!"

We heaved. It took only a moderate pull and the knife severed the quarter-inch wire. The hatch cover flew open. The way to the control room was clear.

Kelley's talker sang out:

"Kelley about to enter the submarine."

We waited silently on deck for several minutes.

I wondered.

Then another message from Kelley:

"Send down a line." It had happened as I feared.

We lowered a line to the submarine; a brief interval, then four jerks on the line, the signal to hoist. We hauled in slowly. A body, clad in pajamas, appeared at the end of the line. The *Falcon*'s motorboat ran alongside, the bluejackets reverently lifted the silent figure from the water. An Annapolis class ring shone on one finger. Shortly, wrapped in the folds of the flag, the body of Lieutenant Haselton rested on the *Vestal*'s quarterdeck.

Kelley reported once more. "I'll make another try to go in." He squeezed through the upper hatch into the trunk.

Anderson's talker called out, "Send down another line!" We sent it down, a short wait, then another call from Anderson, "Hoist away."

We hoisted, and soon another flag-draped body lay beside Haselton's, a seaman this time.

Their fate was clear. Knocked from their bunks by the shock that tore their ship wide open, they had started aft, not waiting to dress, for the open conning tower hatch, the sole exit. They were too late. Already the boat had submerged, a heavy stream of water was pouring down through the conning tower, while another torrent was rushing through from the battery room door behind them.

Haselton remembered the gun access trunk, just overhead. He scrambled up the rungs on the bulkhead, cast loose the dogs on the lower hatch, slipped into the escape trunk. The sailor followed him. The rising flood was just beneath their feet. They slammed down the hatch, jammed home the dogs to seal it tight. For the moment they were safe. Every other man inside the *S-51*, engulfed in the hungry waters, perished at once. These two alone, locked in a cubbyhole at the bottom of the sea, still lived.

But they must not tarry long. There was little space inside the trunk,—two men crowded it. Besides they must escape while yet the ship that sank them remained overhead to pick them up on the surface. They did not know how deep the water was, but they could not afford to bother over that.

It was black inside the trunk. Neither of the unclothed men had any matches.

Haselton felt around the sides of their little prison till he found the air valve. That was luck. There was little air in that trunk, but from the ship's high pressure banks, they could get what they wanted to breathe, to raise the pressure inside till they had equalized the water pressure outside and could open the upper hatch.

Haselton opened the valve. Horror-stricken, he felt a stream of water shoot through into the trunk! The pipe to the air banks led down the port side of the battery room. The bow of the *City of Rome* had cut the line in two!

Hastily he closed the valve, shut off the water.

No words were needed. The two men trapped there understood their situation. It was desperate but not hopeless. They could still build up the necessary pressure inside the trunk to balance the sea pressure outside, by flooding the trunk and thus compressing what little air there was inside. That would probably put them in water at least up to their necks, before they got pressure enough to open the hatch. It would not leave much of a bubble for them to come up in, but there was no alternative.

First, however, they must get the upper hatch cover ready to open quickly when they flooded the trunk. They fumbled for the latch to make sure it would work. It was all right. That they would release as the last step.

But there was another shock in store. They felt for the pulley wire. It was taut! The releasing rod could only be operated from the flooded control room below. No shipmate was alive in that room to cast it loose for them!

Desperation seized their hearts. They tried to unscrew the shackle pin that held the wire to the hatch. The pin would not turn. They had no tools but their fingers. They could not ease the shackle.

Near the floor, the wire led up from the pulley, then to an eye, passed over a hook. Together they strained, trying to pull the eye off that hook. The wire failed to stretch, they could not get enough slack to get over the point of the hook.

Time was fleeting. Their violent exertions were rapidly using up what little oxygen there was in the trunk. They fell exhausted against the side of their prison.

A new ray of hope flashed into their minds. A case of rifles was secured to the port side of the trunk, intended for the boarding party. Haselton ripped a rifle from the rack. If he could get a twist of the wire around the muzzle, he could use the rifle to form a Spanish windlass, and by tightening tear the wire from the pulley. He tried, but unfortunately the trunk was so small he could not swing the rifle in it enough to catch a turn. He tried again, it would not grip.

Their pounding hearts and panting lungs gave notice that the air was all used up. With his last ounce of strength Haselton hammered with the butt of his rifle against the hatch, trying to break the wire. His shipmate, leaning over, gripped the lower end of the wire with both hands just above the eye, and bracing himself heaved his utmost, trying to pull it off the hook. The blows of that rifle butt, ringing feebly out along the ocean floor, sounded tattoo for Lieutenant Haselton and his shipmate. The air was all exhausted, the sounds ceased, the water gradually leaked in through the lower hatch and flooded the trunk.

And thus Kelley found them,—Lieutenant Haselton, a rifle clutched in his hands, butt against the hatch,—the seaman, both hands gripped about the wire, pulling even in death. The sea had conquered them.

Once more, we heard that Kelley was about to enter the submarine. He climbed up the outside, squeezed through the upper hatch, found himself in the now empty trunk. The lower hatch was closed.

In his bulky diving armor, he could not bend over enough in the narrow hole to reach the floor and cast loose the dogs. Kelley felt for them with his feet, kicked them free with his copper-toed shoes, and swung back the hatch cover.

Carefully he passed his legs through the little oval in the deck, reaching for the rungs on the bulkhead below in the control room. Down one rung, then another, and he was half through. He tried another step down but the lead belt round his waist caught in the opening and held him fast.

Kelley tried to push it through, but there was not enough clearance. He dared not take off his belt,—the removal of that eighty-pound weight would destroy his balance and he might find himself floating head down, feet up, inside the control room with no way of getting right side up again. He twisted a little, trying to fit himself to the opening around his waist, but it was useless, he could not go through.

He started up again, and found himself jammed tightly in the hatch, but by pushing hard with his feet against the rungs below, while Anderson, standing on the hatch outside, heaved on his lines, he finally slipped free and climbed through the gun access trunk to the deck outside, where Anderson anxiously awaited him. There would be no entrance to the control room that way.

The divers had been down over their allotted hour,—we had been waiting for Anderson to report Kelley clear before we started them up. Both men looked carefully round to see their lines free of the submarine, then one after the other signaled to ascend, and were hauled up to eighty feet where they climbed on the stage and started their decompression.

Finally we hoisted them aboard. George Anderson had made his initial dive in deep water successfully; a harrowing set of circumstances for a youthful diver to encounter the first time on the bottom.

On the *Falcon*, we held a council of war in the little wardroom and listened to Kelley's story. On the *S-50*, he had barely been able to squeeze through that lower hatch, but with his suit partly inflated with air and the *S-51* leaning badly to port so the opening was on a slant, it could not be done on her. We had no divers smaller than Kelley,—if he could not go through, no one could.

We decided to attempt it next through the battery room. Late that day, Kelley dived again, with Michels for a partner this time. They landed, walked forward of the gun, dropped through the open battery room hatch, the largest one on the ship, and found themselves in the crew's sleeping quarters. Michels carried a submarine lamp, a thousand-watt special bulb with a searchlight reflector. It cast a dim beam through the blackness inside, the light diffusing in the water and penetrating only a short way.

They found themselves practically opposite the spot where the submarine had been rammed. A mass of broken cables and pipes was shoved inboard on the port side; on each side of a vertical hole some three feet wide the torn steel plates of the inner hull were bent inward across the port side passageway till they touched a tangled heap of mess tables and bunks. Escape had been cut off for all the men whose berths were on that side of the ship.

Kelley looked aft. Here a narrow passage twenty feet long ran between the officers' staterooms and some bunks on the starboard side. At the end of that passage was the battery room door. Michels swung the light that way. The passage seemed filled with mattresses and blankets carried there by the swirling waters coming through the hole, as they had first rushed aft. Kelley dropped on his stomach to the deck, started to worm his way under the debris. He went a short distance, when he found that the mattresses, swollen by their long immersion, were filling the passageway from top to bottom. It was completely blocked.

He crawled back to where Michels waited tending his lines, then both came out and we started them up.

I considered the situation. We had to get the forward control room door closed. From Kelley's description it looked as if we could make it by removing the mattresses, blankets, and some bunks we were sure to find in the passage. This would probably take ten or twelve dives to accomplish; in preparation for it I had the blacksmith make us several sets of devil's claw tongs for the divers to hook into the mattresses and haul them out.

Meanwhile, however, it was determined to try the third and last means of entrance, through the after door leading to the engine room.

For this attempt, Ingram and Eadie were rehearsed on the *S-50*. They went down on the *S-51*, climbed down into the engine room, Ingram carrying the lamp, Eadie following. A few steps forward inside brought them to the door leading to the control room. It was a small door, perhaps sixteen inches wide and four feet high. They swung the steel door wide open, lashed it back to hold it that way.

Eadie approached the door, stooped, tried to squeeze through. He failed, stepped back, and started to examine the opening carefully.

Listening on Ingram's phone, I heard him say, "Get out of the way and let me try it." Evidently he pushed Eadie aside, gave him the lamp. Ingram was a smaller man than Eadie.

I listened intently.

Soon Eadie reported:

"Ingram is through. I can't see him any more."

That looked better; at last we had a man in the control room even though he had a long way yet to go to reach the forward door.

Our exultation at this success was very short lived. I got a call from Ingram:

"I'm about five feet inside the room and I'm stuck. I can't go either way. My helmet's caught on something."

I repeated Ingram's message to those around on the *Falcon*. It struck us all cold. There was little we could do for Ingram; it was very doubtful if Eadie could get through to help, even if we asked him to. It was up to Ingram to help himself. If he kept his head, he could probably free himself; if he became panic-stricken he was certainly gone.

On deck, we all sensed that. One man sang out, "Tell him to keep cool!" I refused to transmit that. I had no intention of intimating to Ingram that we doubted his keeping cool. Instead I called to him, in a joking tone, I was far from feeling:

"Use your bean, old man! Wiggle it!"

Ingram wiggled desperately for over five minutes.

On deck no one spoke. Over us, a sparkling sun glittered on the waves as they rolled by the *Falcon*'s rail and splashed about the hoses leading over the side. We breathed in the bright sunshine; at the other end of those lines I could hear the labored breathing of a man struggling alone in the darkness inside the submarine caught on what he did not know, on something he could not reach.

At last the scheme worked, the wiggling dislodged his lifelines from whatever they were caught on. Ingram was free. Very wisely, he came out of the control room, and it was with a sigh of relief that some minutes later I heard Ingram and Eadie report:

"On the stage!"

Kelley and Michels were taken to the *S-50* and carefully rehearsed in getting through the engine room door. Ingram had gone through without a light; he could not tell what had caught him. We determined to give each of the next divers a light, though inside the boat it would hardly cast more than a glow.

Kelley and Michels went down. We slid the submarine lights down to them, guided on the descending line. The divers took the lights but hardly had they entered the hatch and started forward through the engine room when both lights burned out, leaving them in darkness. The heat from the thousand-watt filaments apparently softened the cement on the base of the lamps; under the heavy pressure, water seeped through into the bulb and short-circuited the filament.

Kelley reported the trouble and came out on the deck of the submarine. We pulled both lamps to the surface and told him to stand by while we sent down two more lights that we had already made up. We lowered these, Kelley received them, and entered the boat once more. He kept one light, gave Michels the other. They advanced to the engine room door.

Kelley placed his lamp, shining through the door, on the floor plates, stooped, started to squeeze into the narrow opening when his light burned out.

I had Kelley's telephone. I heard him say:

"My light's gone. Tell Mike to give me his."

Over Michels' phone, I ordered:

"Give Kelley your light!"

Michels handed his lamp to Kelley, who placed it near the door, giving the burned out lamp to his partner. Kelley reported he was ready to try the door again. He was partway through when the last light flared brilliantly and then burned out, leaving the men in complete darkness. Four lights burned out in succession, while they were attempting a passage into the most dangerous part of the boat! In a shaken voice, Kelley reported the latest mishap, and added, "I'm coming up." I hardly blamed him. We had no more lights anyway.

The divers had tried all three entrances to the control room. They had been balked at every one. There was little doubt their nerves were shaken, especially by the latest experience with the lamps. I could see the men feared that they might get well inside the control room, then have their lights go out and be forced in the darkness to try to fight their way out. A man may be brave, but the prospect of being trapped and having to struggle alone in silence and in blackness will shake the stoutest heart. We decided no one would be asked to enter the submarine again until we had a reliable light.

The submarine lamps we were using were frankly experimental. No light of any power able to stand pressure was on the market when the *S-51* sank. The Westinghouse Company, however, had been developing such a light and felt they had the answer. We bought several dozens of their lamps and took them out with us. We shortly discovered their weakness. As lights they were far superior to any previously available, but their bases were not pressure proof. Several lamps had burned out before Kelley's experience in the engine room, but fortunately none had gone out while a man was inside.

We radioed the Westinghouse experts and pointed out the defects. We had considerable difficulty in making their laboratory men believe the water entered through the cement as we said; they refused at first to modify the design and tried various other lamp-making cements without better success. They had finally to adopt the modification we suggested, of vulcanizing a watertight rubber sleeve from the glass base to the rubber electric cable. Several lamps made that way arrived on the *Penobscot* two days later. They went into service immediately, and not one lamp of that design ever burned out on any diver. Westinghouse adopted it as their standard design.

XII

ANOTHER STRUGGLE

Nearly three weeks had gone by since we started work. The divers had toiled steadily down below, we had accomplished a little, but it was plain that the job could not possibly be quickly terminated. October was gone, November was well started. The weather was getting worse, the water colder. The *Falcon* was crowded badly during the day by tenders, telephone men, dressers, and an extra working party from the *Vestal* to handle mooring lines. She was nearly as badly crowded at night to accommodate her own crew and furnish bunks for the divers whom we dared not send off the ship away from the recompression tank, our "iron doctor."

The divers worked below on the *S-51* under depressing and morbid surroundings; they came up on the *Falcon* and found no place outside their bunks where they could rest or even sit down.

This was bad enough while we were diving, but it seemed an aggravation to have to stand it when a storm arose and diving was not possible. Under such conditions, the *Falcon* heaved and pitched as the waves rolled by and we listened to the mournful whistling of the buoy the Lighthouse Service had planted near the wreck. If the storm grew very bad, we sought shelter in the lee of Block Island, fourteen miles away, and rode it out.

What irritated the crew was the fact that Newport was only twenty-five miles away. Practically every diver had learned the art at the Torpedo School in Newport; many of the men still had their homes there; they all had friends (and some sweethearts) in Newport. There was consequently a strong wish to get ashore there, to get a change of scene, to get their minds off the gruesome job below. While the

44

weather was good enough to dive, there were no complaints, but the men could not see why we stayed round when we could do nothing more than pitch and roll at the end of our anchor cable.

That seemed reasonable and several times I tried to get permission to send the divers in for a rest when a storm arose. The squadron commander was, however, opposed to it. He felt that with winter coming on, we dared not lose an hour suitable for diving; that if the divers were sent to Newport during a storm, the weather might moderate, and we might lose half a day before we could get the men back on the scene. This might happen, I had to admit, but even so I believed it was worth it. However, in spite of a number of conferences I was unable to get permission for a liberty for the men.

We went along, riding out the storms, with our divers getting stale, it was quite evident. Several good men failed to carry through what should have been very simple jobs. At last, with a storm raging and our new diving lamps not yet arrived from New London, permission was finally given. I bundled all the divers aboard the *Sagamore* at noon and started them for Newport. They were to leave Newport on the return trip at ten P.M. that same night.

The *Falcon* remained, anchored near the wreck buoy, with the waves breaking over her low rail. In the afternoon, the *Penobscot*, pitching like a cork, came in with stores. It was too rough to transfer anything at sea. We steamed away to Block Island, the *Penobscot* following us. In Great Salt Pond we found smooth water, and put over our boats. The new lamps were in the stores received.

We steamed out to sea again, the waves smashing against our bow, the cold wind whistling through our rigging. We reached the *Vestal*, which rode the seas more easily. A few clusters of yellow cork buoys tugging at the ends of the descending lines, visible occasionally on the crests of the waves, marked the spot where the *S-51* rested. The gray sea, wrinkled like an elephant's hide, cold and forbidding, formed the somber background against which our vessels rolled and pitched ceaselessly to the howling of the wind and the mournful note of the whistling buoy.

Towards evening, the wind slackened, and the waves started to go down. The *Falcon* steadied a little, so that it was possible to lie in a bunk without bracing unconsciously to avoid being pitched out on the deck at every roll.

Before midnight the wind had died out altogether, leaving only a long swell rolling in from the eastward to bother us. By one A.M., when the lights of the *Sagamore* returning from Newport loomed up alongside, the weather was clearing rapidly.

The little party of divers came aboard, transferred in the *Vestal*'s motor launch. They clambered over the rail in the darkness, and disappeared down the hatch. In the divers' compartment, crowded with bunks ranged two high against the bulkheads, they pulled off their clothes, wet from the flying spray on their brief boat ride, and climbed into their berths. In a moment or two, all were sound asleep. All but one, that is. "Tug" Wilson, chief torpedoman and expert diver, seemed very happy after his brief liberty in Newport, and started to sing.

Michels woke up and tried to quiet him. The other divers vigorously backed up Mike. Cries of "Pipe down, Tug," came from every bunk, but it was useless. Nothing could cause Wilson to restrain his exuberance until he finally dozed off about three A.M. Silence reigned below.

When morning came, the wind was gone, and the sea had died to a long swell which rolled ceaselessly by. We could dive again.

With the first glimmer of light, the coxswain and the boat crew scrambled over the stern into the surfboat and stood clear. The *Falcon*'s anchor chain rattled in on deck; with Lieutenant Hartley conning from the bridge, she started ahead and steamed into the circle of buoys, headed for the windward spar. As she neared it, the surfboat ran under her starboard bow, took the end of the first mooring hawser with a pelican hook secured to the eye and ran with it alongside the spar. The bowman speared the ring on the buoy with his boathook; the coxswain threw his helm over to hold position; and as the little boat heaved up and down, two seamen in the boat hanging far out over the gunwale slipped the heavy pelican hook over the ring, dropped the securing link over the bill of the hook, and shoved home the split toggle pin to lock everything. The surfboat backed clear and headed once more for the *Falcon*. Hartley dropped slowly to leeward, while the surfboat came under his starboard quarter, took a second hawser, and steamed away perhaps one hundred yards to the second buoy where once more the bowman clung to the buoy while they shackled up the line.

Back again to the *Falcon*, to run out a headline, and so the surfboat shuttled between *Falcon* and buoys, till finally the *Falcon* lay like the hub of a wheel with seven heavy mooring lines radiating from her to the buoys, out on the rim.

Lieutenant Hartley now paid out on the starboard lines and heaved in on those to port till the little cork buoys on the descending lines floated just abreast the port side, making a lee there with the *Falcon* for us to dive in on that side.

The surfboat tied up astern. The *Falcon*'s crew had breakfast during the centering process. A large motor launch from the *Vestal* drew alongside and the working party, forty men, clambered aboard.

The dressers brought out two diving rigs, the telephone men tested out their circuits, the diving air compressors started up.

Seven o'clock. We were ready for the first divers.

Chief Gunner Loughman looked into the little wardroom where we were having breakfast.

"Who goes down first?" he asked.

I told him. He turned to the dresser behind him.

"Tell Tug Wilson and Joe Eiben to get ready."

I finished my eggs. Coffee with condensed milk did not appeal to me. I drank it black, left the wardroom, and went aft on the lee side. Wilson and Eiben were just ahead of me. In blue woolen union suits, they paraded down the port side. Underneath they each had on two more suits of the same heavy underwear, all tucked into three pairs of heavy woolen socks. They reached the dressing stand on the quarter-deck, sat down on the benches facing me. Wilson was a little pale, Eiben about as usual. I remembered the singing in the early morning and the probable reason for it.

I looked Wilson over carefully. He seemed perfectly sober. Still I wondered whether he ought to go down.

"How do you feel, Tug?" I queried.

"Fine, Mr. Ellsberg, fine! Never felt better in my life!" I thought I had often seen him looking much better, but I decided not to tell him so.

Both men pushed their legs through the openings in the necks of their suits, then stood up while the dressers, slangily called the "bears," pulled the stiff suits over their bodies and helped them get their gloved hands into the sleeves. The men sat down again.

"Listen, Tug; listen, Joe." Both divers leaned towards me. "The new diving lamps came last night and you're going inside the sub. Try to get through the engine room door to the control room. You've practiced it on the *S-50*. Think you can make it?"

Wilson nodded. Eiben looked noncommittal as usual. I paused while their copper breastplates were slipped over their heads. The bears started to bolt the suits to the breastplates.

"All right. When you get in, keep on through the control room, close the forward door, and dog it down hard. You'll take a sledge to set the dogs up with. If you have any time left, on your way out see if you can read how the gyro compass heads. And watch yourself in the control room. Don't get hung up on anything inside. Tug, you go first. Joe, you tend Tug's lines through the room, and follow him up. Tom Eadie will be the outside man on the sub and tend both your lines through the engine room hatch."

Their heavy lead-soled shoes were buckled on. The dressers adjusted headsets, fastened on their belts. Wilson's helmet was held just over his head while he tested out his telephone set, then the helmet was slipped on, given a quarter turn to lock it tightly. A short-handled sledge hammer was tied to his belt. With a sailor on each side to help him walk, Wilson shuffled to the stage. Eadie, in his underwear, took Wilson's place on the dressing bench and the bears swarmed over him. Eiben's helmet was put on.

Wilson went over the side, stepped off the stage, vanished. A stream of bubbles, slowly working away from our side for perhaps a minute, then:

"On the bottom!" came over the phone.

We dropped one of the new lights over the side, turned it on. Eiben was hoisted overboard, and went down taking the light with him. Eadie was ready, and he too went over the side. Wilson had been down about five minutes when Eadie, dropping through the water, landed on the *S-51*.

Silently Wilson left the others, slipped through the open hatch into the engine room. Eiben followed with the light. Only Eadie remained outside, standing on the deck playing out airhoses, lifelines, and lamp cord, almost inch by inch.

Wilson came to the after door. He had minutely scanned the one on the *S-50*; both he and Eiben had a new plan. Wilson squeezed through the door, slid forward a step, felt his helmet hit where Ingram had been caught. He ducked, gave his helmet a sharp twist, cleared the obstruction, was inside the room. Looking back, he could barely make out the glow of the lamp in Eiben's hand.

"On deck! Tell Eiben to come ahead!"

I took Eiben's phone.

"Go ahead, Joe! Tug says he's through!"

Once more Eadie started to pay out line, feeding it carefully to see he did not allow any slack which might get foul of anything.

A few steps, and Eiben was alongside Wilson. A narrow passage, between the galley to port and the radio room to starboard, led forward. Wilson, leading, took the light from Eiben and started carefully ahead. Two steps and he was abreast the door to the little radio room. Wilson shined the light through the narrow door. Inside he could dimly see the radio operator, earphones on his head, still at his key.

Again Wilson started ahead but was halted. A metal bunk, washed all the way through from the battery room, blocked the passage. He seized it, straightened it up, pushed it past him to Eiben. Together they shoved it through the port side opening into the galley. Again they went ahead, cleared the galley, entered the main control space. The sloping deck tended to slide them into the port bilges. Cautiously they moved along, dodging the steering wheels, dodging the periscopes, avoiding the myriad valve handles sticking out from all directions to foul the lifelines trailing behind them and tangle them there forever. Charts, blueprints, floorboards floated round their heads. They passed the compressed air manifolds, passed the ladder leading to the conning tower, entered the narrow passage where the rungs on the bulkhead led up to the gun access trunk. Wilson swung the light up. Over his head was the little oval hatch where Lieutenant Haselton and his companion had struggled and died, where Kelley had stuck trying to crawl through.

Another step forward, and Wilson was at last facing the door that had balked all previous attempts to reach it. He moved close, trained his light on the door. As we had imagined, the door was open, swung only halfway back which was as far as it could go, due to a diagonal stateroom bulkhead behind it.

Reaching through the water, Wilson grasped the handle and pulled on the door. It failed to move.

Wilson carefully played his light all around to find out why. Jammed under the door, one edge projecting toward him into the control room, was a flat brass tread. Evidently the rushing water had washed it through from the battery room.

Wilson passed the light to Eiben behind him, bent low, and pushed on the tread. It was tightly wedged in and refused to budge. He unscrewed his diving knife, cut the lashing which held the sledge hammer to his belt, slipped the knife back in its sheath, and screwed it home. Getting as close to the door as his helmet allowed, he swung the sledge between his legs against the plate. It still refused to come free.

Wilson stepped aside, motioned Eiben forward, and pointed to the obstruction. Eiben took the hammer and tried to drive the plate out, but he had no more success than his companion.

On the surface, I could hear Wilson and Eiben, their helmets touching, talking to each other. Then they reported:

"On deck!"

"Hello, Tug!"

"There's a brass plate jammed under the door. We can't clear it!"

I called the timekeeper.

"How long have they been down?"

He looked at his watch, figured in his notebook.

"Forty-two minutes for Tug. Forty minutes for Joe." Both men would need all the rest of their hour to get safely out of the boat. I lifted Wilson's transmitter to my lips:

"Hello, Tug. Never mind the door. You and Joe come on out!"

Wilson mumbled something. I could not make it out. I took Eadie's phone.

"Hello, Tom! Mind the lines, Joe and Tug are coming out!"

The minutes went by. The tenders on the *Falcon*'s rail "fished" carefully, but no slack came up on the air lines for them to take in.

I listened on both Wilson's and Eiben's telephones, one receiver over each ear. Occasionally I heard the metallic ring of the sledge hammer, some very fluent profanity over Tug's line. The timekeeper called out:

"Sixty minutes for Tug."

No signal from the men below, but I dared not confuse them with useless orders. I waited anxiously till I heard Wilson call at last:

"On deck! We're coming out!"

Ten anxious minutes and the three divers stood once more on the deck of the submarine. First Wilson, then Eiben, then Eadie,—we hauled them up to ninety feet, on to the stage, and started decompression. They had been down nearly an hour and a half. We spent two hours and a half more in decompressing them.

At last the stage broke through the surface, swung inboard. The bears rushed at the three divers, unscrewed their helmets, pulled off their suits. Eiben was silent as usual, Wilson reported briefly:

"We got the door closed." He went below.

Later Eiben told me what had happened. Neither of them had been able to clear the wreckage under the door. The more they pushed on it, the tighter it got. Eiben had heard the order to come up. Both men had started to leave when Tug stopped again, said he had an idea. From the other side of the door, he could probably pull the plate free. The door, however, was the worst in the ship. In addition to being narrow, it would only swing partway open because of the bulkhead behind it. Wilson tried to squeeze through but failed. Then he lay down on his side in the door, and Eiben, pushing on his feet, finally managed to shove him through. On the battery room side was a little space, and there Wilson, on his knees on one side of the bulkhead, pulled the plate off the deck while Eiben, blow by blow from the other side, hammered it free. With the plate gone, Wilson lay down once more, his feet in the doorway, and Eiben finally managed to drag him back into the control room. "Yes," Eiben admitted, "it was pretty hard pulling." Back in the control room, they had swung the door closed, turned down the dogs, sledged them down tightly. Then they came out.

I gasped. Wilson had taken a desperate chance. Seventy feet inside the submarine, with one door already behind him that no one before had been able to get through, to have himself hammered through even a worse trap, where were his senses? Closing the door was important, but none of us would have dreamed of asking a man practically to throw his life away to close it.

I found Wilson, asked him why he had taken such a hair-raising risk. In his deep voice, far different from the flat tone while under pressure on the submarine, he answered:

"Well, Mr. Ellsberg, I know how hard you tried all last month to get us boys a liberty in Newport. And then when we finally hit the beach, oh, boy!"

"So when we couldn't close that door and you told me to come up, I took another look at the door and decided to close it anyway, to try to show my appreciation. And Joe helped me, so we did it."

Not a word about the dangers he had passed through, no mention of the death lurking behind that door to add him to the silent company inside the boat. Wilson had chosen to risk his life to show his appreciation for a little favor.

"Joe helped me, so we did it!" The control room door could not resist that spirit.

XIII

THE FIRST PONTOON

It was getting towards the end of October when some of the pontoons arrived, towed out from New York on the deck of a large Navy derrick, the *United States*. In the wake of the *Sagamore*, the derrick appeared off the wreck buoy in the middle of a fine morning, rolling gently to an easy swell. We might, I thought, have the pontoons put overboard by the derrick, and let them ride to our mooring buoys till they were wanted. But Lieutenant Hartley thought otherwise.

"The barometer is dropping. Looks like a blow to me. Better have them get that baby inside the harbor before it comes."

The skipper of the *Sagamore* agreed with him. He started off with his lumbering tow and gradually disappeared to the northward. It was well he did. By three in the afternoon, it was blowing hard, and the *Falcon*, clear of her moorings, was riding the storm to a long scope on her anchor cable.

No word from the *Sagamore*. Hartley spoke briefly:

"I hope they got inside Narragansett Bay with that tow before this wind hit them, because if they didn't, they haven't got a tow any more!"

There was no argument on that. The *United States*, with her heavy tripod and a boom built to lift one hundred tons at its top, would quickly have capsized in that sea. But luck was with us. Because of its early start, the tug had managed to pass inside the Narrows off Fort Adams before the sea had picked up much, and had steamed on towards Newport. As the wind increased, they had difficulty holding the derrick, and steamed into the inner harbor between the Torpedo Station Island and Newport. Here the tug tied up alongside the derrick which dropped two anchors, its ground tackle being much heavier than the *Sagamore*'s.

But the skipper's troubles had only started. Late in the evening, with the wind blowing hard, we intercepted a radio from *Sagamore* to the Torpedo Station.

"Send more tugboats. Derrick dragging her anchors. Unable to hold her with *Sagamore*."

Even though there were no waves inside the harbor, the sweep of the wind was too much for the moorings. Another tug went to the *Sagamore*'s assistance, but in spite of their best efforts, the derrick dragged through the harbor, hooked and tore away the electric cables and the water line from Newport to the Torpedo Station, and left the little island dark and waterless.

Dawn found the tugs still struggling with their charge,—at least they had managed to keep her off the beach though she was half a mile from where she had first anchored.

When the wind moderated, they managed to work the derrick against a pier, where she was tied up and remained the rest of the winter. It cost many thousands of dollars to repair the damage to the electric cables and water lines crossing Newport harbor.

This experience confirmed our opinion that it was impossible to work with derricks in the open sea.

Alongside the dock, the *United States* hoisted over the pontoons, and the next day the *Iuka* towed two of the pontoons out to the wreck, where we tied them up to a couple of mooring buoys.

No one had ever had any experience in lowering pontoons in deep water,—it had never been tried before. In shallow water, about forty feet deep, it had once proved difficult. The officer who had managed that job had pronounced the pontoons "unmanageable" in lowering; he had found that all he could do was to fill them and let them sink. Having only a short way to go in shallow clear water, they had hit bottom alongside the little submarine he was raising, before they could get out of position. Also his submarine was already so badly damaged he was not trying to make it watertight inside; if a pontoon hit the boat and opened further holes, it made no special difference.

In the *S-51* problem, conditions were vastly different. To lift the submarine with the pontoons built and building, we were required to make the after half of the submarine watertight. We could not afford to let a pontoon weighing forty tons fall one hundred and thirty-five feet on our submarine; that would smash it like an eggshell and ruin our chance of lifting the boat.

The *S-51*, at her depth, was of course wholly out of our sight, yet we had to land our pontoons close alongside her, not more than eight feet away. In addition, to allow us to get the six forward pontoons in position where we needed them for lifting, we were required to plant them one ahead of another with only a six-foot interval between the end of one pontoon and the front of the next pontoon astern.

A somewhat analogous problem would be to lower a heavy Pullman car from the top of a fifteen-story building which was swaying violently, due to an earthquake, to the street, in the middle of a black night when you couldn't see the street, nor the car either after you started lowering; and then land the Pullman car in a vacant space in the middle of a train standing on a track in the dark street below without dropping the car on the diner ahead or the car just behind the vacant space. Frankly, I always had a sinking feeling in the stomach whenever it came time to lower a pontoon.

But it had to be done, so we started out to do it. The stern and the bow of the *S-51* were several feet clear of the ocean floor, since the ship was built somewhat like a rocker, deep amidships with a gradual rise of keel towards each end.

Michels was dressed to go down and pass the first guide line under her stern, just forward of the rudders. We gave him a small manila line with a cork ring life buoy tied to one end. This Michels was to push under the stern from starboard to port, and then let go. The buoy, floating to the surface would bring the line up with it, giving us a reeving line around the stern, with one end rising to the surface on each side.

Michels took the life buoy and was hoisted over the *Falcon*'s side. As he disappeared, Hartley paid out rapidly on the manila line. Michels hit the submarine over the engine room, slid down her side, walked aft along the hard gray sand. A stream of bubbles on the surface marked his progress. They stopped. He was at the stern.

"On deck! Look out for the buoy! I'm pushing it under!"

We strained our eyes, gazing at a spot near the bubbles where that white life buoy should break surface. However we might have spared ourselves the trouble. Another call from Mike:

"On deck! That buoy you gave me was no good. It sank the minute I let go of it! Send me another one!"

It made us laugh to think of Mike's amazement. The trouble had not occurred to me before, though it should have. The high pressure on the sea bottom had forced water into all the air spaces in the cork, making it so heavy it could no longer float. No use sending down another buoy,—it would only get waterlogged and sink also.

Hastily we dressed Kelley, sent him down on the opposite side of the submarine with another line. Reaching under the hull, he took the end of Mike's line, bent the two together, told us to haul away. We did, till the knot came on deck. Then we slipped a new line tied to a shackle down on each side to the divers there; they removed the shackles, bent the lines together, made sure all the lines were clear of each other, and came up.

We now had two small manila reeving lines under the *S-51*'s stern. To the starboard end of each line we secured a four-inch manila line and hauled up on the port sides, till the large lines came up on that side. These new lines were strong enough for heavier work.

To the starboard ends of the four-inch manilas, we shackled in one-inch wire hawsers, and hauled these wires under the stern and upon the port side. We were now ready for the first pontoon.

The surfboat towed alongside a pontoon which the *Vestal* had already rigged for lowering. It was an immense steel cylinder, fourteen feet in diameter, thirty-two feet long, practically a section of a submarine itself. It was heavily reinforced with steel frames inside, had flood valves, relief valves, air valves, and vent valves; pad eyes for towing and for lowering; and two long hawsepipes going down through it vertically to take the lifting chains. The chains, huge battleship anchor cables, ninety feet long with steel links two and a half inches thick, already hung in the hawsepipes, the upper ends held by large clamps on top of the pontoon, the lower ends triced up alongside the pontoon ready for us to shackle into the guide wires.

Floating high out of the water, the pontoon pitched up and down against our starboard rail as we worked on it. We connected the guide wires to the chains and cut the lashings which held the lower ends of the heavy chains against the pontoon; the chains dropped and we hauled up the slack wires on the other side of the submarine.

We secured a six-inch manila hawser to the lowering ring at each end of the pontoon, opened the flood valves on the end bulkheads, opened the vent valves on top of each compartment in the pontoon, and allowed the pontoon to flood. An airhose was coupled to the blowing connection at each pontoon compartment and attached to the air manifold on the *Falcon*'s quarterdeck.

Flooding down proved a slow process,—it lasted nearly an hour. Meanwhile, mindful that we ought to expect trouble in lowering, we determined the position of the *S-51*'s stern by getting our guide lines up and down in the water; then, as it was intended to plant the first pontoon on the starboard quarter of the submarine, we hauled the *Falcon* well over to starboard, so that the guide lines went down at an angle. Hartley estimated that the pontoon alongside of us was probably thirty feet to starboard to the submarine.

It was late in the afternoon and getting dark by the time the pontoon was flooded and nearly ready to submerge. A six-inch lowering line with several turns around a pair of bitts led to each end of the pontoon, the lines a little slack to avoid sudden jerks as the pontoon fell away in the trough of the sea. There was little buoyancy left. The pontoon failed to rise much as the crests passed; the waves started to break over the top and the seamen who stood there left and came aboard.

A little more water poured in through the open flood valves, a wave broke over the forward end of the pontoon and forced it down a little. The awash pontoon no longer had any stability; the water inside ran to the low end and that end went down hard, taking up all the slack in the hawser there, while the other end of the pontoon rose out of water.

For well over an hour, we tried everything we knew to try to get the pontoon to submerge evenly; it was no use, the moment we slacked the lines the pontoon started down on a sharp slant and tended to sink end first, not horizontally. That was dangerous, for the lines and chains were likely to get tangled up before it reached the bottom. But darkness had us and the wind was increasing; we could not hold the pontoon any longer. Reluctantly I opened the vent valves to allow the pontoon to fill a little more and submerge.

The cylinder lost all its buoyancy and started down, forward end first. The men at the bitts paid out on the starboard lowering lines; the men at the winches hauled up on the wire guide lines on the other side as the pontoon sank.

We tried to lower evenly. After only a few feet, the men at the bitts called out:

"She's getting heavier!"

As the pontoon sank and the pressure increased, more water rushed in through the open flood valves, compressing the air inside.

At thirty feet down, the lines started to smoke as they ran out over the bitts.

"We can't hold her!"

"Slack away freely. Let her run!" I shouted. The sailors tried to throw the turns off the bitts. No use. At forty feet the manila lines were going out so fast the men hauling in the wires on the other side of the ship could not take in slack fast enough.

At fifty feet out, Lieutenant Hartley sang out through the darkness:

"Forward line has carried away, sir!"

A second later, a voice came from the other pair of bitts:

"After line has parted!"

The freed pontoon fell eighty-five feet to the bottom. I hoped that we were correct in our estimate that the pontoon was at least thirty feet clear on one side of the submarine's stern before we started to lower it.

On the port side of the *Falcon*, the hauling wires, suddenly released from any strain, came up in loops and snarls.

We took the ends off the winches, ran them well out clear of the submarine, so we thought, and buoyed them off.

Under the piercing beam of the searchlight, the surfboat ran out among the mooring buoys, shot alongside each one in succession. Here the bowman, boathook poised like a harpoon, caught the toggle pin in the pelican hook as the buoy lifted on a wave, jerked out the pin, knocked clear the locking ring, and released the hawser as the bill of the pelican hook flew open. The *Falcon* reeled in the loosened hawsers, took her boat in tow, steamed clear, and anchored.

We agreed that the previous reports had been right when they stated the pontoons were "unmanageable."

When next day, diving started again, Ingram went down first to learn how we had fared. It was a marked relief when he reported no damage to the submarine,—in fact he could not find the pontoon anywhere. It had vanished. He made a short circle on the bottom off the starboard quarter without running into it, but he did stumble across one of the chains, leading away from the submarine. He followed it a distance without seeing anything, then we brought him up. Eadie and Wilson followed him down, located the chain, and walked out along it, finally running into the pontoon standing on one end, looming up from the ocean bottom like a huge water tank. The two chains, twisted and kinked, lay in circles and heaps nearby; the hauling wires led away in a mass of snarls toward the submarine, sixty feet distant; the frayed ends of the broken manila lowering lines floated just above the top of the pontoon, undulating gently in the invisible current like cornstalks in a breeze.

With a Stillson wrench (always the diver's most valuable tool, after his knife) Eadie unscrewed the shackle pin in the end of one anchor chain and released one hauling wire. Wilson traced out the turns and tangles of the other chain in the sand and at last located the end of it, but he was not able to do anything. The shackle was bent, the pin would not turn, and he could not free the wire there.

Before we could attempt to bring our pontoon back up it was essential to get both wires clear of the *S-51*. For the wire Eadie had unshackled, this was easy. We picked up the buoy we had secured to its other end, heaved in, and the whole wire, four hundred feet long, came up, kinked in many spots however.

The other was harder. It was still secured to the pontoon chain to starboard of the boat. Frazer, going down to work on the conning tower, reported that a wire, coming from under the port quarter of the vessel, ran forward and was tangled in the mast of the submarine, and then led away along the bottom at right angles from the port side of the vessel. Frazer climbed the mast, and tried to throw the wire clear, but found it was fouled in the signal yard. We heaved on the buoyed end of the wire, trying to pull it free, but merely succeeded in bending the mast badly over to port.

Several other divers with crowbars and wrenches tried to uncouple the shackle pin near the pontoon but without success. We worked on the job intermittently for two weeks, trying various methods of clearing the wire. I finally determined to try to burn it in half.

Both in Europe and in the United States, various navies had for fifteen years been experimenting with torches for burning steel underwater. A little success had been attained. It was possible then to light a torch underwater and even to keep the flame going awhile. We had with us the American Navy torch, such as it was. Two of our divers, Applegate and George Anderson, had practiced with it in the Navy Yard. Several times on the *S-51*, Applegate had taken it down and tried to burn steel with it, but he had great difficulty in lighting off and he had never succeeded in cutting.

Steel wire is much easier than steel plate to burn, as it takes but little heat to raise to the burning point the small strands which make up the hawser. We had not been able to cut steel; I hoped we might be able to cut this wire.

Consequently we rigged up the torch, brought out the oxygen and gas bottles, hooked up the regulators and pressure gauges, and then dressed George Anderson to go down to burn, with Kelley to give general assistance.

It was early November and getting cold, especially on the bottom. The divers were hoisted over, went down the descending line, Anderson with the torch, Kelley with the lighter.

They reached the submarine, slid off the starboard quarter, and after a brief search found the chain leading to the pontoon. They traced this till they reached the point where the wire, buried in the sand, first showed up across the chain.

They pulled on the wire, trying to get a little slack so Anderson could work more easily, but the wire was taut and they could not move the heavy links of the chain. In order to get a little space, Kelley dug a small hole in the hard sand with his hand, leaving the wire exposed a few inches all around. They were ready.

"On deck! Turn on the igniter!"

I turned the switch on the electric lighting device, while Hartley turned on the gases to the torch and adjusted the pressures.

"Hello, Kelley! The igniter is on!"

There were several flashes below as Kelley sent spark after spark across the tip of the torch which Anderson was holding. Finally I heard a bang. The torch had lighted.

Anderson kneeled down over the wire. Kelley stood close by to help if he could.

On the *Falcon*'s quarterdeck Hartley watched the pressures on his flasks. The minutes went by, the pressures dropped as the gases were exhausted, we switched over to new flasks. I could hear the banging of the torch down below. It was still lighted. We had not much gas left. Nearly forty minutes had gone by and Anderson had not yet reported finished, though occasionally a puff of smoke rose with the air bubbles to the surface, showing some results. I telephoned to Kelley to find out what progress was being made.

I could hear Kelley's teeth chattering. Poor Kelley was evidently very cold, standing by in ice water, doing nothing except to watch Anderson, not daring to move for fear of disturbing his partner, and afraid to leave because Anderson might need him.

"Hello, John! How is Anderson making out with the torch?"

Kelley turned off his air. The roar in his helmet ceased. I could hear him plainly.

"Mr. Ellsberg, if I could only take my helmet off and get my teeth on that wire, I could chew it in half faster than that damn torch is burning it!" Kelley turned on his air again. The conversation was obviously finished.

Hartley looked glumly at the gauges. His last bottle of oxygen was going fast. In about one more minute it would all be gone.

A call from the bottom.

"On deck! The last strand is cut! We're coming up. Take up the torch and the igniter!"

The divers came up, but in spite of decompression, Kelley developed a bad case of "bends" which kept him under treatment in the "iron doctor" all night long.

The next task was to raise the pontoon. Eadie went down, cut loose the broken ends of the original airhoses, coupled a new pair of blowing hoses to the air valves. He found a broken vent valve on the high end of the pontoon. We sent him a wood plug which he drove in the hole, sealing it. Eadie came up.

We coupled the blowing hoses to the *Falcon*'s manifold. A little juggling was required to lift the pontoon. No use blowing air into the high end (the pontoon was divided into two halves by a bulkhead halfway between the ends), for with the pontoon vertical, the air in that end would blow out through the open flood valve there as fast as we put it in. Nor could we put too much air in the low end to lighten it up, for if that happened, the low end would upset the pontoon and make it float on end again, but with the light end up this time; then all the air in that end would blow out the open flood valve there and leave us just where we started, with the pontoon still flooded.

Carefully Niedermair flowed air into the low end, a little at a time, while we tugged continuously on the hoses to get the first sign of motion. Finally it came. The hose to the high end started to run out. Hastily Niedermair stopped blowing. We tried the hoses. They now seemed the same length. Niedermair blew a little air into both ends. No bubbles rose to the surface. The pontoon was now lying in its normal position, horizontally.

Niedermair blew more air into what had been the high end for a few minutes to equalize the buoyancy, then started to blow both ends together. We pulled both hoses taut and waited. For fifteen minutes the air went down. Then the hoses slackened a little, came all slack. The pontoon was rising. In half a minute it burst through the surface at an angle of about 60°, blew like a whale from the end that rose first, then leveled off and blew air violently from the other end. It seesawed a moment, then floated level and rose about eight feet more out of the water as we blew it completely dry through the hoses.

The surfboat ran alongside, bent a line to the broken end of the lowering line trailing astern the pontoon, and took the line to the *Sagamore.* A seaman clambered up the slimy side of the pontoon, closed the flood valves, disconnected the hoses. The *Sagamore* towed the pontoon away to Newport.

It was evident that if we were going to raise the submarine, a new method of handling pontoons would have to be developed. The bottom of the ocean was too far away here to let us play with shallow-water practices.

That same night, another storm broke, the worst one so far. Our little squadron fared badly. The *S-50* suffered the most, rolling and pitching madly. With all hatches secured it was a night of torture for her crew, tumbled about inside, unable to stay in their bunks. At last Lieutenant Commander Lenney could stand it no longer. He signaled the *Vestal* that he would have to seek shelter, and the low-lying lights of the *S-50* quickly disappeared to the westward.

Matters were not much better on the *Falcon*, which was plunging up and down as the waves rolled under her bow. From my little stateroom on the *Vestal* (I usually returned in a launch to the *Vestal* when the last diver was up) I could see the lights of the *Falcon* and the tug boats dancing wildly as they rode the seas. The *Vestal* fared slightly better. She was a large ship and consequently steadier, her motion was much less than that of the small ships. But as the gale increased and the November wind howled through our rigging, a different danger suddenly developed. The high forecastle and superstructure of the *Vestal* caught the wind like a huge sail and caused the ship to tug violently on her anchor. For safety, the cable was paid out to the bitter end, giving us a long scope to swing to; with one hundred and twenty fathoms of chain out we rode as best we could. Captain Tomb and his navigator stayed on the bridge; below, the "black gang" fired up all boilers and the engineers stood by their throttles, prepared for emergencies.

In the *Vestal*'s wardroom, all the furniture was lashed down. The officers ate supper standing up, clinging to the table as we rolled. A squall struck the ship,—she lurched heavily to starboard and the table, breaking its fastenings, shot into the bilges, coming within an inch of decapitating Lieutenant Shinn as it knocked him against the buffet.

The sudden strain on the cable broke out the anchor. We drifted rapidly to leeward, so fast the anchor flukes could not dig in and get another bite in the bottom. Astern of us the *Falcon* started whistling frantically. We were bearing down on her with a rush. On the *Vestal*'s bridge Captain Tomb swung over his telegraphs violently, bells jangled in the engine room, "Full speed ahead!" Slowly the engine started to turn over and then raced madly under a full head of steam as our stern lifted out of water; then the propeller caught the water and we finally stopped. One might easily have jumped from our counter down to the *Falcon*'s forecastle where Lieutenant Hartley, about to trip his cable, stared up at us. The little strip of water between the ships foamed violently as our propeller, alternately buried and exposed, churned the sea; then we gradually forged ahead and anchored clear, steaming slowly into the gale the rest of the night to ease the strain on our cable.

Our plunging ships rode as best they could; we had a pontoon tied to a mooring buoy,—how was it faring? The *Vestal* switched on her searchlight. The beam cut through the darkness, wandered over a world of flying spray and tumbling waves, searching out the mooring buoys one by one. There was no pontoon riding to any of them. Somewhere to the northward, driving before a sou'wester, our pontoon was on its way out into the Atlantic. We dared not send a tug in search of it.

The storm hauled to the southeast, blew all next day. The gray dawn and the bleak day that followed were even more depressing than the darkness. Cold spray, a biting wind, the tumbling seas; the dismal note of the wreck buoy coming to us, monotonously droning a requiem for those below; an occasional glimpse of the mooring buoys as the waves heaved them above the surface; our storm-tossed ships fighting the gale.

We rode it out, the storm blew over, the seas changed to long swells rolling up from the southward. Lieutenant Rundquist and the *Sagamore* were dispatched to search for the lost pontoon.

A radio came to us from Newport. On Horse Neck Beach, some fishermen reported a large cylinder washed ashore. It was probably our pontoon. We directed Rundquist to investigate the spot, on the southern coast of Massachusetts near Buzzards Bay.

The *Sagamore* stood in. Rundquist examined the shore through glasses. Yes, there was the pontoon, thrown a hundred feet up the beach by the storm waves, now left high and dry. Rundquist skillfully landed a boat through the surf, but another blow started and he had to lie off for five days while his boat crew, unable to get back, lived with the fishermen. The weather calmed, the *Sagamore* sent in hawsers, kedge anchors, tackles. With these Rundquist parbuckled the heavy cylinder down the beach, rolling it like a huge barrel till once more it was afloat.

The *Sagamore* towed it back to Newport, tied it up there to the derrick. As expected, the fishermen at Horse Neck Beach, exercising the centuries-old custom of the wrecker, had stolen every portable from the pontoon,— valves, clamps, fittings.

Rundquist returned to the squadron, and reported the success of his little salvage expedition. A good sailor, Karl Rundquist; it was the last act of his long career, for a few months later, forced to retire for age, he died ashore, far from the sea which had been his life.

Meanwhile, we congratulated ourselves on having recovered our two pontoons from the sea bottom and the sea; we brought no more pontoons out from Newport that winter.

XIV

BLOWING THE BALLAST TANKS

Wilson and Eiben had closed the forward door in the control room. They went in again, with Eadie tending outside as before, closed the ventilation flapper valve overhead and screwed down on the open valves going through the bulkhead to the battery room. They came out in less than an hour this time, their work done. Wilson reported in detail what he had closed; I checked the valves off against the plans of the boat.

Wilson had a suggestion.

"I think we can blow the ballast tanks from the control room, Mr. Ellsberg. I noticed on the gauge board that there's still two thousand pounds pressure registering on the gauges to two of the air banks; the other two are zero. If we can open the Kingston valves on the ballast tanks, I can give them the air from the inside."

On the *S-50*, we went over the problem with her captain. Wilson carefully learned what valves to open to hook the live air banks to the manifold and blow the undamaged ballast tanks in the after part of the boat; which valves must be closed to cut off the dead air banks, the broken air line to the gun access trunk, the lines to the damaged tanks forward. We taught him how to operate the master control air motor to the Kingston valves on the ballasts; and in case the master control failed to operate due to long submergence, which Kingston valves he and Eiben were to open by hand in the engine room and the control room.

The work was rehearsed for several days. We borrowed from Lenney on the *S-50* the special wrench needed to open the valves on the high-pressure air manifold. But meanwhile I decided that we would try only to blow the water from the three undamaged ballast tanks on the port side, which was the low side.

This would result in giving the boat a tendency to roll to starboard as soon as she was lightened up, and might help break the suction holding her to the bottom, while at the same time putting the ship on an even keel. Besides there was not enough air left inside the *S-51* to do any more against the sea pressure at the bottom.

Wilson, however, was considerably disturbed when the plan was broached to him.

"That's all right, but what do you think will happen to us if the old sub rolls over on her starboard side while Joe and me are inside the control room playing with those valves? How are we going to get out?"

"Don't worry, Tug. I've already figured it out. Even if we blow those three tanks all dry, that's only sixty tons buoyancy pulling on the port side, and as long as the rest of her is all flooded, it isn't enough to roll her. We'll have to lighten her lots more yet before she can roll, buried in the clay the way she is."

The boys accepted my word for it. Armed with the wrenches, Tug, Joe, and Mike went down. Tug and Joe entered the *S-51*, wiggled into the control room, moved forward to the manifold. When they finally ceased taking any more line, Mike left the deck, slid down the port side to bottom, took station alongside the submarine just above the point where one of the Kingston valves lay buried in the clay down under the bilge keel.

Eiben held the light inside, Wilson manipulated the little wrench, opening this valve, closing that. He put the air on master controller, swung the lever. Nothing happened. The air motors on the Kingston valves failed to operate. Evidently they had been submerged too long. Wilson closed the master valve.

Leaving Wilson standing in darkness, Eiben took the light and went aft. By hand he swung open the wheels to the Kingstons on the tanks abreast the control room and the engine room. Soon he was back. Together with Wilson, he checked over the valve settings on the manifold. They were correct.

"On deck! Tell Mike to stand by! We're going to turn on the air!"

Wilson turned the wrench, opening the air banks to the manifold. With two thousand pounds of pressure behind it, the air started to whistle through from the air flasks buried under the floor on the starboard side of the battery room; the needle on the gauge, submerged though it was, quivered in the dim light from their lamp, and started to fall. The divers could hear the air going through the lines, and the submarine, so long a silent, motionless hulk, seemed to quiver and stir under their feet.

In spite of his faith in my calculations, Tug was strongly tempted to abandon the control room before those port ballast tanks blew dry and caused the submarine to topple over sideways.

"On deck! Tell Mike the air is going through! Say, are you sure she can't move?"

"All right, Tug. I'll tell him. No, there's not a chance in the world. Just watch that gauge!"

But I am sure that if Mike had been on deck to take in the slack of their lines, Tug and Joe would have waited for the ballast tanks to blow dry from the relatively safe position of a seat on the port rail, just outside the engine room hatch.

I called Michels.

"Hello, Mike! The air's on. See anything?"

"On deck! There's a stream of muddy water coming up right by my feet! No air bubbles. I'll look at the other valves."

Mike walked aft alongside the hull, then forward. The same thing was happening in all three tanks. The air was going in, forcing the water out the bottoms of the tanks through the open Kingstons there, where it rose in muddy streams through the clay into the clearer water on the sea floor.

Under the pressure in the banks, the air went through rapidly. In less than twenty minutes, Wilson reported the pressure practically all gone from the air banks. As directed, he shut all the valves on the manifold, turned off the banks. Michels reported that no more water was coming out,—no air bubbles came out at all. There had not been enough air left in the submarine to empty the tanks completely.

Michels climbed aboard again, tended the divers' lines while the men inside wormed their way out. The three divers came up together. Wilson always claimed the boat quivered and stirred while he blew the tanks.

However, so far as we could ever determine, the submarine lay over to port just as much as before.

XV

OUTSIDE THE CONTROL ROOM

We were through inside the control room, but to seal it up we had to close the conning tower and gun access trunk hatches. The ship had sunk with the conning tower hatch open; we had opened the one over the gun access trunk ourselves. Still we could not have relied on these hatch covers even if they were both closed, for they opened outward, intended to be sealed tight by the pressure of the sea weighing on them; whereas we intended to build up an air pressure inside the boat greater than the water pressure outside in order to expel the water. Under such an inside pressure the regular hatches on the boat would spring off their seats and let all the air leak out.

To meet this contingency, I had some special hatch covers made at the Navy Yard before we left, to take the place of the regular covers. The substitute covers were made of steel plate, an inch and a quarter thick, with a rubber gasket secured to the underside to make a watertight joint against the edge of the hatch opening. The hatch covers were quite complicated with blowing valves, test valves, and water valves on top, and a long spillpipe hanging from the underside through which the water was to be expelled from the bottom of the room. Finally, for locking the hatch cover into place, there was a long, thick bolt through the center of the cover, with a heavy steel strongback, swiveled on its lower end, designed to slip through the hatch opening and catch inside the boat.

Due to their thickness and all the attachments, the salvage hatch covers were very heavy, from five hundred to seven hundred pounds in weight, and exceedingly awkward to handle, especially under the handicaps of diving conditions.

Since there were two hatches to seal up over the control room, the blowing connections were fitted only to the cover intended for the gun access trunk; the cover over the conning tower hatch was made a plain plate with no valves on it. As this plate was also the smallest and lightest of the lot (it weighed only three hundred pounds), I decided to have it installed first and let the divers work up to the more difficult cover plates later.

The top of the conning tower opened to the chariot bridge. There was little space inside the bridge enclosure. The forward part was taken up with the binnacle and steering gear, the after part was almost wholly taken up by the housing around the periscopes and the mast. A clear space about four feet by five feet was all there was.

We tried the job out on the *S-50*. Frazer, unquestionably the largest and strongest diver in our crew, was selected for the task, with Smith, who was much smaller, to assist in the confined space.

To help them handle the weight, the *Vestal*'s carpenter made us an oak beam which spanned the bridge rail from starboard to port, with a turnbuckle hook at each end to fasten it down to the bridge framing. In this beam we placed an eyebolt directly over the center of the conning tower hatch, and secured a half-ton chain fall to the bolt.

We brought the hatch cover assembly to the *S-50* in a small boat; the sailors there dragged it up on their bridge. Then Frazer and Smith rigged the beam across the bridge, hooked their chain fall to the strongback bolt, and hoisted the cover and strongback clear of the top of the conning tower. With the cover plate triced up clear of the strongback, they lowered the strongback through the opening, swiveled the bar, caught it inside on both sides of the hatch, then heaved up on the chain fall till the strongback bar was firmly jammed against the inside of the conning tower.

Frazer loosed the lashing on the cover plate, and let it slide down the central bolt. It rested neatly on the turned-up edge of the hatch. Smith slid the nut down, screwed it home. On the *S-50* the rig worked out very well. The divers professed themselves satisfied.

The gear was unrigged and sent back to the *Falcon* with the divers.

George Anderson went down first, on the descending line to the gun forward, carrying a small line with him. He climbed the side of the conning tower, crawled inside the chariot bridge. Anderson tied his line to the binnacle, signaled on it that it was secure. On the new line as a guide, we lowered down the oak beam and the turnbuckles, with lead weights attached to make sure the beam sank.

The material landed inside the bridge. Anderson cut it loose, swung the beam into its intended place across the rails on the *S-51*, hooked in the turnbuckles, set them up. With that done, he reported ready and we next lowered down the chain fall, which he also received, hooked to the eyebolt over the hatch, tried the chains, and made sure the differential purchase was working freely. Anderson then came up, not having been down quite an hour. The stage was all set for Smith and Frazer.

Because of the weight, we hoped for a fairly smooth day to lower the hatch cover, but none came, and we could not afford to wait. Smith and Frazer went down the new line, landed inside the bridge, signaled ready for the hatch. Lieutenant Hartley had it carefully rigged, and swung over the side of the *Falcon* on a line from the end of the port boom. The cover was already triced up near the top of the strongback bolt. We tied a short rope to the bolt, shackled the other end of the rope to the descending line to guide it down. On deck, the boatswain's mate took in all the slack of the descending line, then tended it to hold it taut as the *Falcon* rolled to the seaway. The winchman started to lower slowly, the hatch disappeared, we kept on lowering. I listened on Frazer's phone.

"Hatch is in sight! Hold it!" I repeated the order. The weight was evidently too far to one side.

From far below we got our instructions.

"Take it to port about ten feet!" We swung the boom farther out, lowered a little farther till Frazer caught a small line some ten feet long we had left dangling from the bottom of the strongback. The divers hauled on this, pulled the hatch over the bridge. We lowered a little more till they could touch the hatch on the down roll of the *Falcon*. On the up roll, it went up about six feet. On the next down roll, Frazer yelled:

"Let go!"

We slacked the winch completely. The weight landed inside the little bridge, between the two divers. They cut loose the lowering line, hooked the bolt with the chain fall, swung the assembly from the beam overhead. Just as in rehearsal, they toggled the strongback inside, lowered the hatch, screwed down hard on the retaining nut. The conning tower hatch was completely sealed up in less than an hour. The divers came up, much elated.

To close the gun access hatch was the next job. This trunk was just forward of the bridge. To handle the weight over this trunk, we made another oak beam to project over the bridge, the after end of this beam to be secured to the one we already had in place athwartships, the other end to cantilever forward from the bridge rail and carry an eyebolt for another chain fall. Anderson, with Kelley's assistance, rigged this new beam, shipped the chain fall, secured the guide line, and in a few days we were ready for the next hatch.

This was a much worse job, for the cover to the gun access trunk was larger and in addition was weighted down by valves and spillpipe, as well as being made much more cumbersome by these fittings. It weighed about five hundred pounds. Finally the cover, instead of fitting into a flush deck, had to be installed on top of a trunk some four feet above the deck.

Frazer and Smith, after some rehearsals on the *S-50*, went down on the submarine. As before, we swung the cover assembly over on a line from the end of our boom, shackled to a guide line tied to the gun access trunk below. The heavy spillpipe dangled fourteen feet down from the cover; it was going to be a tough job to get the spillpipe through the hatch.

We lowered away. The *Falcon* was rolling as usual to the ocean swell that never ceased. We plumbed the hatch as nearly as we could with the end of our boom, hauled up all the slack possible on the guide line, lowered slowly. The spillpipe came into the divers' view,—we were twenty feet too far to starboard and a little forward. We swung in our boom, shifted the *Falcon*; we came much closer to the hatch. But with the *S-51* leaning far over to port and thus having no horizontal surfaces to land anything on deck, trouble started. Several times, at Frazer's direction, we slacked off and tried to land the cover on the trunk but each time it promptly slipped off to port. We had no more luck trying to land it on the sloping deck. In desperation, Frazer and Smith finally worked the hatch over to the starboard side outboard of the trunk. Here it heaved up and down with the roll of the *Falcon*.

"Let go!" yelled Frazer. We slacked off. The hatch cover landed in a heap on the high side of the ship.

Laboriously the divers dragged the heavy cover along the side, Frazer heaving his utmost to push the ponderous mass along the edge of the deck while Smith hauled on the spillpipe. They dragged it close enough to hook it with the chain fall and hoisted it over the opening. Smith fed the spillpipe through the upper and lower hatches of the gun access trunk, and made sure the check valve on the lower end fell free through

70

to the control room floor.

Together they entered the strongback, toggled it, centered it in the opening, hoisted on the chain fall to jam it tight. They encountered trouble here, for the spillpipe partly blocked the opening and interfered with their movements. Smith tried to pull out the lamp he had lowered through the trunk to watch the progress of the spillpipe into the control room. It would not come back through the hatch, now the spillpipe was hanging there. Smith asked us to turn off the electricity, then cut the lamp cord. They cast loose the cover lashing and lowered the cover plate. It did not quite go home; they had to readjust the strongback to make it center properly. The second time, the hatch cover slipped into place; Frazer screwed down the nut and together they tightened it with a large wrench.

An hour and a half had gone by. Both men had asked to be left alone to finish the job when their hour expired. Now they came up, with extra decompression to compensate for their overlong submersion.

One of our hardest tasks was done, a harder one it proved than we had anticipated. But in doing it, we lost one of our best men. Frazer never dived again. The strain in dragging that five-hundred-pound hatch cover while under the exhilaration of breathing highly compressed air had dilated his heart. Further work of any kind by Frazer underwater was out of the question.

XVI

A LOST DIVER

November was getting along towards its middle. The water was getting too cold to dive without gloves. The men were coming up with their hands numb and useless. Gloves we knew to be an encumbrance, but there was no escape. Without them, in five minutes a hand projecting from the tight rubber cuff of the diving suit (which in itself partly choked off circulation) became so stiff from cold that the owner was incapable of moving his fingers.

We cemented rubber mittens, canvas covered, onto the sleeves of the diving suits. These mittens were two-fingered affairs,—that is, the pockets took two fingers apiece, though the thumb was separate. It was necessary to wear a woolen glove inside the rubber one for warmth, the rubber and canvas mitten being only for watertightness. By the time all these gloves were on, it was nearly impossible to close the fingers or to handle tools, but without the gloves it was wholly impossible, so we accepted the lesser of two evils.

Divers were getting fewer. Some were lost for good, others were worn out or ill and temporarily unable to work. Even when the day was good enough to work, after a few hours we were forced to quit for lack of men.

We had, after our first trial with men who had no deep-water experience back of them, restricted the work to the eleven men we knew about—Eadie, Smith, Frazer, Eiben, Wilson, Bailey, Michels, Anderson, Carr, Ingram, and Kelley.

Under pressure of circumstances, we decided to try again some of the shallow-water divers and asked for volunteers. Several men indicated a willingness to try. We sent one petty officer, a torpedoman first class, down to secure a line to the bow of the submarine. He landed.

The pressure muddled his head. He glimpsed the bow diving planes, confused them with the rudders, and I was unable over the telephone to convince him that he was at the bow, not the stern. He came up finally without anything accomplished and no special desire to go down again.

We chose Eiben for a job inside the engine room, and picked L'Heureux, the most promising of the shallow-water men, to go down with him, stand on the deck, and tend Eiben's lines through the engine room hatch while Eiben worked inside.

We dressed them both and they went over shortly after noon, Eiben first. He slipped down the forward descending line, landed alongside the gun, went aft into the engine room. L'Heureux's helmet was screwed on. The tenders helped him to the stage, we swung him over the side, dropped a submarine lamp into his hand. L'Heureux disappeared. Shortly he reported:

"On the bottom!"

We turned attention to Eadie, who was being dressed to go down forward. About ten minutes later, Eadie was hoisted out, descended.

On the *Falcon*'s rail, three sets of tenders "fished" their divers' lines. Crouched in the superstructure, getting what shelter they could from the cold wind, three telephone talkers listened intently on the ship ends of the phones going to the divers below. I stood as usual near the telephones, Hartley near the tenders.

The silence was soon broken by Eiben's telephone man.

"Joe wants to know when L'Heureux is coming down with the light. He's waiting in the engine room and can't do a thing till he gets a light."

"Queer," I thought, "L'Heureux's been down there nearly fifteen minutes."

I called to L'Heureux's talker.

"Tell L'Heureux to go aft! Joe's waiting for the light!"

Seaman Schissel had L'Heureux's phone. He transmitted the message several times. Finally he called me.

"I can't get L'Heureux to acknowledge."

I took the telephone, listened a minute. I could hear air rushing through his helmet. I turned to the tender.

"How much line has L'Heureux out?"

"About two hundred and fifty feet. He's taken nearly a hundred since he landed. Still taking a little."

L'Heureux had taken enough line to get back to the engine room, more than enough probably. I called him.

"Hello, L'Heureux!" No answer. I turned to his tender.

"Give L'Heureux 'One' on his lifeline!"

The tender gave the line one jerk. (The signal meaning, "Are you all right?") No answering jerk came back. Something was wrong. I tried again on the telephone.

"H-E-L-L-O, L'HEUREUX!!"

A loud explosive "Ha!" seemed to be the answer.

"What's the matter?" Again I seemed to hear that "Ha!" I tried several times to get a reply, but each time my questions got only a loud "Ha!" in response.

I took Eadie's telephone.

"Hello, Tom!" He acknowledged at once.

"Did you see L'Heureux when you went down?"

I could hear Eadie turn off his air.

"He was standing at the descending line by the gun when I came down, holding up the light like the Statue of Liberty!" Eadie paused, turned on his air a moment to breathe, then shut it off again. "I clapped him on the back, asked him if he was all right. I thought he said 'Yes,' so I left him there and went forward on my own job." Eadie turned his air on again.

I waited a moment for him to catch his breath.

"Go aft and see if he's still there, Tom."

A few minutes went by. I asked Eiben if L'Heureux had shown up yet. No, he had not, Eiben was still waiting in the darkness. I ordered him up out of the engine room, told him to go forward and find L'Heureux.

Eadie called.

"On deck! He's not by the gun! Joe just got here. He says L'Heureux isn't aft."

What had become of him? We had a lifeline to him, but it was not safe to haul on that unless we knew he was clear. If he were fouled in anything, heaving on his line would make matters worse, might even cut his airhose.

Another call from Eadie.

"On deck! I think I see a light out on the bottom. Looks about one hundred feet off the sub's starboard beam and it's going farther away all the time!"

I told Eadie to slide down the submarine's side and chase the light. Evidently L'Heureux had fallen off the submarine and wandered off, trying to find it again.

Eadie started off across the sand, guided by the glimmer dimly visible through the water. Soon he caught up with L'Heureux, walking aimlessly along the ocean bottom, a number of fish swimming curiously about his light. Eadie turned him round, took his hand, led him back to the submarine. Eiben helped him pull L'Heureux back on deck.

It was useless to expect work from any of the trio on that dive. We lowered the stage to ninety feet, told them to stand by, hauled them all up to the stage, and started decompression.

Eiben and L'Heureux had been down fifty minutes, Eadie less time, but knowing that it was L'Heureux's first dive, we gave them all extra long decompression. Over two hours more went by before we hoisted in the stage and landed the three dripping figures on the deck in the darkness.

The bears rushed in. Lead shoes and belts went sailing in all directions; a few strong heaves and off came the helmets. I looked at L'Heureux curiously. Except for the fact that he appeared over-vivacious, he seemed all right. I asked him how he felt.

"Fine, Mr. Ellsberg!" He was positively bubbling over with mirth. Oxygen intoxication, I thought. I did not care to upset him by questioning about his mishap. Surgeon Flotte, specialist in the physiology of diving and our medical officer, strolled by, looked him over. The bears finished the undressing job; in their underwear the three divers went below, changed clothes hurriedly, sat down late at the supper table.

Five minutes later, without a word, L'Heureux slumped forward, unconscious. His knees doubled up, his face became distorted. The men near him dragged him from the table, rushed his tense form up the ladder and out the narrow passage along the deck to the recompression tank. They tossed him through the outer lock; Dr. Flotte scrambled in after, the heavy steel door was swung to. Dr. Flotte sprang for the air valve, opened it wide. Compressed air whistled through, the needle on the gauge mounted rapidly. Thirty pounds—forty—fifty. Flotte's ears began to ring. Sixty pounds. Blood started to flow from his mouth, but still the air roared through. He must get the pressure up on L'Heureux,—never mind himself. Seventy pounds. Still the valve stayed wide open, the needle kept on upwards. Eighty pounds. Enough! Dr. Flotte shut off the air, turned to bend over L'Heureux. He tore off his shirt. L'Heureux's chest was covered with purple splotches, caused by the bursting of innumerable small blood vessels. A bad case of "bends."

The surgeon straightened out his legs, worked over him with hot towels. The high pressure compressed the bubbles again, partly restored his circulation. He began to breathe more regularly. Gradually the doctor released part of the pressure, decompressing him again. But in spite of the fact that Surgeon Flotte worked over him all night, he failed to regain consciousness.

At 3 A.M., the doctor came out of the chamber, wan and weak. He said:

"If we're going to save L'Heureux's life, we've got to get him to a hospital!"

Lieutenant Hartley let go his mooring; soon the *Falcon* was making full speed towards Newport. At 7 A.M., she ran alongside the dock there, where an ambulance was waiting. L'Heureux went over the side in a stretcher.

That was in November. L'Heureux had been a man of average physique, weighing perhaps one hundred and sixty pounds. Partial paralysis set in as a result of "the bends." He wasted away to about seventy pounds and hovered between life and death for months. At last he won the fight. Late the next July, after eight months of struggle in the hospital, L'Heureux came out. He never dived again.

XVII

The Motor Room

I decided it was not worth trying to train inexperienced divers out on the wreck. We would have to proceed with the few men left.

Several days elapsed before we could work again. Then Wilson and Eiben went through the engine room to the motor room abaft it. Here they squeezed through the door, a task they were quite expert at by now, closed a large clapper valve in the ventilation main over the door, closed the other necessary valves on the bulkhead, and then, coming out, closed and dogged down the door. They came out, pushing aside the legs of the engineer officer as usual.

Kelley and Anderson followed them, went aft on the hull over the motor room. They split the nut off a bolt coming through the hull near the motor room hatch, drove the bolt through into the ship, tapped out the hole, and screwed a valve into the hole. To this they connected an airhose to the surface.

Following them, Eadie entered the engine room, picked out a valve on the four-inch drain line coming from the motor room, removed the bonnet from the valve, leaving the drain line open to the engine room. As soon as this was done, we started to blow air into the motor room through the air line Kelley had hooked up. Eadie reported he could feel a stream of water coming through the open valve into the engine room. There was a flapper valve in this line which prevented water from backing through it into the motor room.

Our blowing scheme worked nicely, but only for a brief time. Shortly air started to bubble out, water ceased flowing.

We searched for the reason. One of the *S-51* survivors enlightened us. There was a defective valve on the bulkhead. You could screw down the handle till it stopped, but the valve was still wide open.

77

Wilson and Eiben went down again, once more entered the engine room, undid the work they had done in dogging down the motor room door. Working overhead with Stillson wrenches, they uncoupled the bad valve. It was a slow job. They had to come out before they could put a plug in the line. They tried again next day. Wilson's exhaust valve worked badly and he could hardly keep himself from floating into the upper part of the motor room. With Eiben's help he managed to escape and both men came out. Two other divers tried to enter the motor room; they were unable to squeeze through the door.

Wilson and Eiben went down again, entered, managed to get the line plugged. Back through the door, which they closed and dogged tight for the second time. They started out, Eiben first. I had Wilson's telephone. They came to the engineer officer, his stockinged legs hanging down into the passage. Eiben shoved them aside, passed on. Wilson came up, paused. Evidently the situation was getting on his nerves. He addressed the dead engineer:

"Say you! If you don't rig in those legs, the next time I come along, I'll steal your garters!"

Wilson ducked clear, came out.

Once more we started blowing on the motor room. The water went lower this time, we were making good progress, when the ventilation clapper valve, unable to resist the growing pressure inside, sprang a little off its seat and released the air like a safety valve popping off. We had to abandon blowing. There were no means at hand for holding that valve tight, and indeed few divers left to employ them.

XVIII

WINTER

One day out of three had constituted our average for diving since we started work. Stormy weather put diving out of the question in several ways.

As the wind increased in an approaching storm, the strain grew on the windward mooring hawsers till they were taut as bowstrings. A diver on the bottom absolutely depends for his life upon his airhose. If it parts, he is gone,—left to die in his heavy diving rig when the little air remaining inside his helmet is used up. We had the diving hoses made up six hundred feet long, even though the water was but one hundred and thirty-five feet deep, so that if a mooring line parted or an anchor dragged, sweeping the *Falcon* away to leeward from her position over the *S-51*, we had some reserve airhose coiled down, which the tender could run out to the diver as we swung away, with the idea that the remaining moorings would hold the ship from going more than a few hundred feet before we could get the diver clear and started up.

But with men working inside the submarine, it was unlikely we could get them out if we were torn away. In spite of the reserve airhose we dared not take a chance on being carried away. And so when the wind came up, we always moved a tugboat, usually the *Iuka*, over to the windward side, anchored her there, and ran out an extra mooring hawser to her stern to help hold the *Falcon* up and relieve the strain on the other mooring lines. If the weather got worse, we anchored the *Sagamore* to windward of the *Iuka* with a line to the latter, and then both tugs served in tandem as moorings to hold the *Falcon*.

In this way, in spite of singing mooring lines and seas pounding our windward side, we were able to hang on and continue diving, once we had started, until the wind rose over thirty miles an hour, when the *Iuka* and *Sagamore,*—under the heavy strain on their lines to us—usually started to drag anchor and drift down on us. Whenever that happened, diving had to cease.

We tried to help matters by anchoring the *Vestal* on our weather side to act as a floating breakwater, but never with any great success. She was a large ship, but even so, when she headed into the sea, riding to her own anchor, she formed practically no lee for the *Falcon.* We tried anchoring the *Vestal* broadside, the better to break the wind for us, but in spite of anchors from both bow and stern, the wind hitting her broadside exerted such a force that her stern anchors soon dragged and she always ended by heading into the wind, in which position she was more of a danger than a help, for a big ship maneuvers slowly, and if she started to drag down on us, the storm might easily cause her to drift into and tear away our windward moorings before she could get clear.

With the seven anchors we had, and the use of the *Iuka* and *Sagamore* as portable moorings, we were able to hang on and dive in weather at least twice as bad as diving had ever been attempted before.

There was, however, another feature which made diving in a storm dangerous and uncomfortable to the diver. The pressure of the water on him depended on the depth he was at. While coming up on the decompression stage, he would be required to stand, we will say, twenty minutes at a depth of twenty feet, and he would consequently be subjected to a pressure there of ten pounds. Now when a wave fifteen feet high swept over him, the depth of water on him would for a moment be suddenly practically doubled, and so also would the pressure on him be suddenly increased. These quickly increasing and decreasing pressures as the waves swept by, alternately stretched the ear drums in and out and caused intense pain and severe headaches; a diver who had to stand decompression on the stage near the surface when the seas started to roll high always came in violently ill. This effect was also aggravated by the rolling and pitching of the *Falcon,* for the decompression stage, hanging from her boom, heaved up and down through the water as we rolled, and the poor diver standing on it one minute found himself near the surface and the next roll dropped him perhaps thirty feet down.

It was a particularly bad feature of our exposed location off Block Island, that even when the wind died out after a storm, the swells kept rolling in for a day or more later and prevented diving anyway. For a while we hoped that we might dive under such conditions from the

Vestal, which was steadier than the *Falcon,* but this had to be abandoned when we found that the divers were getting sick from the wave motion alone.

We struggled along, fighting the difficulties inside the submarine; fighting against lack of divers and sickness; fighting the sea which in our minds began to take on a definite personality with an apparent determination to cling to the vessel it had swallowed. The season advanced, the weather grew worse. We had averaged about one day's work in three since arriving; the twenty-first of November came in a storm which blew steadily and from then on, day after day, each morning broke on a wild gray sea. As the wind shifted we sought protection sometimes to the eastward of Block Island, sometimes to the westward of it, and finally were driven inside the stone breakwater forming the Harbor of Refuge at Point Judith, fifteen miles to the northward. Here we lay, as the days dragged on, unable to work, crowded and uncomfortable.

Finally came a smoother day, November 30, bitterly cold, but still calm enough. Ten days had gone by since last we dived. Our little squadron steamed out to the wreck, the *Falcon* sheered in among the buoys, the surfboat shuttled back and forth with the hawsers.

We moored, picked up the buoys to the descending lines. We had only four divers left.

Heavily muffled in woolen clothes and encased in windproof suits, the tenders and dressers worked in the biting cold to dress the first two men,—Eadie and Michels.

They were dressed, hoisted overboard, went down. We knew diving could continue but a few days more at the best. Eadie's job was to enter the engine room, make a last attempt to remove the body of the officer jammed over the port engine. Michels was to attend to Eadie.

"On the bottom!"

Eadie slipped through the hatch, Michels stood by it outside.

A minute went by. Michels called:

"On deck! There's something the matter with my air. I'm coming up."

We heaved on Mike's line. He needed no decompression for so brief a dive. We hauled him in, removed his helmet, tried the air valve. It seemed all right, though Michels said he had received air only in gusts.

Meanwhile I had a report from Eadie:

"I've got him by the legs, Mr. Ellsberg, but I can't pull him free! If I tie a line on him you could pull on him with the winch up there, but I think you'd pull him in half! He's stuck tight!"

"Never mind, Tom!" I yelled back. "Let him stay. Come on up!"

Eadie came out. He had been down only ten minutes; in twenty minutes more he was up, reported a little more fully.

"The water is awful cold down there, commander. It makes it hard to see, because the faceplates on the helmet all fog up from your breath."

I decided to secure the boat for the winter. Bailey, our smallest diver, was dressed, dropped over the side, went down to close the hatches on the submarine's deck, to seal up the boat as much as possible.

Bailey landed near the gun, started forward over the slippery deck to the open torpedo room hatch. Slowly the tender hanging over the *Falcon*'s rail paid out his air line as the trail of bubbles marking Bailey's progress streamed ahead, rose in great clusters through the waves, burst in a fine spray at the surface of the sea.

The clusters of bubbles seemed to grow smaller, then ceased altogether. The lines stopped running out. The tender "fished" them carefully to make sure there was no extra slack. Suddenly the line pulled through his hands again, four quick jerks, the emergency signal!

The tender hastily started to gather in all the slack, when the four jerks came again, feebler this time.

A cry from the tender: "Emergency signal from Bailey! Take him up!"

Eight bluejackets seized Bailey's line. With frozen fingers, as the cold water dripped from the wet lines, they heaved in, hand over hand, at top speed. Bailey had been down only a few minutes, there was no need for decompression; no need for anything but haste. The stage was swung over the side, two men on it, lowered till they stood waist deep in icy water. The tenders hauled, Bailey appeared at the surface, limp, his suit clinging to his body. The men in the water dragged his weighted form onto the stage, the winchman threw in his clutch, jerked the stage and its occupants in on deck. The dressers ripped off Bailey's helmet; his usually light face was blue and distorted, he was nearly unconscious. He murmured weakly:

"No air, no air!"

Bailey was carried into "the iron doctor" given a little pressure, wrapped in hot blankets.

We tried his airhose. Nothing blew through. We increased the pressure. A block of ice blew through, then others, cylindrically shaped to suit the inside of his hose. The cold air going down to Bailey had been further chilled in its passage through the long lead of airhose submerged in ice cold water, the moisture in the air had condensed out, frozen solid, plugged his airhose.

For the moment, the sea had won. We dared not risk further diving. With but few men left and the winter storms upon us, our chance to work was gone. Sadly we pulled up our mooring buoys and anchors, planted a buoy heavily anchored against the bow of the submarine as a marker and dragged the whistling buoy a little closer to the stern to serve as an additional mark.

Then the expedition disbanded. The *Vestal*, the *Falcon*, and the *S-50* went south to join the fleet. The other vessels returned to New York.

XIX

A DIVING SCHOOL

It was driven home on me that if the *S-51* were ever to rise, we were going to need many more divers than we had had. Consequently before the expedition separated, I gathered together on the *Falcon* all the men who had ever had any experience in diving in shallow water. There were some twenty-five of these, seamen and petty officers, who had been sent to us in the beginning as divers. They had served throughout the operation as dressers, tenders, and repairmen, but none of them had actually dived, since L'Heureux's sad experience made it look unwise. These men were all much younger than the group who had done the work so far, but their actual diving experience, even in shallow water, was small.

Surgeon Flotte examined the group. Twenty-two of the men he found physically qualified. These men, together with myself, entered the recompression tank for a pressure test. The surgeon ran the pressure up on us in the tank, a few pounds at a time. At forty pounds, two of the men showed signs of difficulty and they were removed through the air lock. On the rest of us, the pressure was raised to seventy pounds (equivalent to a depth of about one hundred and sixty feet). The remaining twenty men stood this pressure a few minutes without undue symptoms of distress. After examining our hearts and lungs, the surgeon passed us all as qualified for work at the depth in which lay the *S-51*.

When the other ships and divers sailed for Cuba, I kept the twenty men selected for training and started a diving school at the New York Navy Yard.

As instructor, I had Chief Torpedoman John Kelley, who had done excellent work on the submarine and was exceptionally fitted by temperament and previous experience to teach the men. We had a steel tank sixteen feet deep set up in the shipfitter shop; this was fitted with glass ports near the bottom through which the diver could be watched.

There were two primary objects in the training course. The first was to make each man thoroughly at home in a diving suit, so that he could work in any position underwater without having to devote his conscious endeavors merely to keeping himself out of trouble. The second aim was to make each diver able to work with tools underwater so that he might accomplish useful work.

Aside from the need of having more divers, it was also evident that we needed some method of cutting metal underwater if we were to overcome the numerous obstacles to working on the submarine. To this end, I desired to design and develop a torch that would actually cut steel submerged, and to train myself and other divers to use it successfully. To help on this, I also kept with me Chief Torpedoman Frazer and Boatswain's Mate Carr. Frazer had strained his heart and could do no deep diving, but in the shallow tank his diving skill was invaluable during the experiments.

The school started in early December. Wholly forgetting the diving part, the students were given a course in handling air drills, using chipping hammers, running caulking irons, cutting out rivets, and doing various pipe fitting and plumbing jobs with Stillson wrenches. For this work, the mechanics in the Navy Yard were the instructors. No man was allowed to start diving till he showed a fair mastery of the tools. It was obvious that if he could not perform a job satisfactorily in the air and on land, it was hopeless to expect him to do it when hampered by the many difficulties encountered in a diving suit.

So we all drilled innumerable holes in steel plates, cut out rivets, caulked leaks, made and unmade unions, unbolted flanges, assembled valves. Each man became a jack-of-all-trades, for that is what the diver must be.

After a week of intensive tool work, we filled the tank with water and diving commenced. Kelley instructed us thoroughly in the machinery of the diving suit; showed us how to adjust our buoyancy; explained the dangers of "blowing up" and of a "squeeze"; outlined the many other dangers encountered underwater and the best ways to meet them. One by one we dived in the tank, dropped sixteen feet to the bottom. There we practiced adjustments of buoyancy, kneeling, lying down. We tried lightening ourselves by inflating our suits till we were practically ready to float up; and getting "heavy" by bleeding out as much air as we dared in order to get as heavy as possible to stay in position against a strong current.

I found this last trick, which borders on an incipient "squeeze," a most unusual sensation. It is done by shutting off completely the flow of fresh air at the control valve over the left breast, then opening the exhaust valve on the back of the helmet somewhat wider and slowly permitting the air in the suit to escape. As the pressure inside the helmet decreases with the escape of air, the water outside starts to press in on the body, starting on the legs first and gradually working upward. It is as if one were being tightly embraced, hugged all over, and the hug creeps up the body and grows tighter and tighter as the air goes out. When the hugged feeling reaches the chest, it is time to close the exhaust and prevent the loss of any more air. Failure to do so will result in cracked ribs as the water grips you tightly around the body; and the loss of all the air will result in a "squeeze" which even in relatively shallow water is sure to be fatal.

In the tank we were purposely taught to come near the danger line in every operation, that we might afterwards be able to recognize how far we could safely go. And so we "blew ourselves up," took minor "squeezes," allowed water to leak into our suits.

When we were familiar with the diving technique, we started using tools underwater, and I learned at first hand how hampered the diver is in carrying out the simplest task while submerged.

By early January, I was fairly well at home in the water; my underwater torch was designed, and I started experimenting with it. It worked beautifully from the start; we had no difficulty lighting it, and after a little experience found we could cut steel underwater nearly as fast as on the surface. Kelley and I both became expert in its use; but perversely enough, Frazer, who was never going to be able to use it on the submarine, surpassed us both in speed. On a steel plate one inch thick, Frazer cut thirteen feet of steel in ten minutes,—about a foot every forty-five seconds. It was beautiful, looking through the porthole in the tank, to watch Frazer slicing through the steel plates.

We worked along, diving every day. By the end of January, the diving class was reduced from twenty men to twelve, but these twelve gave every promise of being good divers. All young, they were getting to feel at home in their suits, and they were able to make fair progress on underwater jobs.

Through the Navy Department, I made arrangements to have the diving class sent south at the end of January to join the *Falcon,* which was then with the fleet off Panama. We could do no outdoor diving in winter around New York; besides we had no deep water there. I desired to have the students start diving in deeper water to accustom themselves to it, and in the tropics even in January, conditions were ideal to finish their training before spring.

With Kelley as their instructor, the twelve remaining student divers sailed for Panama. I stayed in New York with Frazer and Carr, and kept up in the tank, where we practised with the torch.

In early March, I received a letter from the *Falcon.* The men had been aboard nearly a month, but not once had any one of them been able to make a dive. The admiral commanding totally ignored the character of the *Falcon* as a rescue ship; she was kept constantly employed as a minesweeper, as a tender for the submarines, and as a tugboat for towing or other uses. That she had an unfinished job in raising the *S-51* to prepare for and that divers on board urgently needed training for that task was something the admiral was not interested in. The *Falcon* was given no opportunity to train her men.

After some hasty correspondence which showed it was hopeless to expect anything else, I had the diving class detached from the *Falcon* and sent north again to resume their training in the tank. They arrived late in March, not having been in the water since leaving New York. Seven valuable weeks were lost.

Early in April, we started diving outdoors, in the Navy Yard basin. The water there was cold, muddy, and somewhat deeper than in the tank. We could get thirty-five feet in the basin, and best of all the visibility was so poor that it accustomed the men to working under actual conditions. We used the regular diving barge as our base, and worked from morning until night to catch up the lost diving days.

At the same time, orders went out for the reassembly of the salvage squadron. All vessels were ordered to rendezvous at New York on April 15, to refit for the expedition. The *S-50* was excepted, as we felt familiar enough with the job to dispense with her at the start.

Meanwhile, I combed the records more carefully and managed to pick up a few additional divers, qualified for wrecking work. We got the yard diver from Boston, Joe Madden; and a chief torpedoman, Sanders, from the submarine flotilla at Panama. We were to have all the divers except Ingram we had before, now recuperated,—Eadie, Michels,

Smith, Wilson, Bailey, Carr, George Anderson, Eiben, and Kelley. Then there were twelve men in the diving class, including myself, making a total of twenty-four divers to start the job,—over twice as many as we had originally had.

The middle of April, the *Falcon* and the *Vestal* came into the yard. Quickly we put aboard them the special equipment, boats, and stores needed. We mobilized the divers from their various stations and received a draft of forty extra seamen to act as dressers, tenders, and working party.

XX

LOST, A SUBMARINE

On April 23, 1926, the *Falcon*, carrying the divers, sailed for the wreck. We had better equipment than before, more divers; but we also knew better our enemy the sea and it was a grim group that sailed out of New York harbor on the second expedition. We stopped at Narragansett Bay to inspect our pontoons and the derrick *United States*; then on April 26 we steamed out to the wreck.

The sea had a new surprise for us. Weekly during the winter, a tug from Newport had gone out, inspected our marker buoys, found them safe and in position. The last inspection had come only four days before.

Now, however, as we approached the buoys, we found them five miles apart, the whistling buoy to the southeast of the other one. The blank gray sea rolled in between. Which buoy was correct? We could not tell. Perhaps neither was. The weather was a little hazy. From the *Falcon*'s low masts we could not make out land in any direction to get our bearings. We asked for radio compass bearings from various stations along the coast. We made our radio call steadily,—the stations radioed back our bearings from them. We plotted the positions given. They varied over several miles of ocean—some placed us near one buoy, some near the other. They were not accurate enough for our purposes. We steamed to the southeast and examined the whistling buoy carefully. It seemed as if it were slowly dragging its anchor. We decided it was probably out of position, steamed back to the other buoy.

Here we anchored and hoisted out our surfboat. Boatswain Hawes started to sweep the ocean floor with a grappling hook. All day he dragged, but caught nothing. We worked all around the buoy in widening circles. As evening came, the prospect was depressing. Even using a wide sweep between two ships, there was a tremendous expanse of ocean bottom to cover between those two widely separated buoys. We might be at it for weeks.

Next morning the *Vestal* arrived and anchored nearby. I hurriedly boarded her, sought out the navigator, Lieutenant Sauer. He had the exact latitude and longitude of the wreck, taken the autumn before.

We climbed the *Vestal*'s mast. From that high point, we could make out to the westward Southeast Light on Block Island; to the northward, Point Judith Light; and to the northeastward, Gay Head Light far away on Martha's Vineyard. Carefully we measured the angles between the lights with our sextants, laid out the angles on a three-armed protractor, and swung the protractor over the chart till each arm cut through its proper lighthouse there. We pricked the chart through the center of the protractor; the *Vestal*'s position plotted a quarter of a mile west of the point where the *S-51* lay; the marker buoy apparently was one hundred yards north of it.

With our new position, Hawes ran the surfboat over the indicated location of the ship, and started to drag on an east and west course, as the submarine lay on a line approximately north and south.

Boatswain Hawes grappled all morning without success. Shortly after noon, we put Kelley over from the *Falcon* for a walk, hoping he might find the submarine. He made a circle of about one hundred feet diameter on the bottom but saw no part of the *S-51*. He did, however, bring up some encouraging news. He had run across several heaps of tin cans on the bottom. Apparently we were over old anchorage grounds.

Hawes and the surfboat kept on sweeping. Late in the afternoon, they made a hard strike with their grappling hook. The *Falcon* steamed over, anchored, took the grappling line. Joe Eiben was dressed, hoisted over, slid down the line.

"On the submarine!" he reported. With a cheer, I threw my cap in the air, caught it, jammed it on again. The anxiety of the two days of searching vanished. At least we had found our submarine.

Eiben made a hasty inspection, then cut loose the grappling hook, tied the line to the gun, and came up. The submarine was lying exactly as we had left her on the last November day when Bailey froze his air lines. She was still heeled badly to port, was partly buried in the clay, was considerably more slippery to stand on.

Work started with a rush. We planted our moorings once more, seven anchors in a circle about the boat. The *Sagamore* steamed away to recover the whistling buoy; the Lighthouse tender came out and replanted it with a heavier anchor.

We dropped a thermometer on a line to the bottom, and obtained the temperature. It was 37° F., a little colder than when we left. The divers would have to keep on wearing their cumbersome gloves.

Looking around, we saw the old familiar scene,—the sea restlessly tumbling by, our little fleet heaving at their anchors, a few gulls circling round, the whistling buoy sending out its doleful note as it rose to each passing wave, a glimpse of low-lying land on the distant westward horizon; far below us, the *S-51* lying quietly in the calm peace of the ocean floor, firmly gripped with her cargo of dead by the cold sea.

XXI

PONTOONS AGAIN

Our first endeavor was to lower pontoons once more to the stern. I had a new method. From Boston we obtained a twelve-inch hawser, strong enough to hold the weight of the pontoon even when totally flooded. But there was no intention of letting the pontoon get full. I figured that if we held the pontoon firmly at each end till it just submerged, let the water keep flowing in till the strain on the lowering hawsers reached about five tons, and then shut the flood valves, so no more water could enter while we lowered, we could let the pontoon go down slowly and evenly under control. There would still be the tendency of the pontoon to stand on end if the free water inside all ran to one end or the other, but by using a hawser strong enough for any strain we could hold the pontoon level in spite of that.

On April 30, the *Falcon* steamed in and moored. The *Sagamore*, with a pontoon in tow, came out from Newport. Michels and Kelley went down, passed small manila reeving lines under the stern. We rove around, down one side of the submarine, up the other side, and finished up finally with two one-inch wire lines cut just long enough to handle the chains in lowering. The divers came up; the pontoon was brought alongside the *Falcon*, rigged for lowering. We shackled our heavy lowering hawsers into strong wire straps (endless loops made by splicing together the two ends of a short piece of heavy wire), the wire straps being secured to each end of the pontoon.

The flood valves were opened, flooding began. We secured the two wire guide lines under the submarine's stern to the lower ends of the chain hanging from the pontoon and took in all the slack.

As before, to prepare for contingencies, Hartley held the *Falcon* well

92

clear of the submarine's port quarter, where the first pontoon was to go. The pontoon slowly flooded and sank lower and lower, heaving slowly up and down against our side as the waves rolled by. We slacked out our hawsers to prevent straining than.

Meanwhile we rigged out two stages, one suspended over each end of the pontoon. On these were to stand the men, who with long extension T-handled socket wrenches were to screw down on the flood valves after the pontoon was underwater. We could not use divers for that purpose; there was too much danger of their being caught between the pontoon and the *Falcon*.

The weather was moderate, as good as we could normally hope for, but still there was considerable motion on, and the huge cylinder alongside us moved up and down about four feet as it rose and fell. We kept on flooding, the pontoon grew more "loggy" as it lost buoyancy, soon it submerged, first at one end, then at the other. We held the hawsers on the bitts; the hawsers stretched a little, the pontoon hung three or four feet below the surface.

It was estimated to take about one minute to let the necessary extra water run in.

Badders and Weaver stood by on the stages, their extension wrenches on the valve rods, ready to close them. (Thirteen complete turns were required on each valve to close it.)

Trouble started. The pontoon, its huge mass giving it tremendous inertia, lay dead just below the surface, unmoved by the waves passing over it, but each time the *Falcon* rolled away, the hawsers took up with a snap as they came taut, then slackened slightly as the *Falcon* rolled toward the pontoon. The splices in the wire straps worked as the strains alternated, and gave a little with each jerk.

I yelled to the stages: "Close the valves!"

It was too late. Before either man could get more than a few turns on his valve, an extra heavy jerk pulled apart the wire splice to the forward end of the pontoon. The cylinder promptly took a vertical position, hung a moment on its end, then the other wire strap, now taking all the strain, let go on the next roll. The free ends of the hawsers, with the strains released, shot back on deck. A little cloud of spray, a few waves, and the pontoon disappeared, end first. We took in what slack we could on the hauling wires.

Our second attempt to lower a pontoon had resulted in another failure.

The weather was too bad for further diving.

Next day, Bailey dived to find out how matters were below. He located the pontoon about thirty feet outboard of the stern and a little forward of it, standing vertically on one end. The chains led from it to the port quarter of the *S-51*, and the hauling wires ran clear, rising from under the starboard quarter, to the surface. The situation was not so bad. No serious damage had been done to the pontoon, we had missed the submarine, and the lines seemed all clear. I resolved to attempt to get the pontoon into position alongside the stern.

It was first necessary to have the pontoon in a normal position,—horizontal. The two airhoses to the pontoon were still attached to it. Niedermair blew gently into the lower half of the pontoon till it lightened enough to capsize. Then we took a good strain with our winches on the wire hauling lines, while Niedermair slowly blew air into both ends of the pontoons. When the pontoon became buoyant enough to show signs of floating up, we heaved round smartly on the winches and dragged the lightened cylinder over the sea bottom in close to the port side of the submarine's stern. When we could get no more slack on either hauling line, we vented the air from the pontoon, allowing it to reflood, and then sent Eiben down to examine it. He found the pontoon lying practically in the position originally intended.

This operation took all that day. The following morning, with the weather a little better, the *Iuka* towed out a second pontoon. We rove our two wire lines coming up from the *S-51* through the hawsepipes of this pontoon and hauled them moderately taut to serve as guides on which to lower.

We secured our lowering hawsers to the ends of the pontoon again, except that in place of the spliced wire straps which had failed us, we now used heavy iron rings which the *Vestal*'s blacksmith had forged out during the night. The deck force connected up the airhoses, vent hoses, and opened up the flood valves. The pontoon started to fill. As usual, the *Falcon* was hauled a little clear of the submarine, to starboard this time.

We swung out the stages. Badders and Weaver secured their wrenches to the flood valve rods, and then as the pontoon went awash, leaped from it to the stages.

I waited, watch in hand, a little nervous. The pontoon submerged, the lowering hawsers started to strain. But I must wait one minute to be sure the pontoon got heavy enough to go down evenly. The men on the stages stood poised, the seconds slowly ticked away, the pontoon by the way it strained on the hawsers seemed already far overweight. One minute.

"Close the valves!"

Carefully Weaver and Badders turned, peering down through the water as they worked to make sure their sockets did not slip off the valve stems. Thirteen times the wrenches revolved.

"After valve closed!" sang out Badders.

"Forward valve closed!" repeated Weaver.

Each man gave an extra twist to make sure, then pulled up his extension wrench. The stages were swung in on deck.

I took position at the forward bitts, where my hawser was coiled in figures of eight over the horns. Hartley stood by the after line. The hawsers were marked with a colored ring of paint every fathom, alternately red, blue, yellow, and white.

A few feet below the surface, the pontoon hung from the side, already its outline vague and ill defined.

"Stand by!" The men at the bitts stood ready. Hartley kept his eye on me.

"Lower together!" At the forward bitts the men slacked a little on the hawser; the turns rendered around the bitts, went overboard. A few inches at a time they paid out, till the first fathom was gone.

"Hold it!" They laid back on their end of the line. The turns gripped on the bitts, the line stopped.

"How's your line, Hartley?"

"On the first red!" he replied.

We each had one fathom out. The pontoon was no longer visible.

"Lower together!" Again the lines were slowly rendered out over the bitts. The first blue, the first yellow, and the first white rings went out, when we held again to check. My men were a few feet ahead of Hartley's. He ran out several feet to even up, and then once again we both lowered.

We could feel the lines stretch as the *Falcon* rolled away from the pontoon, and shorten a little as she rolled towards it, but it was not a bad day and our heavy hawsers stood the test beautifully. And so, fathom by fathom, we paid out from the *Falcon*, till the pontoon was sixteen fathoms down, and should have been just above the submarine. We held it then.

Wilson was standing by dressed, all but his helmet. This the tenders screwed on and hoisted him overboard. He slipped down the airhoses secured to the pontoon and landed on it. He walked to the after end of the pontoon, looked over but could see nothing through the water.

"On deck! Nothing in sight yet. Lower some more!" We lowered gradually till Wilson could make out the hull of the submarine below him. We paused a moment, while he got his bearings.

"On deck! She's just clear of the side, but too far aft. You'll hit the diving rudders. Take her forward five feet!"

We hauled ahead on the *Falcon*'s bow moorings, slacked a trifle on the stern lines, till Wilson reported clear. Then we lowered again, till the strain was lost on the hawsers. We had finally planted a pontoon alongside the submarine, just where we wanted it. Wilson checked the pontoon's position, then cast loose the lowering lines at each end by tripping the pelican hooks shackled into the iron rings. We hauled up the hawsers, which came in on deck swelled a little from their immersion.

Wilson was hauled up.

The next business was to see that enough chain was showing through each of the hawsepipes so that we could get the locking bars through the chains at the right points. This was important. The two chains formed the cradle in which the stern of the submarine was to be suspended. The chains were already secured on top of the first pontoon of the pair by heavy clamps, put on before that pontoon was lowered, with the chains hanging from it. We had lowered the second pontoon on the other ends of those chains, dragged under the submarine by the guide wires. We had to pull enough chain through to make the cradle the desired length, and then lock the chains over the top of the last pontoon.

Michels went down to examine this. Both chains were not far enough through, so we heaved on the hauling wires, one at a time, and dragged more chain up through each hawsepipe till twenty extra links showed through above each hawsepipe. We were then ready to secure the chains.

How to lock the chains over the pontoons on the bottom of the sea was a problem that had given us all considerable worry. In shallow water when the pontoons were first used, the chains had originally been secured by heavy split steel clamps, bolted together over one of the links. But each clamp weighed about three hundred pounds, and juggling it into position was difficult. In Honolulu harbor, where the water was shallow, quiet, and warm, it had taken several divers a number of hours to secure the clamps; in deep water we dared not let the divers exert themselves lifting heavy weights. In addition, there was no practical method of holding the chain vertical and steady while the divers tried to bolt up a clamp; suspended from the *Falcon*, the chain would move steadily up and down some six to eight feet as the *Falcon* rolled. A diver standing on a pontoon resting on the sea bottom would have no chance of fitting a three-hundred-pound clamp on the chain as it swung up and down. Besides, there was an excellent chance that the heavy chain as it swung to the *Falcon*'s motions would hit the diver and knock him off the pontoon, if nothing worse.

The clamp method seemed impracticable for us. A better method was to slip a heavy steel bar through a link of the chain just above the hawsepipe, the bar being long enough to bridge across the hawsepipe hole, and heavy enough to stand the forty-ton lifting load on the chain without bending.

This method looked feasible, but to get the bar through a link of the anchor cable, it was necessary to burn out the steel stud in the center of the link. These studs are fitted into each link of an anchor cable to prevent the chain from kinking and jamming; we could not afford to remove the studs before lowering the chain for fear it might kink up in the process of reeving under the submarine.

With the new underwater torch, the task became possible. Where the bar was to go through, the stud could be burned out of the chain as it lay on top of the pontoon; then the toggle could be slipped in the link and locked in position.

The toggle bars were made of special nickel steel; each bar was forty inches long, and weighed one hundred and forty pounds. The ends of the bars were wedge shaped, to facilitate slipping them into the link. Each bar had drilled through it two small parallel holes near its center; through these holes when the bar was entered in the chain link were to be secured two long half-inch bolts, one each side of the link, so that thereafter the toggle bar could not slip back out of the link.

XXII

My First Dive

The second pontoon lay alongside the starboard quarter of the *S-51*, the chains hauled up through the hawsepipes, ready to be secured. Two toggle bars were lashed to the top of the pontoon, waiting to be inserted in the chain. The time had come to put in practical use the new torch.

I elected to go down to do the first burning. Chief Torpedoman Kelley, the only other man familiar with the torch, was to assist.

In my stateroom, I pulled on the usual three suits of blue woolen underwear and three pairs of socks. Looking quite fat with all this on, I came to the dressing bench on the quarterdeck, where the bears started on me. I put on my woolen gloves, slipped into the diving dress. With difficulty I worked my hands down the stiff sleeves and into the rubber mittens. Lead shoes, lead belt, copper breastplate—the weights became burdensome. The telephone receivers were strapped over my ears, I tested out my telephone. A helmet was dropped over my head, given a quarter turn and locked tightly in position. I looked out through the glass faceplates, tried my air valve, tested the exhaust valve. I could not see it, but I felt for the knife on my belt,—always the diver's first concern.

With the helmet on, I could hardly rise. Two bears assisted me to the stage (Kelley had already gone down). I grasped the bails and was swung over the side. A last glimpse of the *Falcon* in the sunlight, the stage was in the water, was being lowered till the waves broke over my helmet. Air began to gurgle out the exhaust valve near the back of my head. The stage paused a moment to give me a chance to test my equipment in the water.

I opened the control valve wider and gave myself a trifle more air. A moment went by; apparently everything in my rig was working properly. I saw the torch dangling in the water in front of my faceplate. I grasped it, slipped the lanyard holding it over my left arm.

"All right!" I bellowed into the telephone transmitter. On deck the tender took in the slack of my lifeline. I stepped off the stage onto nothing, and dangling me by my lifelines, the tenders dragged me forward along the side of the *Falcon* some twenty feet to where the descending line led downward. I grasped this line with both hands, wound my legs around it, took one last look upward at the silvery surface of the sea, gently undulating over my head.

"Lower away!"

They slacked off. I began to descend. The bright light quickly faded to a deeper blue as I sank, the air roared through my helmet. Down, down, it seemed a long way. It was early spring, the water was clearer than it would ever be again that year. I kept my gaze downward, but could see nothing. Down I slid, the light constantly getting dimmer. Would I never reach the bottom? The pressure increased. I began to breathe more rapidly, the air started to feel different, heavy. Then gradually there took shape, dimly outlined against a dark formless background, the stern of the *S-51* below me, peacefully resting. As it loomed up, magnified considerably in the water, it looked perfectly huge. My heart sank. How puny our efforts and our strength were to move such a mass!

That thought passed in a flash, to be succeeded by a thrill. At last I was seeing with my own eyes the object of our labors! With my own eyes I was finally to do something to start that submarine once again to the world above!

Another moment, and my feet touched something. I was standing on top of the cylindrical pontoon. Fifteen feet away was the hull of the *S-51*. At the other end of the pontoon I could see Kelley, looking about ten feet high.

I took a step towards him, along the rounded top of the pontoon, then stopped. My head began to feel very light, queer. I braced my feet a little apart, tried to steady myself. Never in my life had I ever fainted but now my head felt dizzy, my heart strange. I felt that it would be only a matter of seconds before I collapsed. My lifeline floated across the faceplate of my helmet. I fumbled for it, wondered whether I still had strength enough to give the emergency signal to be hauled up, before I passed out. My knees felt weak, my head swam. But there passed across my mind the thought that there were twelve new divers like myself on the *Falcon*; none had yet been down. It would set them a fine example to have their officer ask to be hauled up on his first dive!

I resolved not to signal,—it was better to go up unconscious.

I staggered, grew fainter. Kelley's figure danced before my eyes, a grotesque giant. It occurred to me that as I was still conscious, I might as well do something while I could. Slowly I pushed through the water toward Kelley, came to the first chain, a few links on top of the hawsepipe, the rest hanging down the curved side of the pontoon. I knelt down, Kelley came toward me. I fumbled for the torch dangling from my left arm, lifted it in front of my faceplate. One by one, I turned on the air, the oxygen, the hydrogen, adjusted the valves. A stream of gas under high pressure hissed from the tip of the torch. I raised the electric lighter.

"Turn on the igniter!" I shouted into my telephone. My head began to clear. Apparently I was getting a little adjusted to the pressure, and doing something was taking my mind off how queer I felt.

I held the igniter in front of the torch, pressed the contacts together, let them go.

As they separated, a spark leaped across the gap. There was a sharp explosion, a ball of orange-colored flame appeared, glowing brightly in the water. It burned with a roar like the exhaust of a high speed motor with no muffler. I adjusted the valves, shortened the flame a bit, pulled the trigger on the torch, and watched the flame lengthen suddenly as a jet of high pressure oxygen spurted through it. I released the trigger; the flame returned to normal.

And so had I. The dizziness was gone. I thanked my stars I had not signaled to be hauled up.

I looked around. Kelley was kneeling on the other side of the chain, pointing to the third link from the hawsepipe. He pulled the link a bit, making it lie flatter with the stud more exposed.

I leaned over the link. The stud, a square piece of iron about two inches thick, was firmly gripped between the two sides of the chain link. I brought the tip of the torch close to one edge, with the flame playing against the corner of the iron. In a moment the iron glowed bright red. I pressed the trigger. An oxygen jet, spurting through the center of the flame, hit the glowing spot. The iron ignited.

A beautifully pure white stream of fire shot several feet through the water, with a mass of fine sparks flying off from it,—a sight stranger and more brilliant than any fireworks exhibition I had ever seen.

In way of the oxygen jet, the iron vanished, leaving a gap perhaps an eighth of an inch wide. Slowly, carefully, I drew the torch across the stud, cutting through the two-inch thickness of iron. In less than a minute it was done, the cut was complete. The severed halves of the stud dropped out of the link.

I released the trigger, turned off all the valves. A warm glow went through my veins. The torch was a success! Many jobs previously impossible to us underwater would now yield to that magic flame!

"On deck!" I yelled. "Take up the torch!" I waited a moment, got four jerks on the torch hoses, let go, and watched the torch and the igniter vanish upwards through the water.

I looked again at the pontoon. Kelley had his knife out, cutting away the lashings of one of the toggle bars. He got it free. Together we dragged the bar over the top of the slippery cylinder we were standing on. Kelley entered the tapered end into the open link where the stud had fallen out. He pushed the bar through a few inches but it refused to go farther. The chain was lying at such an angle to the pontoon that on the other side of the link, the toggle bar was digging into the pontoon sheathing and refused to slide through.

We tried to roll the chain so that the bar could go through, but there was nearly a ton of chain hanging down the side of the pontoon beyond the toggle bar; on the other side the chain vanished down the hawsepipe.

That anchor cable, designed to hold a battleship, was nothing we could budge with only our hands. Time was going fast; we had to get the bar in.

I drew Kelley's helmet against mine.

"You lean on it, Kelley, I'll kick it through!" He nodded.

Kelley made himself heavy by releasing as much air as he dared, then pressed both hands down on the long end of the toggle bar. I sat down on the pontoon, and braced myself, my lead-soled shoes against the free end of the toggle.

Kelley suddenly pressed all his weight on the bar, momentarily twisting the links a trifle and lifting the buried end clear of the pontoon. Simultaneously I kicked out, brought the lead sole of my shoe against the end of the bar, drove it through about an inch. Kelley pressed again, I kicked again. Bit by bit we drove it through, till twenty inches of the toggle showed on the other side.

Kelley let go, I got up. He cut away the two small locking bolts hanging by marline lanyards to a nearby eyebolt. We pushed one pin through the toggle bar on each side of the link, screwed down the nuts to hold the pins from dropping out. The first toggle bar was secured.

Together we rose, moved slowly to the descending line tied to the forward end of the pontoon. Over the phone I reported we were done. We looked carefully up our lifelines to see that we were clear of each other, and not foul of anything else.

There came four jerks on Kelley's lines. He answered with four, took hold of the descending line. The tenders above heaved, I watched Kelley ascend, a stream of bubbles widening out in a cone above him marking his progress for a few feet. Then he faded from view.

Alone, I looked toward the submarine. The after end of my pontoon was just touching the diving rudder guard. Lying against the side of the submarine opposite me was the end of the heavy wire hawser with which the derricks had made their futile effort to lift the stern. It had caught on something, the wreckers had not been able to haul it free.

The submarine herself looked perfect. No rust, the paint was all intact in spite of six months' submergence; there was only a very fine marine growth, like moss perhaps, covering the hull. A numerous array of frayed and broken manila lines hung draped over the sides,— remnants of our many descending lines and the hundreds of fathoms of manila the divers had used for various jobs so far.

My observations were interrupted by a jerk, four of them in fact. The signal to stand by to rise. I seized my airhose, jerked it four times, then took hold of the descending line. In a moment, a powerful tug came on my lines, I was lifted off my feet and started up, a few feet at a time, as the tenders hauled hand over hand. I lightened myself somewhat by holding more air in my suit to make it easier for them.

I was dragged up some forty feet, when I heard an order, "Look out for the stage!"

I kicked myself around the descending line, looking all around. About five feet above me was the stage, with Kelley standing on it.

"Take me up a little more!" They pulled, I caught the triangular steel bails which supported the stage, clambered on it. Kelley leaned over, unscrewed the shackle pin which held the descending line against the stage. The line slipped away, clear, and left us swinging freely from the *Falcon*'s boom, ninety feet below the surface.

Kelley was an experienced diver. He was doing every conceivable form of the "Daily Dozen,"—knee bends, arm swings, body rolls—to help his circulation and accelerate his decompression. I followed suit. It made me smile. There we were, buried in the sea, two ludicrous figures engaged in calisthenics while the fish swam round in wonderment. It was too bad we could not tune in on some radio, broadcasting setting up exercises, that we might have a little music to enliven things.

I paused. For the first time I noticed that I had considerable moisture in my suit. My underwear was soaked from the waist down, water oozed out between my toes while I exercised.

It was the old story. While I leaned over the chain to burn through the stud, the water had leaked by on one side of my exhaust valve while the air was escaping from the other side. I had not observed it in the excitement of working on my first dive. Now that everything was over, the clammy feeling of soaked clothing round my legs and cold water round my feet was decidedly unpleasant. I began to feel the chill of the sea surrounding me. I had nearly two hours to wait before I emerged. Exercise was imperative if I were not to freeze. I started the "knee stoops" again, vigorously.

After that, I tried kicking out, one foot at a time, but I found that shoes which weighed thirty pounds were not lightly flung around. I decided to keep both feet on the stage.

A call on the phone:

"Going up!"

We seized the bails and held on tightly. The water seemed to stream down past us. The stage rose twenty feet, stopped. We would stay awhile at seventy feet depth.

Again we started exercising. It grew monotonous. I could hear Kelley singing to himself, vociferously. I started a monologue about nothing in particular. Now I understood why the divers when below swore so volubly. In that solitude any sound was a relief, profanity a safety valve to relieve the strain.

And so, ten feet at a time, we rose slowly to the *Falcon*. At last, at the ten-foot depth, we could see the surface, like a silvery sheet waving over us, the red hull of the *Falcon* close alongside. And finally, the welcome word:

"Coming aboard!"

The stage line creaked, we burst through the surface. Suddenly our suits, no longer buoyed up by the water, became very heavy. We clung to the bails to support ourselves as the swaying stage rose above the bulwarks, swung in, and dropped on deck. I felt a bench jammed in behind me, a pair of hands on my shoulders pressing me down. Thankfully I seated myself.

Two bears grasped my helmet, two others seized my shoulders, held them firmly. A heavy twist on the copper headpiece broke the joint, the helmet gave a quarter turn, was carefully lifted over my head. I took a deep breath, the glory of the sunshine thrilled my eyes. I was up!

XXIII

SEALING UP AFT

We knew now we could handle and secure the pontoons whenever we were ready. We let that matter rest awhile. A more important matter was to complete the sealing up of the interior compartments which had baffled us before.

The motor room was all closed up, but the ventilation valve there had "chattered" and let out all the air when we had put a pressure on it the November before. Then we had no means of sealing it off, now we did have.

The leaking valve led directly from the top of the motor room into a watertight main underneath the deck. If we could get at this main, remove a section of it, and put a blank flange across the end leading to the motor room, the air leaking from that valve could no longer escape.

Kelley went down with the torch, burned away the steel deck over the ventilation main, cut out the steel superstructure between the deck and the hull of the boat so as to expose the pipe as much as possible.

Carr, Michels, Eadie, Wilson, Smith,—followed one after another with wrenches to unbolt the flanges at the forward and after ends of the section of the main we wished to pull out. The divers worked on the job two days. There was a confined space to work in, the bolts came out slowly. Carr, coming up after his second day on the job, reported trouble.

"All the bolts are out that we can reach, Mr. Ellsberg, but there are five bolts left on the underside of one flange, where the pipe bends around close to the hull that are hell to get at. I lay on my ear a whole hour trying to unscrew the nut on the easiest one to reach, and I only got it backed off a little over one turn. I think it'll take the whole gang at least a week to get those five bolts out!"

And I had provided Carr with a set of open-end wrenches, specially shaped by our blacksmith, to make it easier for him to work on those nuts!

If it took Carr an hour, a whole dive, to get one turn on the easiest nut to reach, he was probably conservative in his estimate that a week's work by everybody would be enough to back off all five nuts. We could not afford that much time. I asked Kelley to dress, got dressed myself, and together we went down, Kelley carrying the torch, to see what else we could burn away without ruining the watertightness of the engine room below the pipe, that would make it easier for us to get at those five bolts.

Kelley went down first. I followed him down on a descending line attached to the boat itself this time. Going down the second time was easier, less nerve-racking.

Soon I made out the conning tower of the submarine below me, slipped down through the water a few feet more. Something grazed my side. I held to the descending line, stopped a moment. Jutting out from the after side of the conning tower past which I had been sliding was the ship's bell. I paused to read the inscription:

U.S.S. *S-51*
1921

I examined it more carefully. It was a bronze bell about a foot high. What a wonderful souvenir of the ocean floor that bell would make! I determined to slip it out of its bracket, and take it up with me when I rose.

I loosed my grip on the descending line and slid the remaining few feet to the hull. This time although I noticed the pressure as before, my head stayed clear. With a gleam of elation, I walked aft, for the first time actually treading the deck of the *S-51* herself. But the walking was not easy. The deck sloped so badly to port that each step had to be taken carefully to avoid slipping overboard. I went slowly, hanging tightly to the low railing on the high side.

I came to the open engine room hatch, looked into the engine room. A black hole, nothing more, except slight traces of oily water slowly floating out. A little abaft the hatch, a large valve casting with the bonnet missing marked the spot where Frazer and Smith had struggled a week to close the fouled main engine air induction valve. How long ago that seemed! Poor Frazer, he would not again tread the submerged deck where now I stood.

A little farther aft was Kelley, gazing into the opening he had burned in the upper deck. I joined him, and crawled down into the gaping hole in the superstructure. I must be careful. The jagged edges of the remaining steelwork would quickly gash my suit if I rubbed over them.

We examined the ventilation main. Carr was right. The forward flange was touching the watertight hull of the submarine. The five bolts on the lower side of the flange there could hardly be touched. A diver would practically have to stand on his head to reach them, and as for getting a wrench on them, I marveled that Carr had been able to do even the trifling amount he had accomplished. That flange looked hopeless.

Kelley stood by with the torch, ready to burn away what I indicated, but there was nothing underneath that we could cut out without ruining the tightness of the engine room.

I glanced aft along the main towards the motor room. The pipe rose away from the hull as it ran aft. The after flange on the section we wished to remove was some six inches clear of the hull,—here the divers had managed to remove all the bolts which held the after pair of flanges together.

I saw the answer. As long as that pair of after flanges remained uninjured, it made no difference how we removed the pipe section we were after.

I shut off my air. The roaring in my helmet ceased. "On deck! Send down a wire hawser! Stand by to heave on it when I tell you!" I opened my air valve again.

I went to the descending line. In a few minutes, the end of a one-inch steel wire hawser slid down the line, guided by a shackle. Kelley unscrewed the shackle. Together Kelley and I dragged the end of the hawser aft along the deck, brought it to the point where the fully unbolted flanges lay.

With some difficulty we succeeded in bending the wire around the section of the ventilation main near the flanges and shackled the end of the hawser round its own standing part to form a running loop around the main.

We crawled out of the hole, went forward a few feet to get clear.

"On deck! Take up the slack gently."

The drooping hawser straightened out. The shackle slipped a little down the wire, tightening the loop around the pipe.

"Heave round slowly!"

A strain came on the hawser, it tautened like a bowstring. For an instant nothing happened, then the unbolted end of the twelve-inch pipe bent slowly up, came clear of the rest of the pipe leading to the motor room. Dragged by the hawser, the main kept bending upward. It had lifted at least two feet, when the forward end of the pipe, still held by the flange with the five inaccessible bolts, suddenly tore away from that flange and leaped about six feet over our heads as it swung free, dangling from the end of the wire.

"On deck! She's all yours! Take her up lively!"

In another second, the pipe had disappeared overhead. It was less than twenty minutes since Kelley and I had come down to examine the job that was going to take a week.

Kelley wasted no time. He crawled aft where the open end of the ventilation main leading to the motor room now faced us. Out came his diving knife. Kelley started to scrape away the rough pieces of gasket still stuck to the flange.

Once more I called the *Falcon*.

"Send down the blank and a new gasket!" I waited at the descending line for them and soon they appeared, hanging from a small manila line at the end of the ever-present guide shackle.

I unscrewed my diving knife, cut them loose, and started back to join Kelley. The blank steel plate had already been drilled to suit the flange, and cemented to it was a rubber gasket to make the joint watertight. Kelley took the blank, and while I held it in position against the end of the ventilation pipe, he shoved through a few bolts and set up the nuts. Both of us put in the remaining bolts, some sixteen altogether, and tightened them up with the wrenches. We were ready to come up in a little less than an hour. That chattering ventilation valve in the motor room was sealed off completely.

George Anderson went down while Kelley and I were decompressing on the stage. He slid down near us, clusters of bubbles streaming out of the back of his copper helmet, leaving a trail like a skyrocket. I could see he was carrying an extra airhose.

Anderson secured the hose to the valve over the motor room which he and Kelley had screwed into the hull the autumn before. When finally the stage with Kelley and me swung dripping onto the *Falcon*'s deck, that hose was already connected and Anderson also was on his way up. I shifted from my diving dress to an old uniform and joined the deck force on the quarterdeck. A sailor was coupling the motor room airhose to the blowing manifold just over the *Falcon*'s stern capstan.

It was an everyday scene, but for the men there, a rather tense moment. We had worked for months to seal up that motor room, each time before something had gone wrong, but now we had it and we were ready to blow out the water.

Niedermair opened the air valve, sent air at one hundred pounds pressure rushing down the hose, and in his notebook jotted down the time. He estimated the compartment would take two hours to empty of water.

After blowing a moment, he shut off the air, balanced off on his gauge and read the pressure in the motor room. It was forty-nine pounds. To expel all the water, we would have to drive it down sixteen feet to the bottom of that room, when the pressure in the compartment would have to rise to fifty-seven pounds.

Niedermair started blowing again, stopping every few minutes to balance off and read his gauge. The pressure rose slowly, showing the water was going lower. We breathed more freely.

"Look!" Hawes plucked me by the arm and pointed to a spot just astern of the *Falcon*. A stream of bubbles was rising over the stern of the submarine where a moment before had been only quiet water. Niedermair shut off the air to the hose. The bubbles stopped. He turned the air on again. In about half a minute another stream of bubbles appeared in the same spot.

There was no doubt about it. There was another leak somewhere in the motor room. We blew a while longer but the air pressure inside the submarine rose no higher. The air was coming out as fast as it went in.

Carr went down to investigate. He was below only a short while, and came up with only forty minutes' decompression.

"There's a bad leak in her side, commander. I couldn't reach it from the deck, but I tied my lifeline to the rail and hung down the starboard side just opposite the hatch to the motor room. It's a bad seam in her hull. The bubbles are coming out where two of the plates are riveted together. I could slip the edge of my knife into the joint."

Niedermair broke out the hull plans, and Carr showed us the spot. Halfway down the starboard side, near the forward end of the motor room was a vertical butt where two heavy steel plates joined. Evidently they had not been as closely fitted in building as they should have been and the joint had been caulked by splitting the edges of the two plates and forcing the metal together in a feather edge. The butt must have been tight before the accident, but the long submersion had apparently corroded away the feather-edge caulking and left the joint open nearly an eighth of an inch.

"The seam is leaking for about four feet," Carr added.

There was no help for it. We had to caulk it up.

To make sure of the job, we decided first to fill the open seam with lead, caulked firmly in, then split the steel plate edges again and caulk them iron to iron in the regular manner.

Eadie was chosen for the job, Eiben to help. We made up long strings of braided lead, weaving them from fine electrical fuse wire, and gave Eadie a set of wood caulking tools for that part of the job. He was to caulk the lead braids in between the two plates just as the old-time shipwrights used to caulk oakum in between the planks on the side of a wooden ship. Then with a regular air-operated caulking machine, he was to split the steel plates with his chisels and force them together over the lead with a fuller.

Joe Eiben went down first, taking a small iron stage with him. This Eiben rigged, hanging down the side of the submarine below the leak, for Eadie to stand on. Eadie slid down, taking his large assortment of tools and equipment in a canvas bag. (It was carefully checked before he dived to make sure no possible thing he might want was forgotten).

On the bottom, Eiben tended from the deck while Eadie stood on his little stage against the side of the hull and caulked in the lead braids with the hand tools. String after string went in and was hammered down, before the gap between the plates started to fill up. At last the lead had plugged the opening, and the mallet in Eadie's hands had driven it firmly home. Tom Eadie then took the air-driven hammer, slipped in a chisel, braced it against the plate, and squeezed the trigger. On the *Falcon*, listening on his telephone, I heard the clatter of the chisel against the steel hull. It paused at brief intervals, but otherwise kept up a steady rat-tat-tat for thirty minutes. Then it ceased.

In a faraway tone, I heard Eadie call:

"On deck! Put the air pressure on the motor room again!"

Niedermair turned on the air. We waited a short while. Eadie called again.

"The seam is tight where I caulked it, but it's leaking further down now. I'll caulk that!" His hammer started drumming away again.

We might have expected it. Any boilermaker knows how caulking part of a seam is apt to spring leaks from the vibration in the rest of the seam ahead of the chisel.

Eadie chased the leak along with his chisel, caulking seven feet of seam altogether before he came to the end of the joint and finally stopped the bubbles from escaping. Then loaded down with tools, Eadie and Eiben were hauled up to the stage. They had been down an hour and twenty minutes.

Weeks later, I examined that job. No boilermaker, working with all the facilities of a shop around him, ever did a neater caulking job than the one turned out by Tom Eadie, clinging to a little stage against the *S-51* at the bottom of the sea. And the wonder grew when I remembered that every time he pressed the trigger of his machine, the escaping air, which on the surface cannot even be seen, sent up clouds underwater of bubbles which totally blotted out from his sight the hammer, the chisel, and the steel plates that he was caulking. He had done the job, once the trigger was pulled, wholly by a sense of touch.

Next day we resumed our blowing on the motor room. Again we clustered round the manifold, while Niedermair manipulated the valves. The air went through steadily. We blew for half an hour, tested the pressure, found it balanced at fifty-three pounds. The water in the room had dropped eight feet, leaving the motor room half dry. We blew again, sure now that we had it, when for the fifth time since we had started work on that room, another stream of bubbles began rising to the surface. The bubbles this time were too far aft to be over the motor room itself but they were coming from the motor room without doubt, for whenever we stopped blowing, the bubbles stopped.

A little investigation of the blueprints gave the probable explanation. Just abaft the motor room was a tiny space called the tiller room which held the rudder head and the steering gear. A watertight bulkhead separated it from the motor room. Halfway down on this bulkhead was a hinged manhole plate, just large enough for a sailor to crawl through and oil up the rudder gear.

We had often wondered whether this manhole cover was open or closed. The three survivors of the *S-51* had told us it was ordinarily closed. Now we knew it must be open. We had forced the water in the motor room low enough so that the level was just even with the top of this manhole. Air was passing into the tiller room and leaking out of the tiller room in some manner.

Once more a diver went down to search for a leak,— a new diver this time. Davis, torpedoman third class, one of the men who had trained with me, was sent to investigate. Slowly he crawled aft from the conning tower, came to the motor room, searched along the deck on both sides to where the superstructure and the deck ended. No sign of any leak. He slipped off the deck to the cylindrical hull of the submarine, very fine here as it approached the stem, and straddling one leg down each side of the tail, hitched himself aft, a little at a time.

About twelve feet from the tip of the submarine, he found the leak. Here the smooth hull of the ship had a dent nearly six inches deep and several feet in diameter. In the center of the dent, two rivets had pulled out of the shell, leaving holes an inch wide. From these, two jets of air rushed out, merging into one stream of bubbles constantly floating up.

Davis came up, reported. The leak puzzled us. The *S-51* of course had no such dent in her when she sailed on her last voyage. The *City of Rome* had rammed her forward, and could not have damaged her stern. We had not worked there with any weights which might have made that mark. Finally we concluded that during the winter, while we were away, some vessel had unknowingly dropped anchor right over the *S-51*, and the anchor, bouncing off her stern, had caved it in and pulled two rivets out of the shell. At any rate, there was the dent and the holes, and we were losing air from the motor room as fast as we sent it down.

From Davis' description, we cast a dozen special lead plugs to fit the holes, with their diameters varying slightly, so that in the set, the diver would be sure to find two which would fit. Each lead plug had an oak wedge in its base, which would rest against the steel frame just beneath the shell, and expand the base of the plug inside the boat while the diver riveted the head of the plug over from the outside.

A new, but not an inexperienced, diver was chosen for this task. Gunner's Mate Wickwire of the Panama Submarine Flotilla, whom somehow we had missed before, volunteered and came north in May. His stocky build and cheerful disposition (unusual for a diver, for most of them are quiet men) made him a welcome addition to our force.

He practiced on some holes we drilled in the *Falcon*'s deck till he was quite familiar with the plugs; then armed with a hammer and with the dozen plugs tied to his belt like a string of sausages, he went down alone. Where he was to go, the submarine was so narrow two men could not work together.

Wickwire landed on the submarine, and started out, but like many a diver before him, he lost his sense of direction and went forward from the conning tower, instead of aft. Not till he reached the gun on the forecastle did he begin to wonder. Then he asked:

"On deck! Has this submarine got a gun on her stern?"

I imagined what had happened.

"No!" I yelled. "You're on the bow! Go the other way!"

We started blowing air into the motor room to help him locate the holes. Wickwire retraced his steps, clambered over the deck aft. Like Davis, he straddled the narrow stern and slid out along it till he came to the dent. He tried to fit plugs in the holes. They promptly blew out of his hands.

"On deck! Stop blowing on the motor room! I can't do a thing with that compressed air whistling out!"

Fortunately the plugs were lashed to his belt. He retrieved them. Niedermair shut off the air, but it was several minutes before the pressure blew down enough in the motor room to permit Wickwire to examine the holes.

Again he tried his plugs. A one-inch-diameter plug suited one hole perfectly. Wickwire pushed it through a little till its base touched inside, then carefully riveted it over with his hammer, upsetting it gradually, and filling the countersink left by the old rivet. He trimmed away the excess lead, flattened out the point of the plug, and left it beautifully flushed off with the shell.

Wickwire tried all his remaining lead plugs in the other hole but none would go. The old rivet from that hole was still partly jammed underneath it and the plugs would not slide through. Even the smallest diameter plug I had given him would not enter.

Gripping the submarine tightly between his legs to hold himself, Wickwire hammered desperately at the remains of the old rivet, trying to drive it clear, but it was firmly jammed between shell and frame and he could not dislodge it. He changed his tactics. Making sure his hammer was still lashed to his belt, he dropped the hammer and unscrewed his diving knife. Then, laying a medium-sized lead plug on the hull of the submarine, he placed the blade of his knife on it lengthwise, meanwhile holding the plug between thumb and forefinger. Cautiously retrieving his hammer, he brought it down sharply on the knife, driving it through the plug. Instantly he gripped the two halves to prevent them from dropping overboard.

He tried half a plug in the hole. It slipped through nearly an inch. As before, he peened down the plug, flattening and expanding it out till the countersink outside was flushed off. Then, still straddling the stern, he pushed himself backward till he came to a broader part of the hull and started up the descending line.

Once again Niedermair turned on the air. Steadily he blew. The water went lower, the pressure increased. Finally the gauge registered fifty-seven pounds. Not a leak anywhere. The motor room was dry at last!

XXIV

THE TORCH SOLVES
A PROBLEM

The first week in May, the *S-50* rejoined the squadron. All the new divers were taken on board her, to make them familiar with the *S-51*, while the older divers examined her to refresh their memories.

The work on the first pair of pontoons had taught us something about the troubles handling them. We proceeded with the second pair with the trepidation born of experience.

The second pair of pontoons were to go down alongside the bow. This, like the stern, was a little clear of the bottom owing to the rocker shape of the submarine's keel. Michels and Bailey passed a reeving line under her forward, some thirty feet from the stem, where the keel just started to bed itself in the clay. This line ran just abaft the bow diving planes. The same two divers also passed a second reeving line under about fifteen feet from the bow, then came up.

On deck, we rove a heavier cable down, spliced into the end of the after small line, and with this heavier manila down, we pulled down one side and up the other one of our wire lines. We started to repeat the process on the forward reeving line, but to our disappointment, the line slipped up the curved stem and out from under the bow, and the whole line came to the surface.

We had to dress two more divers and send them down to repass the forward reeving line. They tied two small lines together under the stem, waited while we sent a four-inch manila line down the starboard side and hauled it to the surface on the port side, then had to come up.

Carefully leading both ends of our large line aft to hold it from slipping out, we tied it to a wire hawser, which we fed out to starboard while we hauled up the manila line to port. We had paid out about sixty feet on the wire when, in spite of our precautions, the line once more slipped out from under the bow. It was evident that something positive was necessary to keep our lines then and our chain later from running up the curved stem and getting out from under the boat.

I thought of a trap for the line. About ten feet from the bow, the ship had a mushroom anchor fitted into her keel, with a cylindrical shank that ran about six feet up into a hawsepipe between the torpedo tubes. If we could only drop that anchor, the shank would still stick several feet up into the hawsepipe when the mushroom hit the bottom, which was only three feet below the keel. Any lines rove abaft that point would be stopped by the anchor shank from slipping any further forward. In addition, with the anchor out, there would be a recess left in the keel into which our forward chain would probably slide when the lifting strain came, and that would prevent the chain from slipping forward and out.

Letting go the anchor, however, was a conundrum. The releasing gear was inside the torpedo room forward. While several of our best divers had tried the fall before to enter that room, none had succeeded because the small, peculiarly sloped hatch intended mainly for loading torpedoes into the boat had proved inaccessible to a man in a diving rig. While I believed that in a pinch, Wilson or Eadie might do it, I hesitated to ask. Meanwhile, I looked over the *S-50* for an easier method.

Examining her with Lieutenant Commander Lenney, I found that the cable for the mushroom anchor, which was a heavy wire hawser, ran forward from a reel over the torpedo room through the nonwatertight superstructure forming the forecastle, to a pulley over the top of the hawsepipe. It passed from the forward side of the pulley down the hawsepipe where it shackled into the anchor. From the outside of the ship, the cable was inaccessible except at one point where it passed through a deck locker. The little hatch over this locker, about one foot square, could be thrown back from the deck, and the anchor cable was then visible about three feet below the deck.

The answer was obvious. I sent the surfboat back to the *Falcon.* It returned immediately with Kelley. I showed him the little opening in the deck, explained the task to him. The cable was too far down to touch with his hand, but he was to push the torch through the hole and burn the wire cable in two.

We went back to the *Falcon.* While Kelley was being dressed, we hooked up the torch to the gas bottles. In a few more minutes Kelley went down, the torch dangling from his waist. Landing on a line tied to the gun, he walked cautiously along the forecastle, found the little deck locker near the bow, and threw back the cover. He could not feel the cable as it was beyond the reach of his fingers; he could not see it for it was black inside the water-filled forecastle.

I listened carefully on Kelley's telephone, meanwhile keeping my eyes on the regulators between the gas flasks and the torch hoses. Kelley was turning on the gases; one at a time the air, the oxygen, and the hydrogen started to flow.

"On deck! Turn on the igniter!"

I threw in the switch, called out:

"The igniter is on!" I heard a bang, a steady muffled roar. The torch was lighted. I switched off the current to the igniter.

On the *S-51*'s forecastle, Kelley lay down flat, carefully thrust the burning torch down the opening, shoved his arm through after it as far as it would go. He brought his helmet over the hole. Near the brilliant orange flame, a heavy black streak ran fore and aft. Kelley swung his torch against it, pressed the trigger. A long spurt of white flame shot across the locker with a shower of sparks. Slowly Kelley drew the torch upward. There was a sharp snap, the two halves of the cable flew apart, and with a rumble the anchor let go and dropped down the hawespipe.

"On deck! Take up the torch!"

The tenders hauled up on the torch hoses. I looked at my watch. Only forty-five seconds since Kelley had lighted the torch. Quite a change since the day when he had shouted from the sea bottom that if he could only get his teeth on it, he could chew a wire cable in half faster than the old Navy torch could cut it.

Another minute and we got a signal from Kelley that he was at the gun, ready to come up. He had been down only ten minutes, the shortest dive we ever had on which any work was accomplished. Kelley needed only twenty minutes decompression to come up.

For the third time that day we dressed a pair of divers to pass the forward reeving line. Wilson and Eiben went this time, each with a small manila line tied to his wrist. They landed on the submarine, dropped off, one each side of the bow, crawled in under the keel. As I expected, they found the mushroom anchor buried a few inches in the clay, but its shank still ran up inside the hull. Eiben pushed his line through to Wilson just abaft the anchor shank, Wilson bent the lines together, told us to heave round. Hurriedly, so as to finish while the divers were still there, we rove round the four-inch manila and then pulled through the wire line. All the lines went round without a hitch. The divers came up.

It was late in the day, too late to lower a pontoon, but the weather was good so the *Falcon* remained in the moorings overnight, holding up the wires. Next morning, with no untoward occurrences, we brought alongside, rigged, flooded down, and sank a pontoon with its two chains on the port bow of the *S-51*, though the job took us all day long, and by evening with the weather growing worse, we were compelled to run out and buoy off the two wires which were to act as guides for the second pontoon.

Coming back two days later into the moorings, we picked up the two buoys on the wires. As we feared, the wire cables were snarled and tangled in spite of the care used in laying them out on the sea bottom. It took the whole morning, several dives, and all of Hartley's skill as a sailor to get the wires untangled enough to let us proceed. Finally with only a few kinks left in the cables, we had the *Sagamore* bring another pontoon alongside us, rove the wires up through the hawsepipes in the pontoon, flooded down, and slowly lowered the pontoon on the starboard bow of the submarine. Near the bottom, we held it while Carr went down on it, sighted the submarine to make sure we were clear of her, and then rode down till the top of the pontoon was flush with the *S-51*'s forecastle. Here we again held the pontoon, while we heaved up on the guide wires to draw the chains from the opposite pontoon through under the keel and up through the hawsepipes. Carr counted the links showing above each hawsepipe, but in spite of our heaviest pulling on the capstan we were unable to pull quite as much chain through as we wished. Evidently the other pontoon was sitting on part of the chain and we could not haul it through. When it looked as if a stronger pull would probably break the wires (they were good for about thirty tons each) we decided to take what we had and call it quits. We lowered the pontoon to the bottom, slacked off on the wires till the ends of the chains rested on top of the pontoon, and then sent Kelley down with the torch to burn the wires off the chain ends. We had found that once the screw shackles had a heavy strain on them, the divers could not unscrew the pins to release the hauling wires. Burning off the wires turned out to be the quickest and easiest way of release.

I decided to let the insertion of the toggle bars go till later.

XXV

THE FIRST TUNNEL

At bow and stern we had been able to pass our reeving lines under with no great difficulty, because there the keel, due to its rocker shape, rose clear of the bottom. However, for the other pontoons amidships, the case was far different.

Amidships the *S-51* was buried about six feet deep in a bed of hard blue clay, overlaid with a thin layer, a few inches thick, of hard packed gray sand. To get the reeving lines and the chains through here required that we provide a tunnel for their passage. There was only one way which appeared practicable for digging the tunnel. At that depth it was out of question for the divers to undertake the continued physical exertion of swinging pick and shovel in an excavation, disregarding the mechanical limitations of trying to do it in a diving rig. We all felt that the best solution lay in washing out a hole under the ship with a stream of water from a fire hose.

We coupled up two hundred and fifty feet of the *Falcon's* two-and-one-half-inch fire hose, with a regular hose nozzle screwed to the end. Bailey was selected to go down and start the tunnel. I took him aboard the *S-50* and showed him the spot abreast frame forty-six, where he was to start. A torpedo davit projecting from the deck was the nearest visible mark. He was to spot this on the *S-51's* side, then measure off five feet forward of it, and start the tunnel there.

Bailey was small, but he was an excellent diver and a careful man. We could rely on him to hit the right spot and, in case of any doubt, to ask questions rather than to guess.

Bailey was dressed, went down on the forward descending line, the fire hose dragging after him on a lanyard to his wrist. He found the torpedo davit, tied a small line to it, which he threw over the port side to mark the location, and then slid down the line to the bottom. He measured off the five feet against the side of the submarine, dragged the hose nozzle over, braced it between his heavy shoes against the sea bottom close to the ship's side, and sang out:

"On deck! Turn on the water!"

A sailor opened wide the valve to the *Falcon*'s wrecking pump. The hose swelled out, and throbbing with each stroke of the pump as the water rushed through, disappeared over the rail.

Another call from Bailey:

"On deck! Turn off the water! I'm about fifty feet from the sub and I don't know where the hose is!"

We shut down the pump and the hose flattened out, hanging limply over our bulwarks.

It was easy to imagine what had happened. I remembered in my boyhood days the sight of four firemen clinging to a hose nozzle, trying to direct the stream against a burning building. Bailey, all alone, had tried the same thing except that his stream instead of meeting air, was discharged against solid water, making the reaction worse. The writhing hose had torn itself from his grasp and sent him flying backwards through the water.

Bailey picked himself out of the sand, located the submarine, and after a search, found the hose again. He dragged the nozzle back, braced himself against the hull.

"On deck! Turn on the water again! Easy this time!"

Once more the wrecking pump started to throb. Gently we opened the valve from the fire main to the hose, watched the hose swell out slowly as we gradually raised the pressure. At forty pounds on our gauge, Bailey sang out from below:

"Hold it, that's enough!"

The engineer at the pump throttled it carefully to hold the pressure steady. We watched the stream pulsing through the hose, which was not very hard. A thumb could make a dent in the canvas covering.

Bailey worked his hour and came up.

"I could just hang on the second time, but I didn't get much done. That clay is awful hard, and the stream I had hardly made an impression. I don't think I made a hole a foot deep, and part of that was through the sand on top."

Other divers followed Bailey. We helped matters a little by tying a one-hundred-pound weight to the hose, just behind the nozzle, to assist the diver in holding the hose down. Still the low pressure prevented much progress—the stream had not force enough to cut the clay. We needed more pressure. To get it, we removed the last section of hose and replaced it with a one-and-one-half-inch length and a nozzle to match. With the smaller nozzle, we were able to raise the pressure to sixty pounds before the divers complained. (The usual pressure on a two-and-one-half-inch fire hose is one hundred and twenty pounds.) The sixty-pound stream had force enough to do a little cutting, but of course the smaller hose greatly reduced the size of the jet.

Day after day, we worked on the tunnel at frame forty-six. It was slow work. We were never able to get more than six men in any one day down on the job, because of the loss of time in getting the old diver out and clear before his relief could get down, pick up the hose, and crawl in. Other complications arose. The clay turned out to be so heavy that when cut, it would not stay in suspension in the water, but after floating back a foot or so, would settle down in the tunnel around the diver. Consequently after cutting ahead for a few inches, the diver had to stop, and crawling out backwards, turn his nozzle and wash the cuttings all the way out to the tunnel mouth before he could again advance.

As a final aggravation, after one or two days' work, a storm would drive us away. Coming back, we always found our tunnel filled in with hard packed sand, washed along the sea bottom by the currents, and this had to be removed regularly before we could again drive our bore ahead.

We worked along against constant difficulties. Hoses got fouled in the submarine's superstructure and tore in half when we tried to pull them free. Sometimes the divers could not find the tunnel, and wasted half their precious hour searching out the small entrance hole under the port bilge. Others, lying down in the tunnel, had their suits fill with water, and had to be dragged up, half frozen and nearly drowned.

We made progress, yes, but it had almost to be measured by the inch. As a result of two weeks' desperate work in May, the tunnel had advanced sixteen feet under the port side,—about an average of one foot a day.

We were still two feet from the keel on the port side. Francis Smith was in the tunnel, burrowing his way along. Imagine his situation. In ice cold water, utter blackness, total solitude, he was buried one hundred and thirty-five feet below the surface of the sea. No sight, no sound, no sense of direction except the feel of the iron hull of the *S-51* against his back, as he lay stretched out flat in a narrow hole, scarcely larger than his body, not big enough for him to turn around in. Ahead in his outstretched arms he grasped the nozzle, burrowing his way deeper, while around him coursed backward a black stream of freezing water laden with mud and clay.

He had been working about twenty minutes, when on the *Falcon* the man at the telephone got a call from Smith. He could not understand and passed the telephone set to me.

"Hello, Smith!"

In an agonized voice came the reply:

"I'm in a very bad position, Mr. Ellsberg. Send someone to help!"

Joe Eiben was working aft on the other side of the submarine. I dropped Smith's phone, seized Eiben's, ordered Joe to stop whatever he was doing, climb over the boat to the tunnel, and help Smith. Eiben acknowledged the message, started forward.

Meanwhile I tried to figure out what had happened.

The fire hose leading over the rail was throbbing violently. Perhaps the nozzle had torn itself from Smith's grasp, was thrashing him to death.

I took Smith's phone again, called down:

"Shall I turn off the water?"

Almost a scream came the answer:

"No! For God's sake keep it going! The tunnel has caved in behind me!"

I felt faint. Hastily we coupled up another fire hose, slid it down the descending line for Eiben's use. But it had taken two weeks to drive the tunnel to where Smith lay! On deck we looked at each other helplessly. Over the telephone, I could hear Smith's labored breathing as he struggled in the darkness.

No further messages came. The sailors stood silently around the deck, waiting for Eiben to arrive at the tunnel, wondering what good he could do when he got there.

Eiben reached the descending line at the gun, cut loose the new hose, dragged it forward with him, and dropped over the port side to the bottom. Finally after what seemed an age, he reported himself at the tunnel mouth, said he was trying to enter.

I waited; then over Smith's telephone, I heard Smith say to Eiben:

"I'm all right now, Joe. Had a little accident. You go on back to your own job."

Though he could not turn round, Smith had managed to pass the nozzle back between his legs, and guiding it with his feet, he had washed his way out backward through the cave-in!

Eiben left. Smith sat down on the ocean floor a few minutes to rest, then picked up his hose, crawled back into the tunnel and for half an hour more continued to wash his way towards the keel.

No deed ever performed in the heat of battle with the enemy where thousands cheer you on can compare with Francis Smith's bravery, when in the silent depths of the ocean beneath the hulk of the *S-51*, he washed his way out of what well might have been his grave, then deliberately turned round, went back into the black hole from which he had by the grace of God escaped, and worked his way deeper and deeper into it.

Other divers followed Smith; in a few more days we reached the keel on the port side. Then, marking the corresponding spot on the starboard side as carefully as possible, we started to drift another tunnel from that side to meet the port side hole. As the boat was heeled far over on her port side, the tunnel on the starboard side was not much over half as long as on the low side. While the divers worked on the starboard side hole, we sent one or two men a day into the port tunnel to keep it cleared out.

Only the most experienced of the divers managed to make any headway in the tunnels. Carr, Smith, Wilson, Eiben, Kelley, Eadie, Michels, and Bailey did practically all the work. We tried a few of the most promising of the newer divers on the job, but they never got anywhere at it. The reason was clear enough. Years of experience were necessary to develop the iron nerve and the forgetfulness of surroundings which were essential to allow the diver to concentrate on the job and ignore his situation.

The job proceeded, the divers coming up sometimes singly, sometimes in pairs. Eiben and Eadie, who had been working, one in the port tunnel, the other in the starboard one, met at the gun on the submarine's forecastle, climbed on the stage at the ninety-foot mark, and, according to ritual, began their setting-up exercises while decompressing.

Those two men were safely off the bottom. On the quarterdeck, we turned attention to the next diver, who, except for his helmet, was ready to go over. He was testing his telephone.

A voice came from the superstructure.

"Tom Eadie said something, but I couldn't make it out. I can't get him now!"

Hartley tried, I tried, Gunner Tibbals tried. None of us could understand, though it did sound as if Eadie were shouting something. Eiben was on the stage down there with Eadie. I took Eiben's telephone.

"Hello, Joe! Ask Tom what he wants!"

A pause, then Eiben replied:

"Tom's not here! What did you pull him up for?" Surprised, I looked at Eadie's tender. He had not pulled Eadie up.

"Where's Tom?" I asked him.

"He's still down there, sir. I'm trying to signal him. I've given him 'One' on his line, two or three times, but he doesn't answer."

A shout over the telephone from Eiben. "Eadie just fell back on the stage. His suit's nearly torn in half and he's full of water. Take him up quick!"

Half a dozen bears grabbed Eadie's lines and heaved hard. The weight was tremendous, evidently Eadie's suit was wholly waterlogged. Others grasped the lines wherever they could lay hands on them and we heaved rapidly. Over the side went another stage, two men on it, dropped into the water up to their waists. Hand over hand Eadie's lines came in, then at last Eadie's helmet. The men on the stage seized it, dragged his limp form on the stage; the winchman jerked the stage up, swung it in on deck.

Eadie's suit was nearly completely torn in two just below the breastplate, the leather straps over his shoulders were broken, his lead belt was hanging round his ankles. No need to take off his helmet. We cut loose his shoes, dragged him out of the suit through the hole around his breast.

Eadie was very pale, bleeding badly from the mouth and nose, but apparently still conscious. We did not wait to investigate. The tenders who pulled him out of the suit dragged him hurriedly to the recompression tank and thrust him in together with Surgeon Flotte, who hastily ran the pressure up to fifty pounds.

Hours later, after Eiben had come up, and Eadie was below, wrapped in blankets in his bunk, with Eiben resting in the next berth, I asked them what had happened. Eadie told me.

"Joe and I were on the stage at ninety feet, I was jumping up and down to decompress myself and I guess Joe was doing knee stoops.

"All of a sudden my exhaust valve jammed shut and my suit started to swell out. I tried to reach my control valve and turn off the air, but before I could swing my arm around, my suit stiffened out from the pressure inside, and it spread-eagled me. Both my sleeves shot out straight sideways and I couldn't bend my elbows to get my hand in on the control valve.

"By that time I was so light, I started to float up off the stage and I yelled in the telephone to the man on deck to turn the air off on my hose. I guess he didn't understand me."

I interrupted Eadie and turned to Eiben.

"Say, Joe, didn't you notice it when Eadie started up?"

Eiben looked at us sheepishly.

"Yes, I sort of saw him go, out of the corner of my faceplate, but I just thought he was taking an extra-high jump, and I went right on exercising. I wasn't thinking about Tom and I didn't look around again for him till you called me from the deck."

Eadie went on.

"As I started to float up, I thought fast. Of course I knew if I 'blew up' without any decompression I'd probably get 'the bends,' but that wasn't what worried me most. We were hanging from the *Falcon*, and if I came up from the bottom with all that buoyancy, I'd be going as if I'd been fired from a gun by the time I hit her hull. My copper helmet would flatten out like a pancake and that would be my finish right there.

"As I shot up, I saw the top of the steel bails from which the stage was hanging flash down past my faceplate. I couldn't do anything with my hands, but as I went by, I shoved out the toes of both my shoes, and I managed to hook the brass toe caps on my diving shoes into the tri-angle where the bails join. That stopped me with a jerk, and there I was, hanging onto the bails with my toes and just praying that the caps wouldn't tear off the shoes!

"I tried again to pull my hands in but I couldn't. My suit swelled out some more in a hurry, and burst the shoulder straps holding my belt up and my helmet down. The lead belt dropped around my feet, and my helmet flew up over my head. As it went by, the breastplate hit me a lick under the chin that nearly broke my jaw, and my suit then stretched out so the helmet was nearly two feet over my head. When the straps let go and the suit stretched, that gave me still more buoyancy, and the pull on my toes was awful.

"I tried to yell in the telephone to you to have Joe climb up to me, shut off my air and open the petcock on my helmet so as to let some air out of my suit, but the telephone transmitter was up in the helmet and that was two feet over my head and I couldn't make you understand.

"Then the pressure increased with a rush and nearly broke my ears,* and I started to bleed from my mouth and nose. The strain on my toes was fierce, and I was wondering how much longer I could hang on, when all at once my suit tore apart under all that pressure, let out all the air, and I nearly burst as the extra pressure suddenly disappeared. My helmet sort of dropped back, my suit all filled up with water, and I fell down again on the stage.

"I felt you starting to pull me up. I tried to hold my breath, because there was no more air in the suit. Then I remembered that the lines you were hauling me with were only secured to my helmet, and I could feel that my suit was nearly torn in two just below the breastplate. I was down in the rest of the suit and I could feel my heavy shoes and that lead belt hanging round my ankles. I was afraid that what was left of the suit wouldn't stand the strain and it would tear all of the way across. Then you'd pull up the helmet and I'd just sink with those lead-soled shoes and the lead belt as anchors. I thought how surprised you'd be when my helmet came up empty. I tried to kick the belt free from round my feet. No use, I couldn't get it off, so I just held my breath and prayed that the suit wouldn't rip any more. I tried hard not to swallow any water, and the next thing I knew, they were dragging me onto the stage."

A terrible experience. In less than a minute's time, Eadie had seen death in four different horrible forms, successively staring him in the face,—"the bends," concussion against the *Falcon*, sudden heavy pressure, and drowning had each in turn seemed about to kill him. He came through, saved by his quick thinking, weak and wounded, but with unshaken nerves. A wonderful diver, Tom Eadie. All the world learned what we already knew, when he later won the Medal of Honor on the *S-4*.

We examined Eadie's helmet to see what had jammed his automatic exhaust valve shut and stopped the air from escaping. We found out, but drew little comfort from the knowledge. While Eadie had been stretched out flat in the tunnel, washing, some mud had been carried into the exhaust valve of his helmet by the water that inevitably leaks in whenever a diver stoops over or lies down.

* With no escape for the air, the pressure in Eadie's suit went up till it balanced at the *Falcon*'s compressor pressure of one hundred and thirty-five pounds, equal to diving to a depth of water of three hundred and four feet.

A few grains of sand had entered the sleeve in which the valve stem worked, jammed between the sleeve and the stem, and prevented the valve from sliding open. It was just as likely to happen to the next man working in the tunnel, and added another danger to the multitude we had. We thereafter warned all divers working in the tunnel to leave the petcock on their helmets cracked open a trifle, while they were in the tunnel and later while coming up, so that if their exhaust valves jammed shut, they might have a brief period to shut off their air before the pressure could build up enough in their suits to spread eagle them and prevent them from using their hands. The partly open petcock meant that a tiny stream of water would continually run into their suits while they lay down in the tunnel, but it had to be borne. If anyone ever spread eagled and then had his suit burst inside the tunnel, he was sure to drown before aid could reach him.

There was a little delay on deck after Eadie was hauled up before Carr, the next diver ready, was finally dressed and on his way down, but in about thirty minutes all was quiet again on the *Falcon*'s quarterdeck. The pulsating fire hose hanging over the rail and vanishing in the water showed that far below, Carr, prone in the tunnel, was carrying on. Eiben, hanging at the fifty-foot stage, still had an hour to wait before he came aboard. The *Falcon* pitched easily as the waves rolled by; near at hand the *Vestal*, the *Iuka*, the *Sagamore*, and the *S-50* tugged at their anchors, and far off on the western horizon, a thin wisp of smoke indicated that the *Penobscot* was coming out with the mail. Altogether, the squadron presented a very peaceful scene, with no indication of the swift drama that had just been acted ninety feet below the gently heaving surface of the sea.

A few more days went by, and from the starboard side, the men reported that they could touch the box keel, which extended sixteen inches below the hull, with their hose nozzles. We knew we could do the same in the port tunnel.

To finish the job, Tug Wilson and Tom Eadie went down together, each one taking a fire hose, and each with a small manila line tied to one wrist. They entered the tunnels, Eadie on the port side, Wilson on the starboard side. When both had crawled in as far as they could go, they asked us for the water, and started from both sides to wash away the clay under the keel.

For communication, I wore Eadie's telephone receiver over one ear, Wilson's over the other one, with a transmitter in each hand.

The divers worked nearly an hour, digging steadily. Neither one made any report. On deck we waited anxiously for news, but did not wish to bother the men with needless conversation. Still it seemed as if they should have been able to wash away the barrier under the keel in that time. As the minutes dragged by without a junction, I began to feel that the two tunnels had not met, that one or the other had been drifted at the wrong angle or perhaps a few feet too far forward to meet its mate. Considering the difficulty of locating anything below, and the impossibility of checking up on the tunnel directions once they ran in under the hull, such a failure of the tunnels to meet would be quite natural but nevertheless it would be heartbreaking after all our struggles.

A call in my left ear. Wilson talking.

"On deck! Turn off my water. I think I can feel the water from Tom's hose!"

We shut down on Tug's hose. It hung limply, while the other hose throbbed vigorously.

"Tell Tom to point his hose aft." I gave Eadie the word. A few minutes went by, then:

"Tell Tom to point his hose forward."

I passed that order also down to Eadie. Wilson, lying in the darkness below, fumbled blindly around the keel, trying to locate the direction of the current of water he could feel washing by him. He could find nothing definite.

"On deck, turn on my water again! I'll try to wash further aft along the keel!"

The hour was up, but with the prospect of finishing the tunnel, it looked best to leave them alone a little longer. Alternately, I shut off Eadie's water, and then Wilson's, each one hoping to feel a stream coming under the keel from the other side. Nothing happened, both men kept on digging.

A call in my right ear. Eadie talking.

"Turn off my water, Mr. Ellsberg!"

I ordered the water shut off. Eadie resumed:

"I got a hole under the keel. I'm going to shove my foot under. Tell Tug to look out for it!" I turned off Wilson's water, told him to stand by.

Eadie crawled out of the tunnel, turned round, crawled in feet first, lying on his face, till he touched the keel, and then shoved his right foot, heel up, under the keel till his knee passed through, then bent his foot upward as much as possible.

"On deck! I got my foot through! Tell Tug to look out for it!"

"Hello, Tug! Eadie says his foot is under! Feel around for it!"

Wilson fumbled in the blackness and the mud but encountered nothing.

Two hours had gone by, the men were long overtime. I could hear Wilson cursing volubly as he fumbled in the water-filled tunnel.

"On deck! Tell Tom to wiggle his foot! I can't feel a damned thing!"

I told Eadie. Burying his face deeper in the mud, Eadie struggled to push his leg through a few inches further, and wiggled his foot desperately.

A message in my right ear.

"Something is holding my foot!"

I seized Wilson's phone.

"That's Tom's foot you've got hold of, Tug! *Don't let go!*" and in Eadie's transmitter:

"Stop wiggling, Tom! Tug is going to tie his line on your foot!"

Then to Wilson, "Get a couple of good round turns and two half hitches with your line on that foot before you lose it!"

Carefully holding the foot with one hand to avoid losing it in the darkness, Wilson worked up a little slack in the line tied to his left wrist, wound it round Eadie's foot, then drew his knife, cut away the line from his wrist, and firmly secured the end to Eadie's ankle.

A faraway growl came from Tug.

"All right, tell Tom he can have his foot now! I'm coming up!"

Wilson crawled out backwards from the starboard hole. Eadie crawled headfirst out of the long port tunnel, dragging on his foot the first reeving line under the body of the ship. Outside the tunnel, he pulled through a little slack, cut the line off his foot, bent it to the line on his wrist, and we had a complete line around the ship.

Eadie and Wilson started up, cold and stiff. Their suits were filled with water nearly to their waists.

It was two hours and twenty-three minutes since they had gone down. It took nearly five hours to decompress them. They came aboard finally, utterly fagged out. They had won a point in our struggle against the sea, the first tunnel was at last completed, but on the *Falcon* we spent an anxious night till finally Surgeon Flotte assured us that neither pneumonia nor "the bends" would attack either Tom or Tug.

Another pair of divers took the reeving line, tied it securely to the rail on each side of the *S-51*'s deck, cut off the excess lengths going to the surface, ready for running the larger lines through when a good day offered for pontooning.

XXVI

THE CEMENT GUN

To finish sealing up the interior of the ship, we had two more ventilation valves, one in the engine room and one in the control room, both just like the valve in the motor room, to block off against leakage. The ventilation main leading to the valve located in the engine room we could get to just abaft the conning tower, under the deck, and blank it off as we had the main leading to the motor room valve. But the ventilation main running to the valve in the control room was so buried under pipes of all kinds beneath the superstructure around the conning tower that it practically meant tearing the ship to pieces to get at the necessary flanges on that main. Remembering the trouble that a few inaccessible bolts had given us in sealing off the motor room ventilation main, I looked around for an easier method of blocking the valves against "chattering."

An examination of the *S-50* showed that the valve bodies, inside the hull, each had an inch and a quarter drainage line tapped into the castings just above the valve seats. These drains were intended to remove undue moisture which might leak into the exterior ventilation pipes while the boat was submerged. If we could remove the drain lines and couple hoses to the nipples on the castings, we might force cement in to fill up the valve bodies and the ventilation pipes just above. Once the cement hardened, the valve disks could not possibly spring off their seats and leak when the pressure came on.

Two things were necessary. One was to couple up the hoses, which I was sure the divers could do; the other was to get a cement that while liquid enough to flow freely through two hundred feet of hose from the *Falcon* to the valves in the *S-51*, would still be sure of setting hard after it had forced the water out of the valves below.

For a week, Niedermair experimented with various mixes of cements, but we could find no brand of Portland cement that would do what we wanted. We asked the Navy Yard to help; they sent us out fifty bags of a special quick-setting cement called Lumnite. We experimented with it in various mixes and found it filled the bill perfectly. As a final test, we lowered the piece of ventilation main which Kelley and I had torn out of the *S-51* to the bottom of the sea, with a rubber hose tied inside the pipe and a wooden plug to seal the lower end. We ran down about five cubic feet of cement through the hose, left the pipe submerged all night, and next day pulled it up. The pipe was solidly plugged with hard cement.

That settled the question of the cement to be used.

To plug off the control room valve, it was necessary to enter the control room again. We had sealed it up the autumn before, closed the door to the engine room, and tried to blow it dry, but as we learned to our sorrow, the ventilation valve "chattered" and released the air. Now we had to open the door to the engine room in order to enter.

Eadie went down, entered the engine room, tripped all the dogs with a pipe wrench, and tried to pull the door open but failed to budge it. It had been jammed so tight that the rubber gasket was stuck to the knife edge on the door frame, and pull as he would, Eadie could not tear it free.

We sent down a one-half-inch wire line which Eadie shackled to the door handle. On the *Falcon*, we took the line to the capstan, gave it a jerk. Eadie reported the door had flown open. He let go the wire and came up.

The next thing was to remove the drain pipe and connect up a rubber hose to the large valve. We examined the job on the *S-50*. The control room ventilation valve was just over the gyro compass, immediately forward of the little radio room. Between the valve body and the radio room bulkhead, in a space only about one and one-half inches wide, we must break a union in the drain line, force the drain line out of the way, and insert an elbow with a new half union to match the existing fitting. To the new elbow we would connect our hose.

The *Vestal*'s plumber came over, provided the necessary equipment, and the divers Wilson and Eiben, who were to do the job, rehearsed it.

We fitted them out with the necessary assortment of Stillson wrenches, crowbars, pipe fittings, and lights.

The divers went down on a three-man dive—Eiben and Wilson to go into the boat, Smith to tend their lines outside the engine room hatch.

Eiben went down first with the light, Wilson next with the tools, and Smith last. Wilson and Eiben entered the engine room, squeezed and twisted their way through the little door into the control room, and went slowly forward through the narrow passage there between the galley and the radio room.

They felt their way to the point where the radio room ended. Just beyond it they could feel the gyro compass, with the ventilation valve overhead.

Wilson telephoned.

"Conditions down here are fierce, Mr. Ellsberg. Much worse than they used to be. The water is so black we can't see the light six inches away!"

Wilson fumbled over his head between the valve and the bulkhead for the union that he was to disconnect. After several tries, he managed to get a twenty-four-inch Stillson wrench on the nut, but neither Wilson nor Eiben, nor both of them together, pushing up on the handle, were able to start the joint. It is exceedingly difficult for a diver, on account of the encumbrance of his breastplate and helmet, to use his arms overhead; here it was necessary to reach overhead to handle the wrench, and then to add to their trouble, the union was so set that to break it they had to push up on the wrench handle instead of pulling downwards, which they might have done much more easily. And that was as far as they got that dive. They spent their whole hour on it, but failed to start the union. The three divers came up.

Next day they tried again, this time with a special extension on the wrench handle which bent down so they could exert some force on it. With both men heaving upward, they started the union turning, and then, one-sixth of a turn at a time, Wilson backed it off with a smaller wrench. After that, in went a short crowbar, and he bent away and clear of the job, the drain pipe which he had disconnected.

The next step was to couple up his new half union with the elbow screwed into it. This was tied to his belt. He cut it loose.

Wilson wanted the light thrown on the spot where he was to work, so he could note conditions. He looked toward Eiben, but in the blackness he could see neither Eiben nor the light. Still Eiben must be within a couple of feet of him.

Wilson telephoned.

"On deck! Tell Joe to move closer so I can feel him, and put the light against the big valve!"

I got Eiben. "Joe, Tug says for you to stand alongside and put your light against the big valve!" Eiben acknowledged, moved over till he touched Wilson, and then feeling over his head, found the valve and shoved his one thousand watt searchlight against it. Wilson pushed his helmet over till, touching the light, he could vaguely make out the outlines of the union he was to connect to. Again he telephoned:

"Tell Joe to move the light away a few inches so I can get in and work!" And a few minutes later: "Tell Joe to take the light away! I can't see anything with it anyway, and the reflector is in my road!"

I relayed the message to Eiben. He dropped the light down. Both men stood in utter blackness, unable to see each other, the light, or the job they were working on.

Wilson pushed his new fitting up into place, guided by his sense of touch, but hampered by his gloves, and tried to get the union nut started. It would not catch. He twisted the fitting this way and that, but he was unable to get it lined up so the threads would catch. Several times he asked to have Eiben hold the light against his helmet while he tried to find out what the trouble was. Finally he gave up in disgust.

"On deck! I can't get it started. Tell Joe to try it; I'll hold the light!"

I told Eiben to switch places with Wilson. In the darkness he exchanged his light for Wilson's pipe fitting, carefully felt his way around his partner to avoid fouling on the Kingston valve controls behind them, and feeling in with his clumsy gloves tried to line up the connections. He had no more luck than Wilson, and after fumbling with it for over ten minutes, he informed me:

"It won't go in, Mr. Ellsberg. There isn't quite enough room to get it lined up straight so the threads will start. I'll measure the clearance against my glove. You'll have to make another fitting. We're coming up!"

On deck a few hours later we checked the clearance as Eiben had taken it with the end of his glove. There was only an inch and a quarter room on the *S-51*; the *S-50*, where we had made up the fitting, had a quarter of an inch more space, but the lack of that quarter inch on the *S-51* prevented the assembly. With standard fittings we were unable to make up the assembly in less space than we had the first time; to overcome the trouble, the coppersmith on the *Vestal* made up a specially brazed half union and flat elbow which took up a little less room than the first one.

Eiben and Eadie took this down, screwed it to the drain outlet on the large ventilation valve, and coupled to it a length of hose about thirty feet long, sufficient to reach down the corridor, and out through the engine room hatch to the deck of the submarine, where it ended in a valve which the divers tied to the rail.

In the engine room, Eadie and Smith started a similar job on the ventilation valve, just forward of the port engine. In the engine room there was plenty of room to work; they uncoupled the drain pipe, screwed on the new fitting and coupled up another short length of hose leading through the hatch to the deck outside, where it ended in a valve which was painted a bright yellow to distinguish it from the valve on the hose leading to the control room.

Meanwhile, the *Vestal*'s boilermakers had made us a large tank to serve as a sort of cement gun. It had a special quick-loading hatch on top; a connection on the bottom to discharge the cement into the hose to the submarine; petcocks on the side to show the cement level inside; and an air connection on top for putting on the air pressure to blow the cement through the hose and into the valve castings inside the submarine. We prepared a large cement-mixing trough on the *Falcon*'s quarterdeck, and had twenty sailors standing by with shovels to mix cement and then load it through a funnel into the top of our gun.

When all was ready on the *Falcon*, Grube went down to the *S-51*, taking with him a rubber hose for the cement to run through. On the submarine, he screwed this to the short hose leading into the control room ventilation valve.

As soon as Grube reported this done, the sailors, who had been vigorously mixing the Lumnite cement, now loaded the cement gun and sealed down the cover.

I told Grube to stand by below, ordered Niedermair to put one hundred and thirty-five pounds' pressure on the gun, and opened the valve from the tank to the hose. A stream of cement shot through. In a few seconds, I heard Grube report:

"Cement coming through the hose down here!"

It took but a minute to blow all the cement out of the gun. Niedermair shut off the air, closed the valve to the hose. The sailors opened the tank, hastily reloaded it. Three times we filled and emptied the gun into the control room ventilation valve, sending through enough cement to push out all the water and fill the valve body seven times over.

After the third shot, I ordered Grube to shut off the valve on his short hose, unscrew the surface hose from it, and screw the surface hose into the short hose leading to the engine room valve body.

Meanwhile, Wickwire relieved Grube and finished shifting the hoses. Then we started again to shoot cement, into the engine room valve this time. Meanwhile, Wickwire slipped down the engine room hatch, carrying with him the disconnected hose to the control room. He took this to the door in the bulkhead, gave the valve on the hose end a final turn, to make sure it was tightly closed, and tossed the hose through the door into the control room. This, of course, we had to do before the cement set in the hose and made it so stiff it would not bend. Wickwire swung the door closed, turned down one dog, to make sure the hose was not fouling the door, and then climbed out to his station on the deck again.

We sent four charges of cement in rapid succession through the hose into the engine room valve, which was somewhat larger than the one in the control room. When the last charge had gone through, the diver shut off the valve below, uncoupled the line to the surface, and tossed the short end of the hose with the closed valve down the hatch into the engine room bilges.

On the *Falcon* we dismantled the cement gun and a motor launch took the entire cementing outfit back to the *Vestal.*

Smith went down, entered the engine room, turned down all the dogs on the door leading into the control room, and sledged them tightly home. Michels, going down a little later, connected an airhose to the blowing connection on the salvage hatch which Fraser had long before secured over the gun access trunk.

The control room was ready to blow as soon as the cement hardened.

We waited two days to give it plenty of time to set, then hooked the blowing hose to the *Falcon*'s manifold. Niedermair took the pressure, noted the time, and turned on the air. The pressure steadily rose in the compartment. The cement-filled valve "chattered" no longer, not a bubble of air escaped. In little over an hour, all the water was expelled.

Our second compartment was dry.

XXVII

AN OCEAN OIL WELL

To finish sealing up the interior of the boat, it was only necessary to put a salvage hatch cover over the engine room hatch which had for so long served us as the main entrance to the boat. We started preparing this on the *Vestal*, but I decided that before sealing up the engine room that we could lighten the submarine a little more by removing the fuel which she carried in two sets of double-bottom tanks just above her keel.

The manifold valves leading to these tanks were in the engine room, just forward of the starboard engine.

Kelley went with me to the *S-50*; there he rehearsed carefully on the twelve valves to the tanks, learning to set them so as to blow first the after group of oil tanks, then the forward group.

When letter perfect, Kelley dived on the *S-51*, taking two hoses with him. One of these he screwed to the valve in the deck over the engine room through which the submarine normally took aboard her oil; the other hose he took inside the boat with him and, unscrewing a small relief valve from the fuel oil manifold there, coupled the second hose in its place.

Then it was a case of setting the valves on the intricate manifold, working in a cramped space in the blackness under the floor gratings,— open this valve, make sure that one is closed and so on across the set of valve wheels. At last the task was done, and Kelley reported.

"On deck! All set. Turn on the air!" Kelley started

Niedermair put a pressure on the airhose, watching the gauge carefully to see it did not exceed seventy pounds, as the fuel oil tanks were not heavily built and an excessive pressure would blow them up.

Anxiously we watched the *Falcon*'s end of the oil hose which Kelley had hooked up below. That hose was to form the discharge to the surface from the tanks.

A few seconds after the pressure went on, water started to spurt from the hose to the *Falcon* bilges. Kelley had made no mistakes, the pressure was going through to the oil tanks. Another minute and a dirty mixture of water and oil gushed out, soon followed by a solid stream of fuel oil.

We shoved the end of the hose into a manhole over one of the *Falcon*'s oil tanks. For hours afterwards, the *S-51* spouted oil from the bottom of the sea into the *Falcon*'s bunkers, a gift greeted with smiles by the happy chief engineer of the diving ship. Thirty tons of oil came through the hose by ten o'clock that night, at which time the stream, like many another gusher in the oil fields, turned its owner's smiles to groans by suddenly starting to flow salt water. Evidently the *S-51* had used up over half her fuel before she was sunk.

We pulled the hose from the *Falcon*'s tanks and let it discharge into the bilges for several hours more, when the salt water ceased flowing a steady stream and started to rush out in a spray mixed with air. The tanks were dry, air was coming through. We ceased blowing, disconnected the air hose from our manifold, and climbed into our bunks.

XXVIII

THE ENGINE ROOM HATCH

Everything inside the boat was now complete and we were ready to seal up the engine room. Smith, who together with Frazer had put on the other hatch covers, was selected for the job. Frazer, no longer able to dive, was working on deck in charge of the "bears." Carr was chosen as Smith's mate in place of Frazer.

Together with Smith and Carr, the other divers had rehearsed the installation on the *S-50* of the engine room hatch cover. Several times each pair of divers had lowered the heavy steel cover plate, hoses and all, into place over the *S-50*'s engine room and bolted it down. We could hardly make the rehearsal realistic, lacking the essential feature of working submerged, but to make matters even less like the real job, we were not able to prevent the eager sailors on the *S-50* from helping out the men practicing, whenever the hatch stuck. Below, only two men could get to the hatch and there would be no spectators to lend a hand in the pinches.

The hatch cover for the engine room was the largest and heaviest of the three hatch covers installed on the submarine. Fully assembled, with strongback, discharge valve, air connections, and a heavy suction hose with check valve and strainer box to act as a spillpipe, the thick steel cover plate weighed seven hundred pounds. As an added difficulty, the strongback toggle bar had to be centered inside the boat at the end of a cylindrical trunk three feet below the deck on which the divers worked.

The weight was far too heavy for two men to handle, even if we had not had Frazer's experience to show the danger of overexertion. Here it was physically impossible to manhandle the weight.

There was nothing in the vicinity overhead from which we might hang a chain fall, so we designed and the *Vestal*'s shops made us a small derrick or crane, about seven feet high. As a preliminary step, Michels and Henry descended to the submarine and tied a guide line to the rail near the engine room hatch. Down this line we lowered our crane to the deck below; the divers cut it loose, erected it in a socket in the submarine's deck just abaft the hatch opening, and ran a guy line from the jib of the crane to the rail on each side of the ship to hold the crane head centered over the opening. When the crane was rigged, we sent down a half-ton chain fall, which the divers hooked to the end of the jib, plumbing the hole. Then Michels unhooked the steel ladder inside the trunk which led below into the engine room, down which all the divers had climbed in entering the boat. The ladder would interfere with the strongback. Michels lifted it off the hooks, dropped it into the engine room bilges. The way was cleared for the hatch cover.

Early next morning, Smith and Carr were dressed, and slid down the after descending line to the engine room deck. With only a moderate sea to contend with, Hartley hooked the hatch cover assembly to his boom, hoisted it high above the *Falcon*'s rail to allow the long spillpipe dangling from the underside of the steel plate to pass clear, and swung the bulky mass out over the side. We shackled it to the guide line, and the winchman lowered away slowly. Once the weight was submerged, we kept the guide line as taut as possible, in spite of the rolling of the *Falcon*, in an endeavor to guide the cover down straight. With a little jockeying while the weight surged up and down over the deck of the submarine, we managed to land it close enough for Carr to hook it with the chain fall and drag it over near the open hatch. Smith cut loose all the lowering lines.

The two divers wrestled with the bulky hatch cover, getting the spillpipe through the opening, entering the strongback, lining the securing bolt up on the axis of the trunk, lowering the cover plate down till it rested on the knife edge. It took a long time.

On the *Falcon*, we waited anxiously. The divers made no reports to us. We guessed from hearing over the telephones their brief scraps of directions to each other, when they completed each operation in the job.

Questioning would only annoy them, so no questions were asked and as the divers seemed to be getting along all right we left them alone. But time flew rapidly, the timekeeper warned that the men had been down their allotted hour.

I took Smith's phone.

"Hello, Smith! Time's up. How are you getting along?"

"Fine, Mr. Ellsberg. Nearly done. The hatch cover is touching on one side, and only a few inches off the knife edge on the other side. Leave us alone a few more minutes and we'll have it!"

It was an important job. If they could finish it, it were best to let them stay, as they were thoroughly familiar with conditions. We could give them a little extra decompression on the way up.

I waited twenty minutes, with the timekeeper eyeing me inquiringly all the time. No report from below.

Again I telephoned.

"Hello, Smith! Nearly done?"

"Yes, Mr. Ellsberg. Just another minute now and we'll have it!"

But that minute dragged on to many more minutes and they did not have it. Apparently the strongback bolt was not quite true with the center of the hatch, and it kept the hatch cover from sliding home all around the knife edge. The cover touched on the high side (the starboard side) but it was still several inches off on the low side. The divers were trying to jockey the bolt and the cover this way and that so the cover would drop and touch all around.

At intervals, I called the men, told them to quit, they were long overdue; but each time they were nearly done, a few more minutes would see them finished, let them alone, plus plenty of profanity interspersed with their remarks.

On deck we grew more and more nervous as the time wore on and the men would not report themselves clear and ready to ascend. I took Smith's phone, called down to him:

"How is it now?"

"We nearly got it now. Don't bother us!"

I looked at the timekeeper. "Three hours and twenty minutes now," he said.

I turned to the tenders.

"Take them up!"

Without further discussion, we dragged both men off the deck of the submarine and started them to the surface. They had been down nearly three and a half times the safe limit, on the longest dive ever made in deep water. Our decompression tables had no figures to cover such a case; to be sure, we spent nine hours in decompressing them! It was morning when Smith and Carr went down: it was evening when finally they came over the rail,—weak, wet, and frozen, but principally angry because we had refused to let them finish when success was just a matter of another minute's work! The surgeon put them on the sick list to keep them in their bunks.

Another pair of divers went down to try, but they also failed to get the cover down all around. I decided to modify the assembly, and sent Michels and Grube down to cast the hatch cover loose and send up everything. They slacked off the chain fall to release the strongback and managed to get the heavy cover plate hooked and lifted clear of the opening, when the strongback slipped away from them and dropped into the engine room bilges. The ladder was gone, he had no light, but nevertheless, without reporting anything to the surface, Mike had Grube lower him through the hatch into the engine room bilges where he groped nearly an hour in darkness in a mass of piping before he finally found the missing strongback, tied a line on it, and then after Grube had hauled him up through the hole, asked us on deck to heave on the line and lift out the strongback.

On the *Falcon*, Niedermair redesigned the strongback, added an auxiliary centering bar and clamp to permit the strongback bolt to be lined up and independently held in the hatch trunk before the cover was slipped down.

We drilled another pair of divers on the *S-50* with the new arrangement; then sent them down to try it on the *S-51*. They failed to get it installed.

For three days, every pair of divers we had tried their hands on that hatch and came up without success, some cursing, others nearly weeping. Everything happened. One pair apparently got the strongback lined up squarely, the hatch cover slipped over it, and were ready to screw down on the securing nut when they found they had so burred up the threads on the strongback bolt while sliding the cover down it, that the nut would not engage the threads. They had to disassemble everything, send up the whole hatch rig again, for the *Vestal* to recut the thread on the bolt.

Another pair of divers got the hatch cover nearly down, enough so they felt a few turns on the nut would force it home, when they found that they had lost the nut. They telephoned up the bad news, asked for another nut. Unfortunately, it was a very special large nut, to fit over a two-inch-diameter bolt. We had no spares. Hurriedly we examined the main engines on both the *Falcon* and the *Vestal* to see if we could steal a nut that size from them. There was none. The divers had to come up.

USS S-51

SS City of Rome

The derricks were finally towed to the wreck and heaved down. Nothing budged.

The Falcon *moored over the* S-51.

Chief Torpedoman Smith being hoisted over the side.

I lifted Wilson's transmitter to my lips.

Soon another flag-draped body passed down the quarterdeck.

The S-50 *coming alongside for a diver's rehearsal.*

I asked Kelley to dress, got dressed myself.

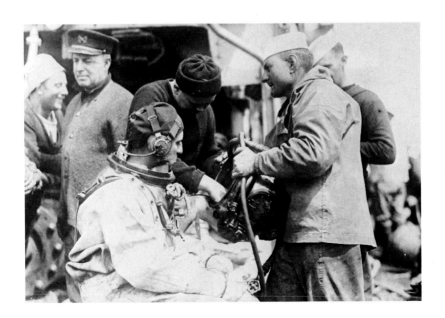

I grasped the bails and was swung over the side.

"The iron doctor." Outside the recompression tank.

Chief Torpedoman Kelley with the Ellsberg cutting torch.

Waldren's special balanced hose nozzle.

*Bow pontoons driven out of alignment by the sea,
June 22, 1926.*

*Wickwire dug his fingernails into the slippery sheathing,
climbed aboard.*

"The bow is up!"

On the Falcon: *Boatswains Hawes and Burnett, Mr. Niedermair, Lieutenant Kelly, Commander Ellsberg, and Lieutenant Hartley.*

We went safely through Hell Gate.

Arrangement of pontoons.

The submarine suddenly stopped, the pontoons bobbed violently.

Bow pontoons below the surface at Man of War Rock. Crew opening valves.

S-51 *entering the drydock.*

S-51 *on blocks. Deck about one foot above water.*

S-51 in drydock. Dock pumped down and bilge shores in place.

"Well, Mr. Ellsberg, have you decided to give back that bell you stole?"

A huge hole in her port side.

Divers who salvaged S-51: Front row—Davis, Michels, Wickwire, Eiben, Frazer, Bailey, Ellsberg, Eadie, Smith, Carr, Kelley, Frank Anderson; rear row—A. D. Clark, McLagan, Dewberry, Grube, Horan, Boyd, Applegate, McNeil, G. W. Clark, Clemens (in rear), Holden, Henry, Sanders. Absent in picture: Wilson, Ingram, George Anderson, Madden, L'Heureux.

The blacksmith and the machinists labored all that night, forging and machining another nut,—two of them in fact, for we made up a spare also at the same time. Next day, two other divers took the new nut down to screw it on and force the hatch cover home, only to find that, after all, the strongback bolt was on such a slant away from true, that when the nut was still six inches away from the cover plate, the bolt came so close to the large discharge valve on top of the plate that the nut would not go by the valve. The divers had to unrig the cover again and cast loose the strongback, ready to start at the beginning.

Three days had passed since we started on the hatch. That cover and its fittings had been down on the submarine and then up again for modifications or repairs three different times.

Smith and Carr were once more out of their bunks and around on deck, still weak but full of fight. They asked for another chance at the hatch. Since everyone else had tried and failed, and the job had to be done, I described to them the new assembly, and let them go down to try again.

They were dressed, hoisted overboard, slid down. For three days and nights they had dreamed about that hatch,—now they had their hands on it again. Carefully they lined up the strongback bolt, sighted it from all sides to get it true. Gently they hoisted the cover plate up over the bolt, and slowly lowered it down over the threaded part of the bolt till it touched the knife edge.

They had been working nearly fifty minutes. I wanted no repetition of a dangerously long dive; it might be fatal to them the second time. I had on both their telephones, one on each ear.

I called Smith.

"Hello, Smith! How are you making out?"

"Fine, Mr. Ellsberg. She's down on one side, only a couple of inches off on the other side, and we'll have it in a few minutes!"

I dropped the transmitter, a little sick at heart, and called the time-keeper over to my side. They would stay no longer than their hour this time.

The divers were talking to each other. I heard Carr say, "I'd better jump on it and jam it down."

"No, don't," Smith replied. "You'll burr up those threads again and the nut won't screw down!"

Silence. They worked a few minutes more, trying to nurse the cover farther down. Apparently no success.

Smith became desperate. I heard him say to Carr:

"All right, go ahead and jump on the — — — —!"

I listened. Carr jumped, there was a clatter of lead shoes on the steel plate, and then I heard a joyous cry from Smith:

"Hooray, Willie! We got it!" As the cover went down under Carr's feet, Smith leaped on the nut, and he afterwards claimed that before it hit the knife edge all around he had four full turns on the nut to keep it from bouncing back!

The fish thereabout saw the strange spectacle of two heavily weighted divers wildly dancing a hornpipe on top of the hatch.

Smith asked for a large wrench, begged to be allowed to stay a few minutes to tighten down the securing nut. We sent an open-ended wrench three feet long, and with that Carr and Smith turned the nut down with such a will that later, when the boat was raised, we had great difficulty releasing it.

The divers started up. They had, after all, been down only ten minutes over their allotted hour.

And so the engine room hatch was finally sealed up, completing all the work inside the boat.

XXIX

MORE PONTOONS

The day after Eadie and Wilson had managed to reeve a line through the tunnel, it being then a little past the middle of May, the weather looked calm enough to proceed with pontoon lowering. We ordered the *Sagamore*, which was standing by in Newport, to come out early with a new pontoon. Meanwhile, we rove off a pair of four-inch manila lines through the tunnel, ready to proceed with the pontoon.

In the middle of a beautiful May morning, one of the smoothest days we ever had, the pontoon was towed to the *Falcon*'s port side, a pair of chains dangling from its hawsepipes, and we prepared to rig it for lowering.

The hauling wires were shackled to the lower ends of the chains. The four-inch manila lines were spliced smoothly into the eyes on the opposite ends of the wires, to make as small obstructions as possible to running under the keel. Then we hauled up to starboard on the after manila line, slowly pulling it through while we paid out to port on the wire cable tied to it.

There was a little difficulty when the eye in the wire reached the box keel of the submarine. The eye caught on the underhanging keel, and considerable pulling both ways was required before it slipped free of the projecting angle bar on the keel and let the wire reeve through. We kept on pulling and at last drew the end of the after wire hauling line in over our starboard rail, where we secured it.

Next we started to haul up the forward four-inch reeving line, spliced to the other wire cable. We had the manila line on the winch coming in steadily and evenly over the starboard rail while we paid out the wire from the opposite side at the same rate to prevent it from getting slack and kinking up. Without warning, the wire stopped running out. I glanced at the winch to see why it had ceased heaving, but the winch was turning as before. Not quite, however, as I saw when I ran over to the starboard rail, for the manila line coming in there was coming up slack, and its frayed end flopped over the rail, the strands looking as if they had been cut with a knife. An extra strain on the hauling line had drawn the manila hawser tightly across the starboard bilge keel and the sharp edge of the rolling chock had instantly cut the line in half.

I knew the starboard bilge keel was about one foot clear of the bottom at a point near the tunnel. There might still be perhaps a foot of the other half of the line sticking out of the mud to which we could bend a new line and pull our wire through. Bailey dived with another manila line tied to his belt. He crawled along the bottom on his stomach, feeling under the bilge keel, and finally found the frayed ends of the hawser just showing clear of the clay, some three feet forward of the tunnel. In the reeving process, the line had apparently sawed its way along the keel, out of the tunnel, and we were pulling it and the wire attached to it through the solid clay beneath the boat. No wonder the line had jammed and cut.

There was hardly enough of the broken end of the line showing for Bailey to get a grip on, but he managed to scoop enough clay away to grip the strands in his gloved fists and pull the line taut, giving him perhaps a foot of unstranded manila to bend his new line to, which he did as well as possible in the cramped quarters and strained position in which he lay.

Over the telephone, he reported the knot tied, and crawled a little clear to observe results. Bailey meanwhile warned us:

"This bilge keel has a rough edge just like a saw. Look out when you heave!"

Seeing what had already happened, it was certainly not safe to pull the line across that rolling chock again. I got the forty-foot motor launch from the *Vestal*, took the end of the line Bailey had tied on, and steamed away from the *Falcon* with it perhaps one hundred fathoms. With that length of line leading at an angle down to the submarine, Bailey reported we were not chafing over the sharp bilge keel.

Three seamen hauled in the slack over the stern of the launch, took a few turns around the samson post, and the coxswain went ahead slowly on his engine till the line tautened out, when we gradually applied more power to pull the line through. The launch suddenly leaped ahead, the line came aboard all slack. We stopped our engine to avoid tangling the line in our propeller. The launch ran alongside the *Falcon*. That attempt was a failure; Bailey reported that the frayed ends to which he had bent the new line had let go. There was not enough left showing clear of the bottom to secure another line to. Bailey was coming up.

We changed our tactics. Once more the fire hose was rigged up, and Michels went down with it to wash away enough clay around the end of that line to let him get a decent hitch on it. We turned on the water, Mike washed a little hole down the line and widened it out somewhat under the overhanging bilge keel so he could, lying down, get his hands in to work. After nearly an hour of washing, Mike exposed about a foot of the undamaged manila; on this he tied his new four-inch line, with a rolling hitch and a couple of half hitches. Mike came out, and we hauled up both Mike and the hose.

Once more I set out in the motor launch and we went ahead till the full power of our gasoline engine was pulling on that one hundred fathoms of line leading away to the ocean bottom. Nothing happened, we could not pull the wire through under the keel. I signaled for a second launch.

Meanwhile the weather was changing. The bright spring sun was gone; the water had turned from a beautiful blue to a dull gray and the wind had started to freshen up. Our little launch was pitching vigorously as the waves rolled by.

The second launch arrived, we took a line from it around the king post in our bow. Both launches went ahead, till their gas engines were running with wide open throttles and their propellers were kicking up a white foam under the sterns of each launch. But we were anchored, the line would not reeve through, and I dared not put any more strain on the line for fear of breaking it. The weather was getting worse, we could not try longer. I cast off the leading boat, and coiling the line down inside the other launch as we ran, we steamed back alongside the *Falcon*.

Conditions were in a dangerous state there. It was now dark, and a storm was blowing up. The sea was rough, the wind already bad, and increasing. The *Falcon* was rolling heavily, and the pontoon alongside was rising and falling violently as the waves rolled by, hammering our side and threatening to crash in over our rail as it rose to the crest of some of the waves. Two three-ton chains, ninety feet long, hung vertically through the hawsepipes of that pontoon down towards the submarine, and from the lower ends of those chains our reeving lines ran under the submarine.

The situation was bad and rapidly growing worse. If we let the *Sagamore* tow the pontoon away from our side, she would pull out from under the submarine the reeving lines that the divers had fought so hard to pass through the tunnel. If we wanted to save those lines, it was necessary to leave the pontoon battering our side while we hooked each anchor chain separately, with our wildly swinging boom, hoisted it up through the pontoon onto the *Falcon*'s deck and unshackled the wires from the lower ends of the chains.

One of the boatswains objected.

"You'll tear the mast out of the *Falcon* trying to lift those three-ton chains while we're rolling this way; and those swinging chains'll kill somebody sure when we try to get 'em in on deck. Let the *Sagamore* take the pontoon away, reeving lines and all, or we'll get sunk!"

He was probably right. The seas were breaking over us, the pontoon was one moment awash, the next leaping over our heads threatening to crash down on our deck. But I thought of the fight Eadie and Wilson had put up to get those lines through. I could not cast their work away without a struggle, and turned to Hartley.

"Will you try it, captain?" Back came the sailor's answer, the old, old call of the seaman unafraid:

"Aye, aye, sir!"

He looked over his men crowded into the narrow passage at the rail, beckoned to one.

"On the pontoon, Badders! Hook on the falls!"

The boom swung over the side, plumbing the pontoon. On the next roll, Badders, poised on the rail, leaped to the top of the pontoon as it dropped away in the trough of the sea. A boatswain's mate slacked roundly on the falls, the heavy block from the boom alternately dropped onto the pontoon and lifted away from it as the *Falcon* rolled. The *Falcon*'s searchlight cast a blue glare through the darkness, framing the heaving pontoon and the man on it against a black background of flying spray and tumbling seas.

A wire strap was flung to Badders; he caught it, slipped it through the end of one chain. On the next roll, as the hanging block shot down on the pontoon and paused a second, he dragged it to the chain link, caught the hook in the strap, leaped clear. The chain rose with a jerk ten feet out of the hawsepipe as the *Falcon* rolled away; the boom flew over and the *Falcon*'s mainmast whipped violently under the sudden strain. Hartley shouted to the winchman:

"Heave round smartly!" The winch groaned under its load, the fall came in, the heavy anchor chain rose through the hawsepipe. Badders rode the pontoon, clinging tightly to the valves.

The falls came two-blocks; we could hoist no more as the boom had only forty feet of clearance over the rail. The sailors slacked one guy, hauled in on the other. The boom swung in over the deck, the chain swayed violently from boom to pontoon. Boatswain Hawes leaped to the rail, passed a stopper around the chain where it crossed our side, secured his stopper to the bitts. The chain could not run back. Hartley slacked away on the boom; forty feet of chain came clattering down on our deck, with all hands standing clear to avoid being brained by one of the flying links.

The block lay slack over the heap of tangled chain; the boatswain's mate unhooked the block, passed another strap around the chain at the point where Hawes had stoppered it to the rail, hooked the block in again there. The fall was taken up. Once more the weight came on the boom. More chain rose up through the hawsepipe; the bight of the chain to the tune of creaking lines, ascended toward the head of the boom, and Hartley as his mast swayed and whipped in the seaway, eyed his standing rigging anxiously and wondered whether it would hold.

Up went the second flight of chain, dangling from the block,—one bight leading to our deck, the other to the pontoon where, link by link, the chain banged the top of the hawsepipe as it was dragged clear. The last link came out, the chain swung in to our side dragging the end of the reeving wire with it. In came our boom again, down came the block, all the chain hanging from it this time, to be dumped in a heap in the passageway.

The block was unhooked, the wire unshackled, a manila line with a number of small cork floats tied onto the end of the reeving wire.

Again the boatswain threw a strap to Badders, who ran it through the top link of the other chain. Once more the boom swung out, the block swung wildly over the pontoon. Badders hooked the block in, jumped aside as the chain jerked out of the pipe.

Again the mast whipped crazily but the rigging held; up went the second chain; finally it also lay in a heap on deck. Its reeving wire was unshackled and a manila line with buoys also secured to it.

A husky seaman heaved the end of a six-inch manila hawser aboard the pontoon. Badders ran it through the towing eye on the pontoon, took a few half hitches, then leaped back on the *Falcon*, thoroughly soaked.

"Man the surfboat!" shouted Hartley. Boatswain Hawes, the coxswain, four seamen, tumbled over the *Falcon*'s stern into the boat, stood off a little from our port side.

A heaving line shot from the *Falcon*'s deck, fell across the boat. A sailor leaped on it, pulled it in. The boat crew hauled it aboard, getting at its end the six-inch towline, which they dragged over their stern as they headed for the *Sagamore*, which was standing by a few hundred feet to leeward. The surfboat, bobbing like a cork among the waves as our searchlight followed it through the darkness, ran close aboard the *Sagamore*, caught another heaving line from her, watched the hawser end being dragged over the *Sagamore*'s rail and made fast to her bitts.

Four sharp blasts came through the night from the *Sagamore*'s whistle; she was under way. The six-inch hawser ran out from our deck in the *Sagamore*'s wake; when it was all gone, two axes swung against our rail on the straining lines which held the leaping pontoon to our side. The pontoon rose over our rail on the crest of a wave; the towline tautened with a jerk and the heaving cylinder fairly jumped thirty feet clear of us as it fell away into the trough. Lieutenant Hartley breathed a sigh of relief as he watched it vanish in the darkness.

"Well, commander, I didn't think the old boat would stand it. Did you see the way the mainmast whipped when the weight came on?"

As the pontoon pulled away, we paid out on the buoy lines and the wires ran back down through the hawsepipes, sinking to the sea bottom. Soon we let go the buoys. They were dragged through the water, up over the pontoon, and shot down through the hawsepipes as the pontoon drew far enough away to take up all the slack in the buoy lines. The pontoon disappeared astern of the *Sagamore*. Our searchlight cut back and forth in its wake. There were the buoys, floating clear, safely secured to the ends of our reeving lines!

The searchlight picked up the surfboat; in its beam, we watched Hawes and his men tossing madly in the sea as, one by one, they ran alongside the mooring buoys, harpooned the toggles with their boathooks, cast loose the pelicans. One by one we dragged in the water-soaked hawsers till only one straining line to windward held us. The *Falcon* steamed ahead on that to slack the strain; the surfboat tripped the hook, the storm swung us flying down to leeward till the ship picked up headway enough to steer, when we steamed up to make a lee for the surfboat. One at a time, the crew tumbled over our rail, wet as usual. Towing the surfboat by a long painter over her stern, the *Falcon* steamed well clear to anchor and ride out the storm.

A day of heartbreaking disappointments.

XXX

A TUG OF WAR

The storm blew for two days. When the sea flattened out somewhat afterwards, we moored again. As expected, we found some kinks in wires when we picked them up, but the divers finally worked them free. After much labor, Michels and Bailey, working from opposite sides of the submarine, managed to saw the forward line, which was jammed under the keel, back into the tunnel, where the eye passed through without much resistance, and we were ready again to lower a pontoon. The *Sagamore* towed back the pontoon we had struggled with before, we took it alongside, secured the hauling wires to the chains (which the *Vestal* had replaced in the hawsepipes), secured our lowering lines, connected up the airhoses. The pontoon was to go on the port side of the submarine. We started to flood down, meanwhile taking in the slack of the wires on the starboard side as the pontoon filled. By early afternoon, the pontoon was awash and ready to sink. We let it submerge, held it just under the surface till it took in about five tons more water, then Badders and Weaver swung over the side on the stages and closed the flood valves. Everything was ready.

With Hartley at the after line and myself at the forward one, we slacked out on the twelve-inch hawsers, and the pontoon started down on our opposite side of the *Falcon*, the boatswain heaving in on the hauling wires as we paid out on our hawsers. The lowering went beautifully,—for the first fifty feet. Then came a cry from across the deck. I ran over to investigate.

Boatswain Burnett, in charge there, explained:

"We can't get any more on these wires. I've given 'em all I dare on the winches, but they won't render. They just stopped coming up."

Others gathered round. Niedermair checked the length of wire that had come in; we knew the length of chain hanging from the pontoon. Everything fitted together. The first link in each chain had reached the box keel and hung up there, that was why the wires dragging the chains through refused to haul up further.

We expected a little difficulty in hauling the chains through, which was one reason we were using plow steel wire cables to pull them with,— each wire was good for a strain of thirty tons and it would not chafe through while hauling over the keel or bilge keel.

We lowered the pontoon ten feet further to make sure the chains were slack going through the tunnel, then tried again to heave up on the wires. No use,—they would not come.

We thought the matter over. We were pulling vertically upward, which would tend to jam the chain links hard against the projecting keel. Perhaps if we pulled out horizontally, the links would drop clear of the keel and run through. We slacked our wire hauling lines a little, and took them off our winches. We bent an eight-inch manila hawser to the end of one wire, a six-inch hawser to the end of the other one. The *Iuka*, which had a very powerful towing winch on her stern, much stronger than our winches, was ordered to anchor one hundred fathoms off our starboard beam. We sent the two heavy manila hawsers to her, told her to heave in on them. With the eight-inch line over one niggerhead and the six-inch line over the other, both leading up nearly horizontally from under the submarine, the *Iuka* heaved round but without result. The afternoon wore on, darkness came with the pontoon still hanging from our side, halfway to the bottom. I ordered the *Iuka* to go ahead on her main engine and see if she could drag the chains through that way. The tug, specially designed to tow large battleships, gradually worked up to full speed, when with her throttle wide open, her propeller was churning up a wake which rushed past us, one hundred fathoms away, as a strong current. But she got no slack through on the hawsers. The chains were firmly anchored against the keel of the submarine. The *Iuka* stopped.

It was getting late. We could not afford to hold the pontoon much longer. As a last-ditch measure, I ordered the *Iuka* to slack off the six-inch line, and put her full towing strain on the eight-inch hawser alone, to see whether she might not pull the chains through one at a time.

We trained our searchlight on the *Iuka*'s stem. The six-inch hawser slacked, sagged away. The eight-inch line tautened, stood out from her stern straight into the sea as the throttle was opened and the engine began to race at top speed. The *Iuka* moved ahead a little; evidently the hawser had stretched a bit under the pull; the *Iuka* came to a standstill, her propeller churning the sea violently. Suddenly the taut hawser leaped free out of the water, a broken end shot in on the *Iuka*'s stern. The eight-inch hawser had parted!

With the strain gone, the *Iuka* jumped ahead as if shot from a gun, brought up on the slack six-inch hawser, parted that as if it were a thread, and ran several hundred yards before the engine could be stopped and the ship brought to rest.

It was ten P.M. There was nothing further we could do. Michels went down on the pontoon with a light to make sure we did not land the pontoon on the submarine. Under his direction, we jockeyed the *Falcon* as best we could to place the pontoon where we wanted it, but we were badly handicapped by no longer having any hauling lines under the submarine to pull the cylinder into position. In the darkness, we made a fair job of it. The pontoon rested on the bottom, touching the side of the submarine at its forward end, and slanting away from it at an angle of about thirty degrees.

As soon as the pontoon rested on the bottom and the lines were slacked, Michels cast off the lowering hawsers, disconnected the airhoses, and came up.

The *Falcon* unmoored and steamed clear for the night. For two weeks we struggled with that pontoon, trying to get the chains dragged through the tunnel. Divers crawled down the tunnel, alongside the chains, to fit large pine wedges between the keel and the chains in an attempt to guide the chains by the point where the first links were catching. It did not work. The divers tried with crowbars to work the first links through, but there was not room enough in the tunnel to swing the bars. We decided to pull the chains out of the tunnel, fit a tapering steel cone over the first link to fill the shoulder between the inch-thick wire and the twelve-inch-wide link. To do this, it was necessary to hook into the chains as they ran from under the pontoon across the intervening fifteen feet to the tunnel mouth. Even this comparatively simple job was difficult. The chain lay in a tangled heap between pontoon and submarine. It was difficult to tell which part led to the pontoon, which went to the tunnel.

Sanders dived to secure a line for hauling back the chains. He slipped over the side of the submarine in way of the torpedo davit, which landed him in the angle between the pontoon and the submarine. The water was murky. He took a step, then lost all sense of direction, could see nothing at all, and stumbled about for ten minutes without knowing where he was, till he accidentally bumped into the submarine. He had informed me he was lost, but I could not then help him other than to advise him to walk in a straight line, and he was bound to hit something. When he reported hitting the submarine, I took him by the hand, so to speak, over the telephone.

"Hello, Sanders! Put your right hand against the submarine! Got that?"

"Yes, sir!"

"Sure it's your right hand?" (Divers are liable to get muddled and not think clearly, when under heavy pressure.)

"It sure is, commander!"

"All right. You're on the port side of the sub, your right hand is touching her, so you're facing forward. Walk along, keep your right hand against the sub, and you'll bump into the pontoon. Got that?"

Sanders walked as directed some twenty feet till he came to the apex of the triangle where the pontoon rested against the submarine's port side. He bumped into the pontoon, reported hitting it.

"All right, Sanders, you're doing fine! Now turn around, keep your right hand against the pontoon, and walk along till you fall over a pile of anchor chain!"

Sanders turned, started along the side of the pontoon, carefully keeping his hand against it in order not to get lost again. Opposite the middle of the pontoon, he stumbled across a length of chain, and a few feet to the left of it was a pile of chain at least five feet high.

He had never at any time been more than fifteen feet away from at least one of the three objects, the submarine, the pontoon, or the chain, yet it took half his dive, with the sun shining brightly on the surface, to locate what he was looking for. That instance was not unusual in working on the submarine.

Sanders passed a strap around one of the chains. We hauled back on the strap till the first link of the chain came out of the tunnel, then pulled the other chain out similarly. When Sanders came up, the weather was too bad for further diving.

A few days later, when we could work again, Bailey and Anderson fitted a tapered cone over one end link, moused the tip of the cone to the wire to prevent it slipping off. They found the eye of the other wire, where it was shackled to the chain, badly chafed and in danger of letting go under another heavy pull. We would have to pull through a replacement wire.

Wickwire tried to unshackle the wire to allow it to be pulled up, but he could not get a solid enough swing with his sledge on the tapered locking pin in the special shackle to drive it free. To help him, we lifted up the end of the chain, draped it across the submarine's deck, where he tried again without any luck.

I went down with the torch, and another shackle, to solve the difficulty. Chief Torpedoman Sanders went down to help me, carrying a four-inch manila line.

I found myself for the first time on the *S-51*'s forecastle near the torpedo davit, with the end of the anchor cable hanging about three links over the starboard side (the high side).

The first part of the job was easy. I turned on the gases, lighted the torch, and burned through the eye of the old wire in a few seconds. Then up went the torch.

Sanders bent his manila line to the remains of the eye on the wire. The *Falcon*'s deck force, at our direction, pulled up on the line, hauling out the old wire, and at the same time reeving around a new wire secured to its other end. When the eye of the new wire came through to us, we dragged it over to where the chain lay and proceeded to shackle the eye to the end link of the chain.

I hung over the side of the *S-51*, with a short manila line from my belt to the rail overhead to hold me in position. Sanders took the new shackle apart, put half of it on the deck, and leaned down to give me the other half. It weighed perhaps fifty pounds. With that in one hand, I struggled with the other to lift some of the ninety-pound chain links a little free of the side so I could engage the end link in one horn of the shackle. With Sanders hanging far over the edge of the deck to assist, we finally managed it, and I then slipped the wire eye over the other horn of the shackle. Sanders carefully pulled himself back on deck, reached for the closing half of the shackle. It was gone. Probably it had slipped down the sharp incline of the deck to port and was buried somewhere in the mud. At any rate, we could not afford to search for it. Sanders went back to the descending line, telephoned to have another shackle sent down, while I dangled over the starboard side and surveyed as much of the boat as my limited vision through the water would allow. No damage in that vicinity but there were innumerable bits of manila lines hanging down all over her. Plenty of cordage had gone down on various jobs; most of it could be seen tangled in a web over the boat.

Sanders moved slowly through the sea towards me with a new shackle in one hand, clinging to the rail with the other hand as he shuffled along. I took the shackle, fitted in place the missing parts, pushed in the locking pin, drove it home with a hammer, peened down a lead plug over the pin to hold it firmly. I was panting hard when Sanders hauled me back on deck. Together we took our decompression on our way up. But Chief Torpedoman Sanders made no more dives after that. He had had tropical fever some time before he joined us; the strain of heaving on the anchor chain put him on the sick list for the rest of the job.

Wilson and Eiben fitted a tapered cone over the first link on this chain, guided the lines while we lowered the chain once more to the mouth of the tunnel.

We dragged one chain into the tunnel with the wire, but in spite of our fairing piece, it still hung on the keel. We tried hauling it with our capstan, it would not come. We bent a ten-inch manila hawser to the wire and once more put the *Iuka* off on our starboard beam to try to pull the chain through. We were sure the ten-inch hawser would not break.

The *Iuka* heaved in on her towing winch, but the chain would not come through. Then the *Iuka* went ahead on her engine full speed, but that also failed to start the chain. Still the hawser held, so as a last resort, I asked the *Iuka* to back down, let the hawser hang in a bight, and then suddenly steam ahead on it full speed, hoping that the sudden jerk might make the chain jump free of the keel.

The *Iuka* drifted down toward us till the line was slack, then jumped ahead with her engine wide open. She brought up on the hawser with a sharp jerk. The chain did not start, but something else did. The *Iuka*'s towing winch, to which the hawser was secured, was torn out of the quarterdeck and went flying over her stern into the sea.

Evidently we were beaten. The chains were never going to go through that way. We sent Eadie down, connected a pair of airhoses to the pontoon, and blew it, chains and all, up to the surface.

Then we dragged the pontoon alongside our rail, and for the second time, but in a calm sea on this occasion, we lifted the chains out of the hawsepipes, landed them on our deck, released the wires, and let the *Sagamore* tow the pontoon away.

I had a new method for handling the chains. We would send them down one at a time, without the pontoon. Each chain, on deck where we could work, had a new tapered steel cone carefully fitted to fair off between wire and link, and the first few links were partly wound with marline to fill the shoulders.

When this was done, we lowered the first chain over the *Falcon*'s rail, hauling up on a wire on the other side. A diver entered the tunnel with the chain; with no pontoon to interfere, and a line on each end of the chain so we could haul it either way, the diver easily worked the first link by the keel, and the rest of the chain, with the diver out of the tunnel, we then dragged through in short order till half the chain hung evenly on each side of the submarine. The second chain quickly followed in the same way, and then with wires leading to the surface as guides on both sides of the *S-51*, we were ready again for another attempt to lower a pontoon alongside the tunnel.

For the third time the *Sagamore* brought back the pontoon we had labored with for weeks. We rigged the lines and flooded it down. In about an hour it was awash; the stages swung over the side with Badders and Weaver manning the wrenches. The pontoon sank a few feet below the surface. We held it there and closed the flood valves.

Then with Hartley aft and me forward, once more, fathom by fathom, we slacked out our twelve-inch lines till the cylinder was down one hundred feet. Kelley and McLagan ready and dressed, slid down the hoses.

"On the pontoon!" A few minutes passed while Kelley peered at the submarine below.

"All clear, lower away slowly!"

We slacked away. With the divers riding it, the pontoon went down about twenty feet more. The anchor chains showed in the hawsepipes as we lowered, till seven links suspended from the guide wires, projected above the pontoon.

"On deck! Hold her!" The lines on the bitts tautened, the pontoon swung from our side. Both chains and pontoon moved up and down together, as the *Falcon* rolled.

We had previously painted with a bright yellow color the links through which the toggle bars were to go. With our new method of handling chains and pontoons separately, there was no longer any danger of the chains kinking up, so before we lowered the chains, we had burned out the stud in the yellow link.

Kelley unscrewed his diving knife, cut the lashings holding a toggle bar to the top of the pontoon. Cautiously he lifted the heavy bar, balancing himself on the swaying pontoon as he approached the chain in the forward hawsepipe. The open yellow link was waist high. He shot his one hundred and forty pound bar through it; McLagan on the other side pushed home the locking pin. The second toggle bar went into the other chain in the same way.

"On deck! Both toggles secured. Lower away!"

Once more we slacked. The pontoon went the last fifteen feet; and the wood-sheathed cylinder came to rest on the bottom alongside the sunken wreck. The lowering lines went slack upon our bitts.

Kelley unshackled the pelican hooks, and one at a time the capstan heaved up the waterlogged hawsers. Then the divers came up.

The *Iuka* was standing by with another pontoon. It was already 8 P.M. but we had no desire to stop. We took the mate pontoon alongside, rigged it, and started it down at 10 P.M. It vanished in the darkness, and we lowered it slowly one hundred feet. There we held it while Carr and Grube slid down the hoses to it. It was clear of the boat; we lowered it till the chains showed through the proper amount and once again held it from our bitts.

Carr cut the lashings on one of the toggles, lifted the heavy steel bar, aimed it at the yellow link. Both pontoon and chain, suspended from the *Falcon*'s side, moved lazily up and down together. Carr shot the toggle halfway through the link, Grube rammed through the locking pin to hold it. A second toggle quickly followed in the other chain.

"On deck! Both toggles in!" sang out Carr.

Again we lowered till the pontoon touched bottom. Grube cast off the lowering lines. I slid the torch down to Carr. Then one at a time we slacked off on the guide wires till the ends of the chains rested on top of the pontoon. Carr lighted the torch, rapidly burned the wires off the chains, climbed across to the mate pontoon and cut the wires there. Meanwhile Grube closed the air valves and disconnected the hoses. The divers reached the surface, just at midnight. With our new method, in one day they did what two weeks of heartbreaking labor with the chains in the tunnel had previously failed to accomplish.

XXXI

THE LAST TUNNEL

There was still one more tunnel required to take the chains for the fourth and last pair of pontoons, abreast the conning tower.

For some weeks, I had looked forward to this task with dread. We had had a terrible time in the first tunnel. It seemed doubtful that the divers could last through another such ordeal, especially as the new tunnel, being amidships and therefore under the widest part of the submarine, would be even longer than the first one.

It was nearing the end of May. On the surface the weather was growing milder, storms became less frequent. But on the bottom the water still retained its intense chill and conditions for the divers were as bad as ever. Our first-string divers displayed no enthusiasm about starting the second tunnel.

Meanwhile a machinist's mate on the *Falcon*, Waldren, had been thinking over our tunneling troubles. He visualized the divers sent flying over the ocean bottom by the "kick" from the nozzle and he remembered that he had once seen a different type of nozzle which had no kickback. Waldren said nothing, but getting a heavy brass bar, he busied himself for some weeks on the lathe in the engine room, machining out a nozzle which, when completed, looked like nothing anyone in the salvage squadron had ever seen. In addition to a large opening which discharged water ahead, it had a number of smaller ports which discharged water at an angle astern; the whole nozzle was so proportioned that the kick ahead and the kick astern practically balanced each other. I learned months afterwards that this nozzle had already been patented years before for other uses, but so far as we were concerned off Block Island, it was a brand-new idea.

Waldren brought out his handiwork just before we were about to start the new tunnel. It was a full-sized nozzle, so we used a two-and-one-half-inch fire hose again for the first time since the day Bailey had started the other tunnel.

Eadie went down with the new nozzle, carefully spotted his position on the port side abreast the conning tower, braced himself with the nozzle pointed at the clay close to the buried hull, and sang out:

"On deck! Turn on the water!"

Slowly we opened the valve from the fire main to his hose till the pressure rose to thirty pounds, then held it there. The hose swelled out moderately. Far below, Eadie started washing. He worked a minute, then I heard:

"On deck! More pressure on the hose!"

The valve was opened a little wider, the pressure went to fifty pounds. Shortly another call:

"More pressure!"

We had never been above sixty pounds, even with the small hose, but if Eadie could stand it, we could, so the gauge went up to seventy pounds. Still not satisfied, Eadie called for more, and we opened the valve wide, gave him the full force of the pump, one hundred pounds. The hose stiffened out, became hard as iron, in a long bend swept over the rail into the sea. At the valve, a seaman stood by to close off hurriedly if the nozzle tore from Eadie's hands. I listened anxiously. Another call.

"On deck! Give me some pressure!"

"You've got one hundred pounds already!"

"Give me some more then! I'm just starting to do some real digging!"

I yelled down the hatch where an engineer stood by the wrecking pump.

"Speed up on that pump. Give her the limit!"

He opened the throttle. The needle jumped,—one hundred and twenty, one hundred and thirty, one hundred and forty, one hundred and fifty pounds,—the limiting pressure for which the wrecking pump was built.

A terrific pressure for any man to try to hold. But no complaint came from Eadie. The pump labored on.

Another call from below:

"More pressure!"

I looked down the hatch where the engineer waited.

"Shove her up till she breaks!"

The chief engineer screwed down on the safety valve, shot more steam to the pump. Up went the pressure again. One hundred and sixty, one hundred and eighty, two hundred pounds. The gauge needle would go no further. We paused there. The domed cast iron head over the pump cylinder was pulsing back and forth with each stroke as if it were made of rubber, not iron. The pump was laboring far over its normal capacity. I dared go no further. We stopped there.

Another call from Eadie.

"On deck! Give her some more!"

"Sorry, Eadie! You'll have to get along with what you've got. If I give her another ounce, the pump will blow up. You've got two hundred pounds now!"

Eadie, handicapped by only two hundred pounds of pressure, was nevertheless making famous progress. The hose on deck was so stiff it would have been impossible to make a dent in it with a sledge hammer. Under that pressure, a jet of water, hard as a crowbar, was shooting out of the nozzle, cutting through the stiff clay easily, while the side jets shot a cone of water astern that widened the hole made by the main jet and at the same time carried backward the broken clay. In less than an hour, Eadie had tunneled six feet under the boat and disappeared beneath the hull.

Eadie turned over the hose to Wilson and started up. Wilson continued the job. The wrecking pump pulsated, threatened to let go at any minute, but the divers were doing so well it seemed unwise to cut the pressure. Wilson finished his hour, advanced another six feet. Eiben relieved Wilson, Kelley succeeded Eiben, Carr followed Kelley, and when darkness fell and Carr, the last diver for the day, finally started backwards out of the tunnel, he had reached the keel. Five divers in one afternoon had done what had taken weeks on the first tunnel.

The pump stopped, we pulled up the hose, admired the shiny brass nozzle. Eadie explained the secret.

"There wasn't any kick at all. I could have held everything you could send. And the harder the water came, the faster the clay went. She's a wonder!"

Everyone on the ship braced up. Instead of weeks of work and hours of terror, the last tunnel would go through in a few more hours. Eagerly we waited for the dawn.

Next morning, Wilson took the hose, went down to start the tunnel on the starboard side. With great care he noted the tunnel entrance on the port side, and then threw a weighted line down the starboard side of the ship, exactly opposite, to mark the location. There he braced himself, directly below the huge "5" of the "*S-51*" painted on the side of the conning tower.

"On deck! Turn on the water!"

The valve was opened wide, the pump speeded up. The gauge needle spun round to the two hundred mark and steadied there. The pump started to pant once more, as the fire hose, swelled to the bursting point, carried the pulsating stream to the nozzle in Wilson's hands.

Twenty minutes went by. A loud crash from the hold, a fountain of water shooting from the pump room hatch. The fire hose went limp. The wrecking pump was racing like mad when the soaked engineer finally worked his way through the deluge and shut off the steam. The expected had finally happened. The cylinder head on the pump had blown up! The cast iron plate lay in pieces all over the fire room.

We started several smaller pumps, put all of them on the fire main, but could get no more than sixty pounds on the hose. Wilson worked with that a few minutes, asked for more. He learned there was no more.

"On deck! I'm coming up. I can't work without any water!" And only a few weeks before, sixty pounds on a small nozzle was all we had dared give the divers. Wilson came up.

We surveyed the wrecked pump. A new casting, twenty inches in diameter, to fit the cylinder, would probably take several weeks to cast and machine. We could not afford to wait. A boat raced to the *Vestal* for her repair officer and the boilermaker. Shortly they came aboard and we pointed out what we wanted. Back again to the *Vestal* with all hands taking the pieces of the broken head as a pattern. We found a boiler plate one inch thick. From this the boilermaker cut a disk the size of the old cast head, and a ring liner to make up for the curvature of the broken casting. Hurriedly these were marked out, rushed to the drill presses, while several lathes turned out a new set of longer studs to bolt up the double thickness of liner and plate. Back again on the *Falcon*, where the pump waited, the old studs removed. The new studs were screwed in. On went gasket, steel liner, gasket, steel cover plate, retaining nuts. Socket wrenches spun round, the head was tightened up. In four hours from the time the pump blew up, a jury head was on, the pump was running again. Today, two years since, that makeshift head is still doing duty on the *Falcon*'s wrecking pump.

The pump was ready again, but the weather turned bad and we ran for shelter.

Next day, Kelley took the hose down to work in the hole Wilson had left. He came up an hour later, sure he was not far from the keel. Michels and Wickwire followed Kelley, and Carr followed Michels. The pressure pounded from the pump. The new head pulsated even more than the old one, but being boiler plate instead of cast iron, had much more elasticity. Carr worked away steadily.

Thirty minutes went by. Carr should have reached the keel. We dressed Eadie ready to go down in the other tunnel and try to pass a line under the keel to Carr, as he had done in the first tunnel.

A message from below.

"On deck! Turn off the water!" We stopped the pump. The minutes went by. No word from Carr, though evidently he was moving around as his tender was kept busy hauling in and paying out on Carr's lifelines.

Another call, repeated by the telephone man perched in the superstructure:

"On deck! Send me down a line!"

Hartley rove off a small manila line, shackled it to the descending line going down to the submarine's gun, and paid it out. It reached the bottom, Carr cut it loose from the shackle, became active again. What, we wondered, had gone wrong with him?

Soon we learned.

"On deck! Hoist away on the hose, pay out on the line!"

We obeyed. Hand over hand the tenders heaved up the hose, which came in over the rail while the manila line ran out. Finally the nozzle came up, the small line tied firmly to it. We stopped, asked Carr what next?

"On deck! That's all, I'm coming up. You got a reeving line through the tunnel!"

Carr had worked his way to the keel, washed a hole under it into the tunnel on the other side, and then crawled all the way through, dragging the fire hose and his own lifeline under the boat. Coming out on the opposite side, he found the broken radio antennae dangling there. Dragging some slack on his lifeline through the tunnel, he climbed the antennae to the bridge, and then crawled to the deck. Here his airhose made nearly a complete loop around the submarine, down the starboard side, through the tunnel, and up the port side,— a risky thing, for a tunnel cave-in would have blocked off his only avenue of retreat.

Standing on the *S-51*'s deck, near the gun, Carr had received the manila line; with this he had slid down the side and tied the new line to the hose nozzle, then crawled back through the tunnel and ordered us to haul the hose up.

And so the first reeving line went through the amidships tunnel, a far different scene from the one in the forward tunnel, when Wilson struggled for hours to find Eadie's foot wiggling in the darkness and the mud under the keel!

Smith and Eadie dived next, each carrying a line. They met under the keel where Smith backed out, taking both lines which he bent together. I had no desire to have anyone repeat Carr's stunt of crawling all the way through,—the cave in danger was too great when we could play it safe by using two men.

We rove round stronger manila lines, and with them pulled through our pair of wire hauling lines. On deck, we shackled the anchor chains to the wires, carefully fitted the tapered steel cones over the shackles. The weather turned very bad, but we were determined to get the chains down before our reeving lines got tangled up; in spite of seas breaking over our rail, we lowered the heavy chains one by one, and managed to drag both through successfully.

The tunnel was larger this time,—the chains slipped through under the boat with comparative ease. That done, we unmoored in a hurry and ran for shelter.

Four stormy days went by before we could dive again. At last, in a moderate swell, we finally moored.

The surfboat drew alongside towing a pontoon obtained from the *Sagamore*, while nearby the *Iuka* anchored with the last pontoon in tow.

The pontoon was flooded, the flood valves closed, and the cylinder lowered. Grube and Carr dived, put the toggle bars through the chains, saw the pontoon land on the bottom, then cast off the lowering lines. Carr burned off the wires from the chains, leaving only a pair of airhoses secured to the blowing connections on the pontoon, which lay on the port side of the submarine.

The divers came up in a rougher sea. The breeze was freshening from the east, and the *Falcon* moved uneasily. We had another pontoon riding astern of the *Iuka*. If we hurried we could get it down. We brought it alongside, rigged it for lowering, opened the flood valves. It took an hour for it to go awash, and spray was flying over the pontoon when Badders and Weaver swung out on their stages and closed the flood valves.

The twelve-inch hawsers groaned and stretched as we slacked them away on the bitts and the pontoon sank. On each up roll, the *Falcon* jerked heavily on the hawsers, and with each jerk, the diameter of the manila line shrank a little.

Hartley watched his line, I controlled the forward one; fathom by fathom slipped out. The pontoon was down one hundred feet. Kelley and Boyd, dressed and ready, were hoisted over into the waves and disappeared down the descending lines. It was getting dark.

"On the pontoon!" came from below.

At the bitts, we held the hawsers. The *Falcon* was rolling badly, her side moving some twenty feet up and down every few seconds. Far below us, the pontoon, straining on the hawsers, was compelled to follow our motions, and the divers were having a desperate time trying to maintain their footing on top of the slippery cylinder as it heaved irregularly, jerking them up and down with it. They cut loose the toggle bars. Kelley managed after numerous misses to shoot them through the yellow links and Boyd finally got the locking pins through. We sent down the torch. Kelley burned free the wires and we pulled them up.

I had an idea that we might level off this last pair of pontoons afloat just above the submarine, in the position they would occupy while lifting. To do this, it was necessary to open the flood valves, so we could blow out some water and make the pontoon buoyant enough to float up against the toggle bars in the chains.

Boyd and Kelley had taken a set of wrenches in a canvas bag with them for this purpose, and as soon as the wires were burned clear, were to open the flood valves, but matters began to go wrong.

Boyd's tender got a signal on his lifeline to take him up. The telephone man asked him his reason. It came back in broken sentences, interrupted by expressive pauses.

"On deck! I'm seasick from [gulps] trying to ride this pontoon! If you don't take me up [another pause] my insides are coming up anyway!"

We started Boyd up.

Smith was waiting, dressed except for his helmet, as the emergency diver. I told him to stand by.

Meanwhile Kelley, alone now, crawled on his stomach along the top of the pontoon to its forward end. Stillson wrench in one hand, he tried to cling to the pontoon with the other, as he attempted to get his wrench on the valve stem just beyond the edge of the cylinder. The pontoon plunged erratically, sweeping him through the water and bouncing him up and down as he clung to the lowering ring. He was unable to steady down on the pontoon. Finally he telephoned:

"On deck! This pontoon keeps falling away from me. I can't hang on long enough to get the wrench on the valve. If you can send someone down here to sit on me, maybe I can make it!"

"All right, Kelley. Smith is coming right down!"

We put on Smith's helmet, hoisted him over and watched him disappear.

"On the pontoon!" Smith crawled to the forward end where Kelley lay, sat on Kelley's legs. With this extra ballast, Kelley tried again to adjust the wrench, but on the back of that pontoon, which in spite of its huge size, was heaving up and down just above the submarine like a bucking broncho, it was like trying to brand an untied mustang. Smith could hardly hang on himself, let alone hold Kelley down.

Another minute, and Kelley could stand it no longer.

"On deck! Take me up! I'm sick!"

Kelley started up.

Smith took the Stillson wrench, stretched himself out and tried, unaided, to get at the valve. Over the telephone, I listened to him, heard his heavy breathing, his gasps as he was thrown against the pontoon, his curses as he was flung back from the valve stem. Smith was the mildest tempered diver we had, a very quiet man, but after a few minutes of tossing up and down in futile efforts to turn the valve, he was swearing profusely. At last he ceased long enough to call:

"On deck! I can't make it. The — — pontoon won't stay still long enough to get a look at the valve; and I'm damn near flying off every roll! Lower her to the bottom, or I'm coming up!"

If Smith couldn't do it, nobody could. We lowered the pontoon the last twenty feet, and slacked out the lowering lines when the pontoon came to rest. With the pontoon lying quietly on the sea floor, no longer hanging from the *Falcon*, Smith cast off the lowering lines, disconnected the airhoses, and then crawled aboard the submarine and started up.

Our day's work was over. The *Falcon* unmoored. The last pontoon was down.

As Smith was hoisted over the rail, I noticed casually a canvas tool bag upside down on the stage at his feet. Queer. Had he lost his tools? I lifted the bag. There, neatly hidden, lay the bronze bell of the *S-51*!

I remembered that I had intended to bring that bell up myself once; I had often directed other divers to retrieve it when their work near it was done, but always the men were so worn out that the extra minute's work on the bottom to uncouple the bell was never undertaken. Now Smith had it, apparently intending to make away with the trophy unnoticed.

I sent Lieutenant Kelly to the *Vestal* with the bell, directing him to lock it safely in a chest under my berth there.

Some hours later, Smith came out of the recompression chamber, found me and asked for the bell.

"I'm sorry, Smith, but that bell is going to Annapolis as a trophy of this job. Nobody is going to have it personally. But I'll be mighty glad to have your name put on the nameplate as having recovered it and as being the donor."

"No, I want the bell myself, Mr. Ellsberg. If it goes to the Naval Academy, it'll be lost in a crowd of other things in a museum. If I take it back home with me to Pittsburgh, it'll mean something. Come on, be a sport. If you hadn't seen that bag for another minute, I had one of the bears all set to take it away, and you'd never have known. Besides, the bell had pulled out of its socket and was lying against the sub's rail, ready to fall overboard and get buried in the mud, and then none of us would have had it. Come on, I rescued it, it ought to be mine!"

But I was adamant. The bell was government property, the Naval Academy should have it. Smith left disappointed. For weeks afterward, my usual morning greeting was a grin from Smith, and the query:

"Well, Mr. Ellsberg, have you decided to give back that bell you stole?"

My stock reply was:

"No, Smith, it's going to be presented to Annapolis with your compliments."

Gradually we both forgot the affair.

XXXII

LASHING UP

The *S-51*, when we lifted her, was bound to come up one end first. Even on a submarine in commission when running submerged, it is a delicate matter to maintain her properly trimmed fore and aft. With no free water in the boat and all the machinery available for balancing, it is not unusual for boats to rise at a considerable angle. For us to attempt to bring the *S-51* up horizontally was wholly out of the question. We could only choose which end we should raise first, and we elected to bring up the stern first, as in that position we could expel the most water from the rooms inside. Our spillpipes were in every case located in the forward ends of their compartments. With the stern at the surface, all the water left in the bilges of each compartment would run to the forward end of it where it would blow out through the spillpipe hanging there, and thus lighten the boat still more.

But if the submarine was to come up one end at a time, there would be a period during which the boat would lie at an angle of thirty degrees, with her stem in the mud and her stern at the surface. In that position, all our pontoon chains would slip up the hull under the pull of the buoyant pontoons and would float away, letting the boat sink again. To prevent such a catastrophe, it was necessary to lash each pair of pontoons to the submarine so that when the stern came up, the pontoons would still stay where they belonged while we lightened up the bow till it also floated. We intended to bring her up stern first and designed all the lashings with that in view, but recognizing that there might be a slip, we also decided to provide a few lashings to prevent the pontoons from sliding forward off the bow, during the long tow to New York.

But before we could do any lashing, it was necessary to float all the pontoons off the bottom into their lifting positions, which meant the pontoons must float just above the deck on each side of the submarine; the cradle chains would then be heaved taut under the hull by the pull of the pontoons.

The end of May found us engaged in this task. Memorial Day came round. The weather was rough but diving was possible, and we dived. We forgot it was a holiday, till shortly before noon a small ship, the *Triton*, stood down from the northward towards us and circled under our stern. We hoisted our colors and half-masted them. The *Triton* passed close aboard, flung flowers and wreaths into the water as she swung slowly over the spot where lay the *S-51*. Several black-clad women, leaning over the *Triton*'s rail, wept as the bugler sounded "Taps." A moment later one of them was carried below unconscious. Her husband lay with his shipmates, inside the motor room of the submarine. Sympathetically, we gazed after those to whom the *S-51* meant more than a ship's name, till the *Triton* disappeared over the horizon, then turned once more to our diving.

We lay that night in the moorings. The weather report was fair, the sea calm. But weather off Point Judith follows no settled rules. By midnight it was blowing hard; by three A.M. it was blowing a gale.

Lieutenant Hartley slacked his moorings, allowed the *Falcon* to head into the sea. He dared not put over a boat to unshackle the buoys in that storm. A half mile away, the *Vestal* rode to long scope, rolling heavily. The *S-50* got underway for the Harbor of Refuge. The *Sagamore*, anchored to leeward, was pitching like a cork; the *Iuka*, anchored to windward, was behaving likewise.

Through the darkness came the scream of a siren,— rising sharply, falling away to a moan. The lights of the *Iuka* were rapidly getting closer; she was dragging down in the gale.

On the *Falcon*, the shrilling of the boatswain's pipe brought the watch. A hoarse order from Hartley:

"Stand by each mooring line with an ax!"

The *Iuka* swept closer. Down the teeth of the gale we caught the rumble of a chain,—the *Iuka* was letting go her sheet anchor. No use; she dragged two anchors as easily as one. Resistlessly she came on, rising and falling sharply as the waves rolled by her. She loomed up not fifty feet from our bow, her lights gleaming through the storm, her siren shrieking out a warning; two more surges in that seaway and she would smash down on the diving ship.

Hartley's voice rose above the din of storm and siren:

"Cut the hawsers!"

Seven axes flashed through the darkness onto the heavy manila cables stretched out across the *Falcon*'s rails. Strands parted as the steel buried itself in the hemp. One blow on each hawser was enough. The remaining strands snapped, the broken cables jerked from our side. The *Falcon* shot down the wind, and in a few seconds was a hundred yards to leeward of the *Iuka*. Clear of the mooring buoys, we dropped anchor to ride out the storm.

Meantime the *Iuka* stopped dragging and remained practically in the spot the *Falcon* had just vacated, a strange thing to happen as the storm kept increasing. Nevertheless there she remained, while all the other ships dragged slowly to leeward.

Morning came, the gale howled on. We watched the sea, a tumbled mass of huge waves and flying spray, while the wind whistled through our rigging and our vessels tossed wildly in the sea. The radio told us of ships driven ashore all up and down the coast. We thanked our luck that we were well off shore and safe and as the foaming crests swept by our sides, congratulated ourselves on having sunk our last pontoon before the storm hit us.

The day went slowly by. No chance to work at anything. I braced myself in my bunk, grasped the chance, the first in months, to read and rest. I had a new book, presented by a friend just before the expedition sailed. I hauled it off the shelf, opened it for the first time.

On the flyleaf was written:

"When the weather is too rough for sub raising, you may find this book interesting!"

I plunged into the story of "Beau Geste." The donor was right. In a few moments, I was far away from ship, storm, and submarine. In the middle of the burning African desert before Fort Zinderneuf I followed Beau Geste, and not till the mystery of the disappearance of the "Blue Water" was explained (which point I reached at two A.M.) did I suddenly return from Africa to my heaving bunk.

The worst gale we ever experienced finally blew itself out. The *Vestal* literally had the paint blown off her topmasts. Our airhoses, which we left buoyed off from the pontoons, were a tangled mass, but worst of all the *Iuka* found she could not lift her anchor and get clear of the spot where she had so securely ridden the gale. She finally had to slip her anchor cable in order to get free.

On the *Falcon*, we had a job to do before we could resume work. All the mooring hawsers which we had cut to dodge the *Iuka* were hanging from the mooring buoys, ruined. We had to fish up the ends attached to the buoys, remove the pelican hooks, and reeve off a new set of eight-inch hawsers. We were not willing to splice the old hawsers and trust them to hold the *Falcon* for diving.

When after two days' work, we finally steamed over the wreck, moored, and sent down Michels to inspect, we also found conditions in a mess below. The *Iuka*'s anchor was jammed in between the port forward pontoon and the hull of the submarine; the *Iuka*'s anchor chain was looped around the pontoon and from there led aft where it was tangled in the conning tower and finally was draped down the starboard side where the bitter end lay in the mud. Michels cleared the chain from the bridge and tied a line to it; we hauled up the free end, but in spite of all our heaving, we were no more able to get the anchor up than the *Iuka* had been.

George Anderson dived with a crowbar and a four-inch line. He bent the line to the chain; we heaved first forward, then aft on the line under his directions and at last managed to get the chain clear and leading up and down, but the anchor would not drag free. It took a strenuous effort with the crowbar by Anderson to trip the flukes and a desperate struggle by which he wedged himself under the bilge of the pontoon to secure his line around the crown of the anchor, before we were able to drag the anchor out with the line and heave it up on the cable. Then we were ready once more to work.

The struggle was too much for Anderson, however. He had been feeling none too well for weeks. Now, threatened with pneumonia, he had to be sent ashore for observation and treatment.

The weather turned bad again, and from June 1 to June 9, we were unable to dive. But finally it calmed, and we entered the last stage of the job,—lashing the pontoons.

If we had thought the pontoons were troublesome to handle before, we now found our former pontoon difficulties were mere trifles compared to those we daily encountered in the lashing process. To lash the pontoons, we had first to get each pair afloat over the submarine.

We secured two hoses to each pontoon, one hose to each compartment. In the leveling process, we took a pair of pontoons at a time, blew air into both ends of both pontoons simultaneously and as evenly as possible. We supposed both pontoons, when slightly buoyant, would float up horizontally alongside the submarine till the chains stretched taut and stopped them.

Actually, what happened was far different. We started in to level off the pontoons abreast the first tunnel. In spite of Niedermair's best care, it was found impossible to blow evenly through four hoses at once. The forward end of the starboard pontoon got light before the others; that end rose. As it lifted off the bottom, the water pressure on it decreased a bit, the air inside expended and blew out more water, lightening the compartment still more and sending it up faster. Before we, on the surface, could stop blowing, that pontoon was standing vertically, forward end up, after end flat on the bottom. The high end dragged all the slack chain through under the submarine from the corresponding half of its mate pontoon on the opposite of the boat, preventing that pontoon from rising horizontally, even if it wanted to, which it never did, for it also rose vertically, but with its after end up.

Considering the nerve-racking time we had had in getting the pontoons down, it was nearly a knockout punch to learn that they would not level off so we could lash them. We broke several six-inch manila hawsers trying to lay out horizontally the up-ended pontoons, but could not tip the huge cylinders over. Finally we did it by lightening the bottom ends till they capsized,—a process which did not add to our peace of mind for fear that the pontoons might fall against the submarine and smash it in.

We got them flat again, flooded both pontoons completely to make sure everything was equal, and tried it over, but with the same result. Once more we tipped the pontoons, and I looked around for a new method of leveling off.

We tried the following scheme next. Eadie went down on the starboard pontoon, and shackled a strong wire hawser to the lifting pad at each end. Then he came up. On the *Falcon* we took the wire hawsers over our side to the capstans. As a trial we heaved in till each wire had a good strain on it, about ten tons, but of course this failed to budge the pontoon, which weighed forty tons. We eased off the wires till they were slack.

Niedermair then blew both ends of the starboard pontoon together. Every few minutes he stopped blowing and we heaved on the wires. After the fourth blow, we were just able with a pull of about ten tons on each wire, to lift the partly lightened pontoon off the bottom.

When this happened, we blew no more, but lifted slowly on both lines till the marks on the wires showed we had lifted the pontoon about twenty feet, at which time it was hanging just above the submarine's deck. At that point we ceased hauling and left the pontoon hanging suspended from our side. This placed a considerable strain on the wires, for on every up roll, the wires received quite a jerk, but it was unavoidable.

Part two of the process was then started. Niedermair turned the air on both ends of the opposite pontoon, which still lay on the bottom, and blew steadily till one end, which turned out to be the after end, started to rise. It floated up, leaving the forward end still in the mud; but this time, when the pontoon reached an angle of about forty-five degrees, the light end brought up with a jolt on the chain through its after hawsepipe and was unable to rise further, since there was no slack chain obtainable from the other side of the boat. Niedermair continued to blow, but to the forward end only, and shortly that end also floated up till it was halted by the chain in the forward hawsepipe. The port pontoon was now floating horizontally above the submarine on its own buoyancy, and tugging on the chains which ran through the tunnel to the other pontoon. Niedermair ceased blowing.

The strains on our wires to the starboard pontoon were now much increased, for in addition to the weight of that pontoon, there was added the buoyant pull on the chains from the opposite side. With every roll, it seemed certain the wires must let go or our capstans tear away. We hastened to finish the operation.

Niedermair started blowing again, this time into the starboard pontoon which hung from our wires. As he expelled water from it, the strains on the wires gradually lessened. Soon the pontoon was itself buoyant,—the wires quit tugging and when slacked off a little, remained slack. Both pontoons were floating evenly in position above the submarine, ready to be lashed.

On the *Falcon*, things brightened up considerably; the new scheme had worked. If we broke no wires in the process, all would be well, though it was obvious that we needed better weather for leveling off than we had needed for lowering or the wires would promptly snap.

We repeated our leveling-off method on the midships pair of pontoons, the pair abreast the conning tower, with good results. Then to lighten up the submarine, we blew this pair of pontoons completely dry, giving them their maximum lift of one hundred and sixty tons. The engine room and the motor room were also dry, as were the port side ballast tanks. These ballasts had been blown partly dry by Wilson inside the control room the winter before, using the *S-51*'s own compressed air; the job had later been finished by Michels from the outside of the boat. Michels had used a fire hose to wash down under the port bilge keel till he came to the open Kingston valves in the shell; then he had inserted an airhose through the Kingstons and blown air up into the ballast tanks, meanwhile expelling water through the Kingstons, till the tanks were empty.

I had hoped that with two pontoons lifting amidships, two stern compartments dry, and the port side ballast tanks dry and tending to roll the boat to starboard, that the *S-51*, which lay with an eleven-degree port list, would straighten up. As she lay, tightly buried in the clay, she was gripped by a suction force far greater than her weight. The *S-51* weighed one thousand tons, but the suction holding her to the bottom was about eight thousand tons, a force so large we could never hope to overcome it by a direct lift. I hoped to get around this and break the suction by letting water in between hull and clay in two ways,—first by rolling the boat to starboard, and second by lifting her one end (stern) first.

The difficulty is easily demonstrated. If a flat plate is placed on a smooth table top with a film of water between to exclude air, it will be found impossible to lift the plate straight up off the table. However, if one edge of the plate is grasped and lifted ever so slightly, air works its way under, breaks the suction, and the plate comes away easily.

A similar condition, except that the force to be overcome was six times as much per square inch, and was spread over a vastly greater area, the whole bottom of the ship, existed on the *S-51*. This suction, amounting to eight thousand tons, was the one unknown we had to deal with, and it lay in the back of my mind always as a constant dread, that we might not be able to break the suction and lift the boat. The fear was well founded in fact; some partly buried torpedoes that our war vessels had lost in years before had broken in half under a heavy pull rather than come out of the mud; and some ten years before the British had had two different experiences where, in shallow water, they had been wholly unable to drag two small but partly buried submarines clear of the bottom, and those boats are there yet. We had a submarine far larger, and a suction many times greater, to deal with.

Wilson and Eadie dived to measure off lashings for the second pair of pontoons. Hanging over the sides of the boat, they stretched small manila lines across the deck between the chains on the starboard and port pontoons,—one line on the forward chain, one line on the after chain. They sent up the lines cut to proper lengths, and while we on the *Falcon* made up sections of wire hawsers with eyes in both ends to suit their measurements, the divers attached strong steel clamps to the chains just under the floating pontoons.

Eiben and Michels went down after them to measure off the lashings for the midships (or third) pair of pontoons, which floated abreast the conning tower. On the submarine, Eiben went to the starboard side with one end of a small measuring line. Michels, on the port side, took the other end of the line and walked slowly aft through the water between the port pontoon and the conning tower. As the boat lay heeled to port, the pontoon was fairly close to the submarine. Michels walked between the two, the pontoon looming almost as large as the submarine. Abreast the conning tower he paused a moment, peering through one of the eyeports out of curiosity. It was black inside, he saw nothing, but while he looked, he felt a strong push shoving him against the tower. At the bottom of the sea, that is disconcerting. Startled, he jumped sideways, clear of the tower, then stopped as he remembered Joe Eiben was down with him. He looked around to see why Joe had pushed him. There was no one in sight. And then his blood froze as he saw that the pontoon, which he had thought as immovable as the submarine, was swaying irregularly in and out like a huge inverted pendulum, occasionally crunching against the conning tower. And he had been in between! If that sweep he felt as a shove had been one of those wider swings he now watched, he would have been smashed in a huge nut cracker.

Fascinated, he watched the swings of the pontoon as slowly and inexorably it swung in and out against the conning tower; though Michels did not know it, he was receiving the first definite proof of a much-disputed point in science,—that the effect of surface waves is felt far deeper in the sea than previously had been considered possible.

Michels soon returned to normal; he had his job to do but wisely decided not to tempt the jaws of death again. He slipped over the side of the submarine, clinging to his line, and, keeping beneath the pontoon, stretched the lines over to the chains and marked off their lengths. Cautiously keeping low, he crept back on deck and clear of the superstructure where Eiben waited; together they started upward. On deck at last, Michels told what he had seen. All the divers were warned to keep out from between the pontoons.

We finished making the wire lashings that night. They were heavy pieces of wire, which when stretched across the deck and clamped to the pontoon chains would form a loop completely encircling the submarine, and in connection with other lashings passed around the gun and the conning tower, would prevent the pontoons from sliding off the submarine, either forward or aft, while we were raising her.

Carr went down next morning to install the first wire lashing. In a somewhat choppy sea he was hoisted overboard, dragged to the forward descending line (attached to the *S-51*'s gun) and started his descent.

Carr was perhaps halfway to the bottom when on the surface, over nearly the whole length of the submarine, there was a sudden burst of bubbles lasting a few seconds, then solid water again as the waves rolled on. Something had happened below. We wondered what.

Carr stopped taking out lifeline. Evidently he had landed but the customary "On the bottom!" was conspicuous by its absence. Grube, his partner, stood on the stage, helmeted, ready to go overboard, but till Carr reported himself safely down, we could not put another diver over. The minutes went by, Grube sagged under the weight of his equipment. I took Carr's phone.

"Hello, Carr! Are you all right?"

"On deck! The descending line is tangled in the bridge and I'm mixed up with the periscopes! There's something wrong with this boat, I don't know what. Send Grube down to help clear the descending line!"

We hoisted Grube over, he landed near Carr and reported. Both worked in silence for ten minutes when Carr bellowed up excitedly.

"On deck! I just doped out what's wrong. The submarine has rolled over! Instead of heeling to port, she's listed way over to starboard, a lot worse than she used to be to port! I'm down on deck now, hanging on to the gun. The boat's leaning about twenty degrees to starboard. You can't walk on the deck any more!"

I heard the report with mingled joy and alarm. At last we had moved the *S-51* and broken the suction! The one unknown was conquered. If we could move the boat, we could lift it.

The alarm was due to the uncertainty as to what damage might have occurred when she suddenly rolled to starboard and also how her new position would effect our future work.

"Lucky we got that engine room hatch secured," I confided to Hartley. "We'd never get it in place with the deck sloping the way she is now!"

Carr went ahead with the lashing job. One wire he got secured, the other would no longer fit with the changed position of the submarine. He came up with a new measurement.

Eadie went down to inspect. He found the stern of the submarine had lifted perhaps five feet off the bottom, while the bow had buried itself a few feet deeper. In its present position, the submarine's stern was lying over, partly covering the after starboard pontoon as it rested on the bottom. In going from bow to stern Eadie had walked on the high side of the ship which was level now; he had not been able to walk along the deck.

I was fearful that if the submarine or the buoyant pontoons lost any air, the stern of the submarine would settle down again and crush in the pontoon on which it was resting, or at least jam it down so tightly that we could not float it up and level it off.

The pontoons which we had afloat over the submarine were all leaking and we could see air from them constantly bubbling to the surface. When they left the boiler shop at New York, the steel cylinders had all been tested and made tight, but their journey from the Navy Yard to Newport on barges, the strains they had undergone in being hoisted overboard by derricks at Newport, the towing from Newport to the wreck, and finally the heavy pounding by the seas against the sides of the *Falcon* which they had undergone while being lowered, had all combined to spring seams and rivets. Every pontoon leaked,— the wonder was that they held air at all.

A storm was blowing up and the sea was getting rough. We would soon have to leave and perhaps before we could get back, the floating pontoons would lose enough air to let the stern sink down hard on the after pontoon. To get that pontoon clear was important. Niedermair connected its hoses to the *Falcon*'s manifold and blew enough air into it to make it just float off the bottom, in the hope that it would slip clear, but it failed to move. We gave it a little more air, but still it remained imprisoned. More buoyancy was not wise. It might suddenly come clear, float upwards with a heavy pull, and jerk the port pontoon, its mate, hard enough against the other side of the submarine to dent in the motor room and ruin its watertightness.

By now the wind was blowing harder and the seas rolling up. The *Falcon* began to strain on her regular moorings and the additional ones run out to the *Iuka* and the *Sagamore*, anchored to windward. It was too late to send more divers down, but a new dilemma presented itself. In the storm coming up, the lightened submarine would probably roll a little from the disturbance set up in the water on the bottom. If it did, the stern pontoon, released, would float up on the starboard quarter, till it brought up on the chains and stopped just above the motor room deck. And there, projecting above the stern of the submarine like a spear, was a heavy steel mast, six feet high, to which the after radio antenna and net clearing lines had once been attached. With the boat lying far over on its starboard side, this mast was pointed so that when the pontoon floated up and swung to the currents, it would be driven against the top of the mast and be punched full of holes.

The mast had to come off before we left. Kelley, who knew best how to handle the torch, and Carr, who had some experience with it, had both been down already. None of the other divers had had any training with the torch, except myself. There was strong disagreement on the *Falcon* over any further diving. The weather was such that ordinarily we would have unmoored and steamed clear before the sea reached the state it was in. If it had been a case of any other diver going down, we would have left, but I could go myself when I couldn't ask anyone else to go and I settled the argument by electing to dive. I dressed hurriedly, was hoisted overboard, seized the torch, and slid hastily down the descending line to avoid the surging pressure of the surface waves in my ears. Forty feet down, the sea was calmer, and I went a little more slowly till I landed on the port side of the submarine.

"On the bottom," I reported, and walked aft on the port side of the hull, clinging to the rail till the rail ended, and then balanced myself on the curved side of the submarine as I went some fifty feet further aft to where the stub mainmast rose from the center of the narrow deck. I tried to sit on the high edge of the deck to work but slid downwards and only by grabbing the tall light set in the deck just abaft the mast did I keep from going overboard.

I straddled the mast with both legs, and lighted off the torch. It burned with the usual roar, especially noticeable in the silence of the deeps. Hanging down the steep deck, with one hand clinging to the tail light, I swung the torch to the base of the mast, just above the deck planking, and burned into the steel. A stream of white sparks flashed through the water.

It was slow work. I had much trouble hanging on and was unable with only one hand to guide the torch very well, but I succeeded in getting a ragged cut completely across the starboard half of the mast. From where I hung, I could not reach the opposite side of the mast at all, and had to drag myself up the deck and on to the port side, where I stretched out flat on the steel side of the submarine and tried to reach down to the mast.

Half an hour had gone by since I had dived, and but half the job was done. If only I could have reached it decently, I might have burned the whole mast off in five minutes, but as I lay I barely touched the near side at all, and that only by stretching out the torch to the limit. I started on the port side, cut half an inch when my arm slipped and I had to start over. Meanwhile, every few minutes I was getting phone calls from the *Falcon*, which I tried to disregard, but which nevertheless annoyed me.

"Are you done yet?"

"No, let me alone!"

I burned another inch. Again a voice in my ears:

"Sea very bad up here. We're afraid the mooring lines will break any minute."

Where I was, everything was calm. The water was quiet, the submarine immovable, no sign of life except the blazing torch and myself. It did not seem possible a storm was raging overhead.

"On deck! Don't bother me. I'm nearly done!"

I reached for the mast again, cut across the port side of it to the after end, leaving only about an inch of metal unburned where the inaccessible steel curved away from me. I rolled over, tried to find a position where I could reach it, but failed. I shifted the torch to my left hand, hung on with my right, and clumsily managed to burn through another half inch. Another call came from on deck, Hartley's voice this time.

"Are you done, commander?"

"No, another minute or two! Leave me alone!"

"Sorry, but I can't hold on another minute. The seas are sweeping our stern and the mooring hawsers are singing like bowstrings. They'll let go any second now!"

I looked at the mast. Just a thread of steel left uncut which kept it from toppling over. If it touched the pontoon, it would snap off without doing any damage.

I put out the torch, gave four jerks on my lifeline. In a trice, I was jerked off the boat, hauled up forty feet well clear of everything. Dangling on my lifelines as I went up, I could see that already we were rapidly swinging away from the submarine. Apparently Hartley was slacking off his weather lines and heading into the sea to relieve the strain.

I got only a few minutes decompression at eighty feet, a few more minutes at sixty feet, where I began to feel the sweep of the waves, and then I was hastily run up the rest of the way to the surface without any more decompression, to avoid the danger of burst ear drums from wave pressure variations.

It was an amazing change from the calm of the bottom to the breaking crests and the tossing waves as I was jerked through the surface and swung drunkenly in on the swaying stage. A huge wave broke over our counter as I dropped on deck, and soaked the bears as they struggled with my helmet. Through my faceplate, I glimpsed the port quarter mooring line, taut as an iron bar, going over the rail. Off came my helmet. Still cumbered by the rest of my diving rig, with a bear on either side I hurried for the recompression tank. Off to port I could see Hawes and the surfboat crew lifting high on the waves, trying to trip the pelican hook on a mooring buoy.

I reached the recompression tank, crawled through the door. Two bears followed to undress me. Slam went the steel door, and a loud hissing followed as the air shot in and quickly built up to a pressure of forty pounds. My decompression started.

Stripped of my suit, I lay down on the floor of the inner chamber, and as the pressure was gradually reduced, exercised vigorously.

Soon the throbbing of our propeller indicated we were unmoored. We steamed away. I found it a little difficult to exercise with the *Falcon* heaving so erratically in the storm.

Ninety minutes later I came out. No ill effects from "the bends." Hartley was in his bunk, but he turned out to give me hell nevertheless.

"That was the worst weather the *Falcon* ever had a diver down. It made me sick to watch our mooring lines, I never thought they'd last, the way the waves kicked up a few minutes after you went down. We were taking green seas over our stern. And you can bet I started to let go the minute I had you off the bottom!" He clung to his desk to avoid sliding away. I hung on to the wash basin.

"Well, skipper, that mast will never hurt anything now. One touch and away she'll go. I'm sorry I couldn't come up sooner, but the job was tough going, and it was so calm down there, I hated to leave and come up to this pitching tub!" And as the little *Falcon* did her stuff during the night while I tried to stay in my berth, I half wished myself back in the unearthly quiet that rules on the ocean floor.

The *Falcon* went to Newport to give the divers liberty till the storm blew over. Several days later, on June 17th, we came back once more and started to secure for raising. Kelley went down with the torch, burned holes in the starboard ballast tanks, low down, where we had been unable to reach and open the Kingston valves from the inside. He crawled over the boat, tried to get under the bilge keel on the port side, and burn just below the bilge keel into a tank there. He could not squeeze under the projecting keel, and failing, came up. I thought I could do better, being a little smaller. Down I went with the torch, and McLagan with a light to tend me from the submarine's deck. We landed just forward of the conning tower. I slid down the port side, walked forward a few steps. There was not much light anyway, but with the pontoons overhead, they cut off what little light ordinarily filtered down to the bottom. McLagan dropped the light to me; with it I could see a few feet. I was standing opposite the ragged gash cut in the hull by the *City of Rome*. Curious, I shined my light through it. A torn mass of steel plates, broken pipe lines, and blackness beyond.

The tank just aft this hole was my job. I paced off ten feet back, swung the light over the hull. The bilge keel stuck out from the ship, perhaps a foot above the sand. Putting the light on the bottom ahead of me, I lighted the torch, lay down in the mud, and tried to squeeze in under the bilge keel to the hull, but with my bulky helmet, I had no more luck than Kelley had. I wasted an hour on it, but it was useless, I could not get under and reach the hull. McLagan hauled me back on deck, and we went up together on the stage. I decided to let Kelley burn a hole higher up, above the bilge keel where the ship was accessible, and on his next dive, he did it.

Michels followed Kelley with an airhose, and reaching in through the holes Kelley had burned in the starboard ballast tanks, blew all the water out of them.

This made the buoyancy of the boat symmetrical, as it balanced the side pull exerted by the dry port ballast tanks, but the submarine still lay far over to starboard.

We finished installing lashings on the two pairs of floating pontoons amidships, and turned attention to the stern pontoons. Wickwire was hoisted over, and crawling aft on the submarine, dropped to the bottom and walked around the starboard pontoon to inspect its position. The stern of the submarine seemed to be resting lightly on the wood sheathing of the cylinder; the top of the pontoon was inclined away from the ship as if the submarine had rolled it partway over.

Wickwire made a complete circuit of the pontoon, reported that he thought by hooking on a hawser and having the *Sagamore* heave that we might pull the pontoon out sideways. From the *Falcon*'s deck, we watched his bubbles in the water as Wickwire circled round the pontoon and searched along it for a line by which he might pull himself up.

"On deck!" Wickwire called, "are you blowing any air in this pontoon? It's starting to roll around a little."

"Hello, Wickwire," I answered, "we're not touching it. You must be seeing things!"

"The pontoon's rolling a little more, commander." A pause. Then excitedly, "The submarine's moving too! She's rolling. There she goes! She's over on her port side again the way she used to be! Say, you ought to see her go!"

I imagined Wickwire, leaning against the pontoon, the solitary spectator. A magnificent sight to watch a large ship resting quietly at the bottom of the sea suddenly come to life and lazily roll in her bed from one side to the other! I clung tightly to his telephone. What next?

"Mr. Ellsberg, this pontoon is moving again! Say, she's on her way up! Going faster now. You'd better stop her! So long, I'm leaving!" My eyewitness reports ceased. Wickwire, in spite of lead shoes and heavy ballast, sprinted through the water across the sea bottom, away from the ship.

Wickwire's faith in my ability was impressive, but I saw no way of stopping that pontoon till it fetched up on its chains. But Wickwire himself must be in a precarious position, with both the submarine and the pontoon doing acrobatics around his lifelines.

I called him. No answer. The tender jerked "One" on his lifeline. No jerk in return. No "give" to Wickwire's lines. They were obviously caught on something, no signals were going by the obstruction. I tried again on the telephone, but still no answer. Five anxious minutes passed with no news from Wickwire. Hastily we put Smith, the stand-by diver, into his helmet, placed him on the stage, were hoisting him overboard—

"'One' on Wickwire's line!" sang out his tender. He answered with one jerk. I telephoned again.

"Hello, Wickwire!"

"All clear now, Mr. Ellsberg! I'm sitting on the sub's tail. I'll come up as soon as I see how she lays! I was too busy to answer before."

Wickwire was safe.

Hartley belayed the stage, swung Smith back in on deck.

Wickwire had run some thirty feet when he was stopped with a jerk.

His lifelines were taut, stretching back towards the submarine and he could go no further. He turned round, walked back along his lines, till he came to the submarine. The pontoon was nowhere in sight, but its two chains led vertically upward against the stern, and there alongside one of the chains, his lifeline hung. Wickwire grasped the chain, started to climb the links. He went up twenty feet, came flush with the deck of the submarine, was just able through the water to discern the pontoon as a dark mass perhaps twenty feet higher. Up he went, climbing the stiff chain, like Jack up the Beanstalk, a queer sight. There, just under the pontoon looming over him like the bottom of a ship, his airhose was caught in a loop round the chain. He circled round the chain, unwound his line, hastily slipped down again, and then swung round to the stern, where he climbed the rudder and sat down on the after torpedo tube to rest. The pontoon was now plainly visible to him, floating a little above the *S-51*.

Wickwire had cleared himself none too soon. The top air valve had broken off the pontoon in its gyrations and air was escaping from it fast.

Wickwire, resting himself on the narrow tip of the stern, was galvanized into life as the pontoon above suddenly started to sink and shot downwards past him, resting heavily on the chains from which a few moments before he had been hanging.

That was too much. Wickwire changed his mind about a further inspection.

"On deck! I've had enough this dive. Take me up!" Smith made the inspection. The *S-51* was lying about ten degrees to port. We flooded back the engine room, and the submarine then settled practically erect, with a list of only a few degrees to port.

A heavy fog and a bad swell prevented diving June 18. With a somewhat lesser swell on June 19 and 20, we started to level off the bow pontoons. The motion of the *Falcon* was bad and three times the wires or the shackles broke, spoiling the job. Finally we succeeded; and then transferred our gear to the stern, where lay the last pair of pontoons. Here we had a little better luck, as only one wire broke in the process.

It was June 21. We were almost done, and working like beavers. All blowing hoses were attached to pontoons and submarine and buoyed off at the surface. Two pontoons, which had lost so much air from leakage that they had sunk again, were leveled off once more and all the lashings put on. The divers, working in relays, secured a towing bridle, made of one-and-one-half-inch chain, around the bow, and a heavy wire towing hawser led forward from this; a similar chain bridle was fastened round the stern with a wire led aft as a sternfast.

We worked till 10:30 P.M., when the last lashing was secured and everything was in readiness to raise the boat.

All hands were dead tired from the hard drive of the three days past, coming on top of months of arduous labor. When the last diver came up in the darkness, Hartley unmoored, steamed clear, and we climbed into our bunks, determined to finish the job next day.

XXXIII

JUNE 22, 1926

But we had reckoned without the sea. June 22nd dawned in a storm. Diving was out of the question; raising the submarine in such weather not to be thought of. Ordinarily, I might have welcomed the storm as giving us a chance to recuperate before undergoing the strain of the raising, but not then. In the foam capping the waves, we could see clusters of air bubbles rising from the bottom. Our pontoons were leaking, losing the precious air which kept them leveled in position above the submarine. If the storm kept up a day or two, as well it might, we would return to find our pontoons sunk on their noses alongside the *S-51*, the chains and lashings tangled, and a big leveling job to do over again. We must get enough air into the pontoons to make up for the leakage till the weather cleared.

The need was urgent, so in spite of the storm, Hartley took the *Falcon* in among the mooring buoys. Over went the surfboat. Boatswain Hawes and his seamen battled the waves to get the hawsers shackled to the buoys. Finally we were in position over the wreck, with our bow, heading south into the storm, over the *S-51*'s stern. In fifteen minutes we would be through, ready to start for Point Judith and rest.

We fished up the buoyed hoses leading to the stern pontoons, coupled them to our manifold. Carefully Niedermair blew through them for one minute, then shut the valves. The sailors disconnected the hoses, and tossed them, buoys and all, back into the sea. Then we blew through the hoses to the midships pontoons the same way.

The storm was getting worse, we could not stay much longer. We skipped the hoses on the next pair of pontoons, which were not leaking so badly, and tried to pull aboard the hoses to the bow pair, which were

186

buoyed off just under our stern. The hoses would not come in. Leaning far out over the rail, I looked under the *Falcon*'s counter and found the hoses caught in our propeller, swept under no doubt as we tossed about. The hoses had to be cleared. If they cut in two, all the air would escape from the bow pontoons and quickly let them sink.

Into the surfboat tumbled the crew, I with them. We steered in under the overhanging stern of the *Falcon*, armed with boathooks. The storm was a help now, for as the trough of the sea swept by, the propeller was partly exposed. Leaning over the side of the boat, I speared the hoses with my boathook, between each pair of waves, dragging them a few inches up the top propeller blade, while the rest of the boat crew held the boat in close so I could work.

"Duck!" yelled Gunner Tibbals from the *Falcon*. A huge wave was sweeping by. Instinctively I dropped my boathook, ducked down below a thwart. The boat rose to the wave, crashed her rail, where a second before my head had been, against the stern of the *Falcon*. My boathook, still poised over the side, snapped in two and drifted away.

The wave passed, we sank into a trough. I took another boathook, resumed my fishing job, but kept a wary eye on the waves as they swept up. I lost another boathook, we stove in the rail of the surfboat, but after some twenty minutes' work, the hoses pulled free of the propeller, undamaged. The boat ran out from under the stern, came alongside. On the top of a wave, I leaped easily over the *Falcon*'s bulwark.

The sailors pulled the last hoses aboard, and connected them to the quarterdeck manifold. Niedermair was getting ready to blow, when looking over our port quarter, I saw a huge mass of bubbles, foaming up and spreading out right under the *Falcon*'s stern!

It flashed through my mind that, after all, the hoses had parted and were releasing the air, but a second look made me drop that idea. No such geyser of air could come through a few small hoses.

Probably the pontoon chains had broken and the bow pontoons, free, were shooting to the surface, under our stern. When they hit us, we would be sunk right on top of the *S-51*.

There was little time for action. The winchmen were standing by the capstans, ready to let go the mooring lines as soon as we had finished with the hoses.

"Let go the port quarter mooring line! Heave round like hell on the starboard winch!" Hartley shouted.

The port line slacked, the starboard winch raced as a seaman jerked the throttle wide open. Our stern began to swing slowly to starboard. We had cleared the patch of foam about twenty feet, when the broken water suddenly widened out and four pontoons, with the bow of the *S-51* between them, burst through the surface of the sea!

The rolling of waves, felt far below the surface, had rocked the submarine on the bottom, destroyed what little suction grip was left; the lightened bow had broken free and risen with increasing speed. There in the middle of a storm, when we had no desire at all to see it, one end of the submarine, and the wrong end at that, was once again afloat!

There was no choice. Storm or no storm, we must raise her now. The *Falcon*'s siren shrieked a warning to the other vessels. A boatload of extra hose came from the *Vestal.* We connected all the hoses to the submarine's after compartments and to the stern pontoons, dragged them on board, coupled them to the *Falcon*'s blowing manifold. We started to blow air into the stern. There was no chance of getting her into port even if we lifted her, but I hoped that when, during her stormy tow, she finally broke loose and sank again, it might at least be in shallower water, where raising her next time would be easier.

The pontoons, weighed down by the submarine bow cradled in chains between them, rose and fell sluggishly as the seas rolled by, occasionally exposing the stem of the *S-51* in their midst. Niedermair turned the air on the after pontoons. The *Falcon*'s air compressors labored their utmost to force the air through rapidly.

Meanwhile the *S-50* maneuvered close aboard on our starboard side, dropped anchor just clear of our mooring buoys and endeavored to send us an airhose to help us out with the compressed air stored at high pressure in her banks. It was useless. Time after time, the storm swept the *S-50* down to leeward as if her anchor were a feather. The hose never came on board.

The *Falcon* was left to fight the battle out herself. With all her compressors running, she was still not able to keep up much pressure on so many lines at once.

The storm grew worse. The pontoons swayed back and forth in the sea, battering each other. Wood sheathing came off in large patches, floated away. An hour went by, full of feverish activity, but it was passed in silence by the men on the *Falcon*, watching the wreck of all their hopes.

Everything was wrong. The blowing connections were all set to expel the water from the submarine with the stern, not the bow, at the surface first. With the bow up, it was impossible to drive more than two-thirds of the water from the sealed compartments in the submarine. Then the pontoon lashings had been put on with the main purpose of holding the pontoons from sliding aft when the stern rose. Now the bow was the high end. How long would they hold in that position? Evidently not indefinitely, for the two pairs of pontoons, which had risen properly lined up, were now a huddled group at the bow, pointing in all directions.

There was nothing to do but pump air and hope. We pumped steadily.

Some bubbles appeared aft, foamed on the surface, spread out.

I watched them, thought gloomily: "Well, here's the stern! I wonder what luck we'll have towing in this sea?"

But instead of that, a pontoon shot through the froth, leaped free of the water like a tarpon, dropped back, and floated away with some broken ends of chain dangling from the hawsepipes! A few seconds later, its mate appeared, sparkled a second as it rose dripping above the sea, then lazily drifted to leeward with its companion.

The anchor chains under the stern had slipped upward a little under the lifting strain, had struck the point where the box keel began, had broken under the impact. The released pontoons racing upward under full buoyancy had left the partly flooded stern resting in the mud. The *Sagamore* chased the pontoons through the storm, some miles away got lines on them, and started slowly for Point Judith.

Our chance of raising the stern was gone. Mechanically, we continued blowing air into the engine room and the motor room, but I knew that with the bow end up we could not eject enough water to make the stern lift. Shortly, a moderate amount of bubbles showed over the spot where the spillpipe in the engine room was buried in the sea. The engine room was venting air, we could get no more buoyancy aft.

The stern did not rise.

The situation was now desperate. The four pontoons at the bow were charging back and forth as the seas swept by, battering each other like mad bulls. The stem of the *S-51* rode heavily between them; we could hear the groaning of the chains under the keel as the submarine swayed. The stern pair of chains had broken; it would not be long before the forward chains parted under the terrific punishment they were getting. When that happened, the heavy bow, with no internal buoyancy of its own, would go crashing one hundred and thirty-two feet to the bottom, making a complete wreck of all our work. The prospect sickened me.

There was one way to save the situation,—flood the pontoons before the chains broke, and let the whole mass sink gradually. But to do that meant getting out on that chaotic mass to open the pontoon flood valves. It looked like suicide. I could not ask any man to try it.

Niedermair stopped blowing aft, the compressors came to rest. The rumor got out there was no hope of bringing up the stern. The divers clustered round, as sick at heart as I was, anxious for information.

Eadie voiced the unspoken question:

"Can't we sink the bow?"

"Yes, Tom, that'll do it, but who is going to open those valves?"

Silence. No orders, no comments.

None were needed.

Wickwire stripped off his jumper, threw away his shoes. Seizing a wrench, he leaped overboard, swam fifty feet to the nearest pontoon, dug his fingernails into the slippery sheathing, climbed aboard.

He was in the midst of a raging cauldron. The sea swept over him, the pontoon rose and fell wildly under his feet. He reached the flood valves, turn by turn, he swung them open. The sea swept him away, he swam back, battered but determined. Carefully he clung on, opening a turn at a time, when he was not buried in a wave. Again he was washed off, fortunately to the side away from the submarine. If once he fell into that devil's churn where the bow of the *S-51* ground between the pontoons he would quickly be mincemeat.

Another sea caught him, took him off again. His strength was gone, he drifted to leeward, paddling feebly to stay afloat. The surfboat picked him up, brought him in, exhausted, nearly strangled from salt water. The valves on one pontoon were open.

Badders went overboard from the surfboat, battled the seas on the second pontoon; Weaver tried the third and broke his arm; Boatswain Hawes, with no one else available in his boat, himself leaped into the sea, wrench in hand, clung to the third pontoon while he swung the wrench. Like the others, the green seas swept over him as the wild pontoon plunged sickeningly up and down. He stuck, one second buried, the next high above the sea as he rode the pontoon, turned the valves. The sea tore him away; fortunately, like the others, he drifted clear to be hauled into the surfboat.

No one ever got aboard the fourth pontoon, but it was unnecessary. The other three, valves partly open, were beginning to fill and ride more sluggishly. In another minute, we got what sad comfort there was in seeing the bow of the *S-51*, with the four pontoons still clinging to it, slowly vanish beneath the waves and sink gently from our sight. A few bubbles, a little froth, marked the spot.

The sea had won again.

As best we could, we cast loose our moorings, and with the rest of the squadron, the *Falcon* slowly steamed northward through the storm to the Harbor of Refuge at Point Judith, where hours before we had expected to go for a rest before raising the submarine.

The disappointment and gloom in the salvage party need not be described. The sailors were worn out, the divers literally burned out by months of toil under heavy pressure on the bottom, the officers haggard from the physical and mental strain. Silence reigned on the *Falcon*. No one spoke, except for the routine orders of the ship's work. We dropped anchor behind the stone breakwater in the early afternoon, crawled wearily into our bunks.

June 22, 1926,—a day no one there off Block Island will ever forget!

XXXIV

STILL MORE
PONTOONS

The storm abated during the night. At noon we steamed out
again, moored.

We put two divers over together to inspect, Eiben forward,
Smith aft. A silent hour went by as the divers worked along the wreck
from opposite ends, finally meeting amidships, when we hoisted them
up, cast loose the moorings, and again headed north for Point Judith.

In the little wardroom of the *Falcon*, a silent group of officers listened
to the report from Eiben and Smith. It held little comfort.

The *S-51* was lying far over on her starboard side, her bow some
thirty feet to the right of its old position. Three of the pontoons which
had been at the surface were clustered round the bow, resting on the
bottom vertically, in a tangled mass of chains, wires, and hoses. The
fourth bow pontoon, the one on which the flood valves had not been
opened, was floating horizontally some six feet above the forecastle,
tugging hard on its chains.

The pair of pontoons abreast the conning tower, which had risen
only halfway to the surface and had consequently never been exposed
to the waves, were still afloat over the submarine and apparently the
lashings were intact, but, owing to its heavy list, the bridge was now
jammed hard against the starboard pontoon of this pair, and was crushed
in. The conning tower just below the bridge seemed undamaged.

The pontoons at the stern were, of course, missing, and the stern
itself was covered with mud from having sunk into the bottom when the
rest of the boat, at a sharp angle, rose to the surface.

The bow plating was badly damaged, the bridge was smashed, but
neither one of these spaces contained any essential buoyancy. We lost

perhaps ten tons of lift in the damaged bow buoyancy tank, but the three precious main compartments,—the motor room, the engine room, and the control room, on which we had spent months of work, all seemed undamaged from the drop of the bow when we sank the boat.

Taken as a whole, the physical condition of the submarine was not hopeless, but the work on the pontoons had all to be done over again, except on the midship's pair. Indeed it was worse even that that,—we would have to untangle the battered pontoons at the bow, get them to the surface, and repair them, before we could even start to lower pontoons again.

Their story told, Smith and Eiben returned to their shipmates in the messroom below. In the wardroom, each officer sized the problem up to himself. It looked bad. How could a set of divers, already worn out, who had been kept going for some weeks past on their nerves only because they were able to see the end of the job in sight, now undertake all that work again plus the unknown but obviously dangerous job of clearing away the wrecked pontoons? No one spoke.

In Hartley's stateroom, Captain King, Hartley, and I considered it. It would be difficult, but if only we could get the divers to work, not impossible.

Smith came later into my room, where alone I was pondering the problem. Of all the divers, Smith had I think faced the most risk, been in the most danger. Always he worked like a Trojan, unsparingly and intelligently. For some weeks he had not been well. Weakened by the strain, he had not dived much in the week just gone by. Wan and pale, he sat on my bunk.

"Mr. Ellsberg, I want to leave. I can't dive any more anyhow, and I've got to get away and rest."

I looked at him, surprised. I knew as well as he that he was knocked out, that his diving days were over, and I had hardly expected ever to ask him to dive again. But Francis Smith was an outstanding figure in the diving crew, a natural leader and an inspiration, especially to the newer divers. If we let him go, I could see our diving crew disintegrating. Most of the others were physically not quite so badly off as he, but mentally they were farther gone. If Smith went the rest would want to go also, ostensibly only for a rest, but once our gang broke up, and their wounds, so to speak, stiffened, never would we get them back. Diving in the Navy, in peace or war, is a volunteer effort. No man can ever be ordered to dive.

The situation was critical. I could see our expedition melting away, failure our portion. A repetition of the *S-5*, which still lies buried where she sank twenty-five fathoms deep, abandoned by the Navy six years before, after nine months of struggling by many of the same divers whom I had with me.

I pointed this out to Smith. I would not ask him to dive; but I could not let him go. He was obdurate.

"I'm sick of it, Mr. Ellsberg. I just can't stand it here any longer. I can't work, and on the *Falcon* I can't rest. There isn't any deck space; if I crawl in my bunk, this bucket tosses around so badly I nearly turn inside out. I want to go back to Pittsburgh, my home's there. Maybe if I rest there a month, I might be able to come back. I'm sorry, but I can't stay."

I did not argue with Smith. I asked him to think it over a few hours, promised that if he still felt the same way then, I would get him the leave he wished. Smith left.

Something was wrong. Francis Smith! I thought of the day he was buried in the tunnel while I clung in agony to his telephone! He was no quitter. I started from my stateroom to find the reason. In three steps I bumped into it.

The wardroom was deserted except for one officer. He buttonholed me. I listened. He was totally discouraged, worn out, physically ill. He spent some time trying to make me see that we had failed, the job was hopeless, the divers unable to work again. I knew the last claim was true, but refused to admit it to anyone else. I escaped from the wardroom, a suspicion rising in my mind.

I circulated a little among the divers, made a few inquiries. As I expected, they were all disheartened, dead tired, anxious only to get away and forget, but I learned also what I was looking for. The officer who had spoken to me had already gone among the men, told them the task was hopeless, assured them the only way we would ever raise the *S-51* would be to bring out a few tons of dynamite and blow her up!

Action was quick. A hasty conference with Captain King and Lieutenant Hartley, and within thirty minutes a tugboat was on its way to Newport bearing away the ill-discretioned officer, on leave for his health.

A few hours later, I invited Smith back to my stateroom, went over with him exactly how the submarine lay, carefully explained in detail each move we would take in repairing the damages, replacing the pontoons; and shortly convinced him that the job was far from the hopeless task he had been told, if only the divers stuck to it then. Smith was not only convinced and ready to stay to the finish, but he became so enthusiastic over the prospect that he begged for permission to dive again, weak as he was! I sent him out to talk to the others.

That evening, all the divers gathered in the *Falcon*'s wardroom. As with Smith, I explained the situation, pointed out the possibilities. But taken as a body, they were tired, discouraged. If they could go ashore for a week or two, they might return then, rested enough to finish.

"I'm sorry, men, we can't do that," I explained. "If we get away from here, most of us will never come back. We've got to drive it through now for our own sakes. The country has forgotten us,—it will never know if we quit, but we'll know. Stick! We can do it! And because we're men, we are going to stay here and fight it out with the ocean if it takes us the rest of our lives! Who's with us?"

They all were.

We sailed out again next morning, moored, prepared to dive. With the midship pair of pontoons pulling up, and one pontoon still lifting on the stem, the forward end of the submarine was off the bottom nearly all the way back to frame forty-six, where after weeks of digging by numerous divers, Eadie and Wilson had once before driven through a tunnel.

Once more we needed a pair of chains there. Before the ship should bury herself deeper, Eadie went down with the hose; in one dive, with the vessel only slightly in the clay, the new nozzle drilled a hole through. We rove off new lines, hauled our wires, lowered down and stretched out on the bottom a new pair of anchor cables to take the pontoons there later.

That done, we turned attention next day to the tangled heap around the bow. That pontoon floating over the forecastle had to come down before we could release the others. It was floating athwart the deck. We could not sink it there or it would drop onto the forecastle. Smith investigated. One of the lashing wires, leading to a sunken port pontoon from under the floating one, was holding it athwartships. But the wire was some seven feet to port of the deck edge, and out of reach. He could not cast it loose.

Kelley had a method. With McLagan to assist, he dived, taking the torch lashed to the end of a squilgee handle some six feet long. They landed, straddled the rail on the high edge of the deck, groped their way forward. It was nearly as easy to walk on the side of the ship as on the deck.

Under the pontoon, Kelley lighted the torch, pulled the trigger, lashed it back with a rubber band. Then with McLagan holding him, he leaned far out to port, thrusting out the squilgee handle with the torch spurting a jet of flame through the water at the far end. He balanced himself precariously on the edge of the deck, McLagan hanging on to steady him. With both hands he swung the tip of the torch to the wire, held it there a moment. A white stream of sparks shot out, the wire snapped.

Glancing through the side faceplate over his shoulder, Kelley saw the pontoon, freed from the wire, swinging towards him. He dropped the torch, jumped over the side, grabbing the rail and clinging there. McLagan tried to run. There was nothing to run on. The pontoon swirled by, hit him, sent him flying overboard through the water to the bottom where he landed in a heap in the mud twenty feet below. The pontoon came to rest in a fore and aft position on the starboard side.

Kelley scrambled back on deck, gripped his partner's lifelines, and hauled him up again. Bruised and shaken, he escorted McLagan aft to the descending line at the gun. They rose, came aboard. Neither would say much.

We dangled Boyd from the surface till finally we landed him on top the pontoon which Kelley had cut free, as it floated in its new position. Boyd cut loose the old hoses, then secured a new pair, and opened the flood valves and the vents to sink the pontoon to the bottom where we could release the chains. We returned next morning to find this pontoon also standing on its end on the bottom alongside the submarine, thus completing a trying situation.

Meanwhile in the Harbor of Refuge at Point Judith we had set up a floating navy yard, consisting of the *Vestal*, which provided the shop facilities, and the floating derrick *United States*, of one hundred tons lifting capacity, which was towed from Newport to Point Judith and anchored behind the stone breakwater. The derrick was the dry dock for the pontoons.

With Lieutenant Kelly to run it, the derrick hoisted out of water the two pontoons which had broken loose from the stern. The *Vestal*'s crew quickly overhauled both pontoons, after which they were dropped overboard, leaving the derrick clear to repair the bow pontoons when we raised them.

The divers were a source of concern. The spirit of the men was excellent, they were doing their utmost, but most of the older divers were burned out. Wilson soon had to be sent to the hospital in Newport. His stomach could no longer hold food. Madden had long since been sent back to Boston with burst eardrums. Kelley came up with a minor case of "the bends" after every dive. He could dive only for brief periods now, when a torch expert was needed. Eiben went around with a permanent limp. I suspect he had a "bubble" in his knee, but never said anything about it. Bailey no longer could dive at all. George Anderson had been sent back to New York to save him from pneumonia. Holden and Sanders had been ordered to stop by the doctor and were acting as tenders. Smith was diving, but I dared not keep him down long.

Only Carr, Eadie, Michels, and Wickwire of our older group were still in fair shape and able to stay down an hour.

So far as the rest of the older and more skilled men were concerned, they were going along on their nerves, a bunch of eager cripples. But I was thankful for the youngsters whom Kelley had trained to dive the winter before. They had done their best through the first spring months, assisting the more skilled divers on the easier jobs. Now the burden fell on them. They were the reserves. Young, eager, with more power of recuperation, they swung into the breach left by the disabled veterans, and carried the job along.

On Albert Grube, only nineteen years old, fell the main task of releasing the bow pontoons. With Davis to assist, he landed on the round top of starboard number two pontoon where it rose some sixteen feet above the forecastle. Halfway down its vertical side, the chains hung from the hawsepipes, secured in place by the heavy steel toggle bars, with a locking pin holding the toggles in the chain links. Carefully Grube slipped down the side, Davis lowering him by his airhose, for all the world like a mountaineer going down a precipice. His breastplate came opposite the upper hawsepipe. Davis ceased lowering, clung tightly to the lines to hold Grube suspended. Swinging across the face of the pontoon, Grube gripped the dangling chain between his knees to steady himself, lay against the chain with the toggle pressed against his chest. With a small wrench he unscrewed the locking pin on one side of the link. Then he grasped the one-hundred-and-forty-pound toggle on the other side of the chain, braced his lead shoes against the link below, and hauled with all his might. Slowly the heavy bar started out of the chain till it came clear. Grube dropped it. The bar disappeared in the sand below, while the freed chain rattled back through the hawsepipe.

Davis eased him down sixteen feet farther to the lower hawsepipe where Grube cleared the other toggle bar after a struggle, for the weight of the chain had it jammed against the pontoon. At last he dragged it out of the link and the chain vanished with a roar while Grube spun round like a top in the swirl that the flying chain set up in the water. Davis pulled him back on top the pontoon, gave the rising signal, and the two young divers started up.

When we had them aboard, we hauled the *Falcon* clear and Niedermair blew the pontoon they had been working on. For eleven minutes the air went down; then the pontoon floated up and we hauled it alongside. Its sheathing was gone and it was leaking through numerous rivets. The *Iuka* took it in tow after we had expelled all the water, and sailed with it for our repair base at Point Judith.

Working continuously during the next two days on the tangled web of chains, wires, and hoses around the bow of the submarine, the divers finally succeeded in freeing the three remaining pontoons there. We brought two more cylinders to the surface, battered and leaking, and started them for Point Judith. Finally we started to blow the last pontoon, but immediately large air bubbles showed on the surface, indicating that the pontoon was leaking like a sieve. We blew on it for nearly half an hour before it finally rose, the most battered of all the pontoons, with two large holes punched in its side where the pontoon astern of it during the storm had continuously charged into it as the seas rolled by.

The pontoon barely floated. To get it to Point Judith, the *Falcon* unmoored and steamed away with it in tow, pumping air to it all the way to keep the waterlogged cylinder from going down again. We dragged it inside the breakwater, against the derrick, where huge wire slings were passed under it, and the derrick lifted it out of water. Meanwhile, I seized the opportunity to send all the divers on the *Sagamore* to Newport for a few hours' change of scene, while the *Falcon* returned to the wreck. The *Sagamore* rejoined us there late at night.

Matters began to look brighter. All the damaged pontoons were up. At Point Judith, the *Vestal* was working night and day, patching holes, welding up leaks, replacing sheathing, renewing broken valves. The tired divers, with the wreckage cleared away, saw the promises made to them fulfilled, and turned to with renewed energy.

On June 29 we had a storm which drove us off, but gave all hands a much-needed rest. The last day of June the weather was passable, and the divers removed the damaged towline from the bow. Working steadily on the narrow deck at the very stem, Boyd and Davis succeeded in slipping a heavy shackle into the bullnose at the stem and then coupled a towing wire to it; while Kelley, Grube, Henry, Wickwire, and Michels, working in relays, fastened another towing chain round the base of the gun, led it forward, secured it to a chain bridle under the bow, and then ran it out over the sea bottom to a buoy well ahead of the ship.

July 1 dawned with a light breeze, but with heavy swells from the southward. The *Falcon* moored nevertheless and rigged for lowering pontoons. The *Sagamore* and *Iuka* steamed out from behind the breakwater at Point Judith, each towing a rebuilt pontoon, while the divers started to pick up the wires to the pair of chains we had run through a week before. The last storm had carried away the buoys and snarled the wires; Eadie and Eiben cleared them.

The first pontoon came alongside, pitching heavily. We rigged it, strained the lowering lines severely as the pontoon jerked on the lines till we got it submerged. We lowered to ninety feet, when Carr and McLagan went down to insert the toggle. Both became so seasick riding the plunging pontoon that they could do nothing till we lowered the pontoon to the bottom.

We brought the mate pontoon alongside, rigged and lowered it to ninety feet. Here Kelley and Boyd went down. Boyd tore his suit open trying to insert a toggle bar, and had to be brought up, leaving Kelley alone. Kelley managed to get both toggles in, catching the chain on the fly, but came up sick. Smith, Henry, Clark, and Davis followed in succession to cast off the lines which ordinarily one diver could do in a few minutes. Finally at 10 P.M. we had the pontoon down and free. Our twelve-inch lowering hawsers were so badly stretched we threw them away and broke out a new set.

July 2, the sea was still running a heavy swell. We turned to on the stern of the submarine. Michels and Grube dived together, passed a line under the stern, and we hauled down a four-inch manila. The wire line followed as usual. We were reeving it through when in some way Grube's lifelines became tangled in the wire and he was jerked halfway to the surface before we could stop. Michels climbed the wire, helped Grube unwind himself, and both men came up. Eiben and Davis passed the second line; we got wires, chains, and both pontoons down on the bottom and toggled to the chains without accident, in spite of the rolling of the *Falcon*.

July 3, we moored in the same swell, prepared to lower the last pair of pontoons at the bow.

At this point, we obtained a new recruit to our diving crew. Chief Torpedoman Ingram, who made the first dive to locate the *S-51* just after she was sunk, had worked with us through the fall operations, and had expected to rejoin in the spring. However, as he was the station diver at Newport, and one expert diver was required there to recover torpedoes lost on trial runs, the inspector at the Torpedo Station had refused to release Ingram in the spring. As we had already stripped the station of all its other divers, we could do nothing about it, though Ingram tried every method he knew to get sent back to the *Falcon*. Finally on July 2, he succeeded in getting his discharge from the service; on July 3 he showed up on the *Falcon* as a civilian volunteer ready to dive, and begged us not to let his presence be known, as he thought it might possibly get him in trouble! We welcomed him with open arms, promised to say nothing about the way he had bootlegged himself back on the job.

Immediately he went into a diving suit and, going down with Carr, he helped put in the toggles and let go the lines on the pontoon which we lowered to the port side of the bow.

We had only one pontoon left. We brought alongside the last one, rigged it, flooded it till it went awash. Over went the stage with Badders on it to close the flood valves. He got the after valve closed, but the sea swung the forward end of the pontoon in under the counter of the *Falcon* and the wrench on the valve became inaccessible. Before we could haul the pontoon clear by a line to the *Sagamore*, so much water entered the open valve that the pontoon became heavy and its forward end sank far enough to carry the handle of the wrench about four feet below the surface.

Badders jumped from the stage, dived repeatedly underwater and closed the valve half a turn at a time, but before it was fully shut, the wrench fell off the valve stem and sank. Badders could do no more.

The pontoon was getting very heavy on that end as the water flowed in. I recalled several cases where our pontoons had broken away and sunk end first; it seemed about to happen again on our very last pontoon. But if we could not close the valve, I could at least prevent further flooding. Niedermair turned on the compressed air, blew into the hose to the forward compartment, drove some of the water out till the strain on the hawser eased up. Meanwhile Eadie, who had been nearly dressed, had the rest of his rig put on, and was dropped over on the pontoon, going down about eight feet. He closed the valve with a Stillson.

I had jumped overboard to help Badders when the trouble first started, and now stood in a soaked uniform at the forward bitts. Hartley manned the after line.

Together we lowered on our hawsers, dropped the pontoon to ninety feet and held it just above the starboard bow of the submarine while Grube and Eadie dived to insert the toggles in the chains. Then without bringing up the divers, we leveled off the pair of pontoons.

It was the first and only time on the *S-51* that we ran through our chains, lowered a pair of pontoons, and succeeded in leveling off the pontoons afloat over the submarine in one continuous operation.

We had, moreover, in three successive days, lowered three pairs of pontoons, which was a far better performance than we had been able to do when the divers were fresh on the job.

The *Falcon* unmoored in a fog and steamed clear for the night.

July 4 came on a Sunday, but in spite of both holiday and Sunday, we celebrated by making an early start on the job. We had two pairs of pontoons to level off, and three pairs to lash.

We tried leveling first on the second pair of pontoons from forward. Boyd and Henry did the diving; the job worked fine.

The *Falcon* then shifted aft to get over the submarine's stern, where we leveled off the pontoons there without much difficulty, while Wickwire and Davis handled the lines on the pontoons.

Michels, Eadie, and Eiben, going down in succession, washed the mud away from the buried Kingston valves, and once again blew the water out of the starboard and port ballast tanks, using an airhose shoved through the open valves or the holes Kelley had burned weeks before.

Ingram cleared the towline round the stern and secured a buoy to it from a point well astern of the vessel.

Carr and Grube went down on the bow, secured wire lashings across the deck on the forward pontoons, and were putting the lashings on the chains of the second pair when the pontoons started moving. The forward end of the port pontoon suddenly dropped to the bottom of the sea, while the corresponding end of the starboard pontoon shot up twenty feet. The leveling job was ruined; they could not install their lashings, and were lucky not to be hurt. The port pontoon had apparently leaked enough to grow heavy on one end and sink.

It was dark, too late to do anything. We hauled up the divers and unmoored.

XXXV

July 5, 1926

We moored especially early on July 5, in a choppy sea with a southeasterly breeze and a moderate swell.

Our weather reports indicated a storm next day. As the submarine was practically in the condition it had been in two weeks before when a storm brought up the bow, we decided if possible to finish and get out that day to avoid a possible repetition of the accident.

Our important job was to refloat the sunken end of the second port pontoon. Eadie took down the necessary wires and airhoses. We went through the leveling-off job quickly, completed it without mishap. Carr and Grube dived to install the final wire lashings. Carr noted that the submarine had straightened up during the night, and had only a slight port list instead of the heavy heel to starboard with which she had landed on the bottom after the storm.

Eiben dived to check the position of the bow pontoons, and to secure a line on the bow as a telltale. He came up after a short dive.

One more dive and we would be through.

Wickwire went down aft to check up on the pontoons there, and to secure a telltale line to the stern. He slipped down the descending line abaft the conning tower. For the last time, I heard the call:

"On the bottom!"

Wickwire went aft along the slimy deck of the submarine, set the valves on the stern pontoons, slid down her side to the sea bottom, and secured his telltale to the stern. He was through. I waited impatiently for his signal to be hoisted up. It was nearly noon. We must lose no time.

No signal came. I raised his telephone to my lips to order him to hurry, but desisted. Over the telephone, I heard Wickwire's helmet clang against the stern of the *S-51*, I heard him murmur:

"Good-bye, baby! I'll see you next in the Navy Yard!"

There was a loud "Smack," and then the tender on Wickwire's lifelines felt four vigorous jerks. We hauled Wickwire up quickly, shoved him into the "iron doctor" to decompress.

Captain King mounted the *Falcon*'s bridge, ordered all ships to take stations for raising. The *Falcon* hauled about one hundred feet to starboard of the submarine, with twenty airhoses running into the sea from her manifolds to the pontoons and compartments on the *S-51*. The *Sagamore* moved in ahead and picked up the buoys to the two tow-lines the divers had secured on the *S-51*'s bow, while the *Iuka* ran in aft and took the towline around the submarine's stern. The *S-50* anchored perhaps two hundred feet away on the *Falcon*'s starboard beam and sent over a hose to carry compressed air from her airbanks to help out the *Falcon*'s compressors, while a second submarine, the *S-3*, stood near by to take the *S-50*'s place when required. The *Vestal*, which had come out from Point Judith, was anchored one thousand yards to port.

It took but a few minutes after Wickwire was hoisted in to complete the readjustment of all ships,—the salvage squadron stood by.

At 12:17 P.M., I stepped to the air manifold and swung open the valves on the hoses leading to the motor room and to the engine room of the *S-51*. The rubber hoses bulged; the air shot through under the full pressure of the *Falcon*'s compressors. Niedermair opened the valve on the hose from the *S-50*, and we started to drain her banks, but even so, the pressure on our manifold quickly dropped from one hundred and twenty-five to ninety pounds, which was the highest our laboring compressors could maintain.

The air ran through for exactly an hour. At 1:17 P.M., bubbles started to rise over the engine room. We blew a few minutes longer to make sure both engine and motor rooms were dry; then tested each room separately on the pressure gauge. The air had reached the bilges; the rooms were dry.

Niedermair shut off both compartments and turned the air on in the hose leading to the control room. That hose stiffened out under the pressure as the air went down, but within a minute I got a severe shock, for a multitude of bubbles streamed through the surface over the control room. The air was coming up as fast as we sent it down.

Niedermair and I looked at the bubbles sadly. The control room, the sealing up of which had cost the divers so many desperate hours of work, was not holding the air. Whether the hose had torn away, whether something else had broken, we could not tell, nor could we find out. The *Falcon* was no longer in diving position over the submarine. To get her there would waste several precious hours of daylight; even aside from that we dared not put the *Falcon* over the submarine and risk having the lightened stern rush to the surface under us; not to mention the danger the diver would run if the stern started to rise while he was down.

Together Niedermair and I figured hastily. We had lost sixty tons lift in the control room; in addition we knew we were going to lose some of the buoyancy in the forward pontoons when the stern rose, but it still figured that we would have a margin of a few tons over. We said nothing about the control room, turned off the air, and decided to go ahead.

At 1:55 P.M., we resumed blowing, sending all the air to the pontoons at the stern.

Eleven minutes elapsed.

A cloud of bubbles spread over the sea. A moment later the stern pontoons broke surface, riding gracefully as the waves swept by. Seamen lined the rail, looked at the stern eagerly, but in silence. They had seen one end of the boat before; that much meant nothing.

All the air was immediately concentrated on the six pontoons forward. Here we blew for forty minutes, when air started to discharge over the surface, but nothing followed.

Blowing ceased, while one by one, we tested each compartment of each pontoon. The forward pair of pontoons vented air all around, the midship pontoons showed the same. We would get no more buoyancy in them. The after ends of the second pair of pontoons also lost air as fast as we supplied it. Only the forward halves of this pair showed any water left that might be expelled, and there could not be any great quantity left there.

I started the air again in these last two compartments. The *S-50* reported her air all gone,—the *S-3* maneuvered to get alongside her and transfer the airhose to her fresh banks. Meanwhile the *Falcon*'s compressors had to take the whole load,—they throbbed continuously.

Niedermair and I looked at each other glumly. Another failure. I wondered what had gone wrong with the control room of the *S-51*; how long the weather would stay good and let the stern float. There was a pair of small pontoons in Newport. I could get them out in a day, attach them somehow to the bow to make up for the lost control room if only the weather held out. But we had a storm warning.

Captain King came by, evidently perturbed by the long wait with the bow still down.

"How are things going?" he asked anxiously.

"Still fine, captain!" I replied. He knew they were not, but he left without any more questions. A peach of a commanding officer! He was not going to add his anxieties to ours. He felt we were doing our best, and left us alone.

Slowly the air pulsed through to the pontoons while Niedermair jotted down gauge readings and I made meaningless notes, trying to appear calm and businesslike as the worried divers one by one came up on the bridge to ask questions.

"Everything is going according to schedule," was the reply to them all, and I scheduled busily. How long would it be before a stream of bubbles showed the last pontoons dry, our hopes dashed?

An hour had gone by since the stern rose; the divers lined the port rail, tense, anxious.

Niedermair made the round of the gauges, for the tenth time noted down the unchanging pressures. Both of us paused in front of the last gauge, that to the port forward pontoon. It registered forty-eight pounds, had been steady on that for half an hour. Niedermair tapped it aimlessly, not hoping for any movement, but to our surprise, the needle promptly dropped to forty-four pounds, then to forty-two pounds, and continued to drop steadily. The water pressure was decreasing on that pontoon!

I rushed to the rail, looked over. No bubbles, no sign, but I needed none.

The divers clustered round.

"Gentlemen, here comes your bow!"

They looked, nothing showed, but an instant later the sea boiled violently and broke into huge geysers of water, then six pontoons broke through the foam and the *S-51* was afloat again! My cap went into the sea, followed by a hundred others. Cheers, tears, and the happy feeling:

"Now we can go home again!"

XXXVI

THE TOW

S oon we were under way, a strange procession. The *S-51*, still enclosing the bodies of eighteen of her officers and men, hung between the pontoons, with only her periscopes and part of her bridge showing above water. One hundred and fifty feet astern of her, holding to the line fastened around the tail of the submarine, came the *Falcon*, steadily pumping air to the pontoons and to the submarine to keep ahead of any leaks. One hundred fathoms ahead of the *S-51*, the *Sagamore* towed both submarine and *Falcon*, with two towlines on the bow of the submarine and one line going past her to the *Falcon*'s bow. Ahead of the *Sagamore* was the *Iuka*, with a line to the *Sagamore*, helping her along with her burden.

The *Vestal* steamed on ahead of the *Iuka*, navigating for the squadron.

The speed was slow, only two knots, partly on account of the difficulty of dragging the submarine and its unwieldy pontoons through the water, partly to avoid straining the pontoons and their chains by the pounding of the waves as we steamed along.

Captain King, from the bridge of the *Falcon*, directed the tow. Gradually we moved to the northward for Point Judith, to get over shallow water as soon as possible. At dusk we passed inside the hundred-foot mark, turned westward. With the sea astern, we increased speed to three knots and steamed on through the night, the pontoons lighted up by the *Falcon*'s searchlight.

Off Westerly, Rhode Island, near midnight, the tow struck a strong adverse tide, which we bucked for nearly an hour without making any progress before the current slacked off and we could go ahead again.

After getting clear there, the *Vestal* adjusted her speed so as to bring us to the first danger point, The Race, off New London, at slack water. Trouble was especially not desired there, as the deepest spot on the whole trip, three hundred feet to the bottom, lay in The Race. We had no desire to have to dive there.

The *Vestal*'s navigation was accurate. At about 4 A.M., we passed through The Race at dead slack water, meeting no currents at all, and in the early dawn of July 6, we slipped at last into the smooth waters of Long Island Sound. The worst was over.

In smooth water, with no ocean swells to cause jumping of the pontoons, the *Sagamore* and *Iuka* worked up to full power on their engines while the *Falcon* went ahead slowly on hers. The tow soon reached a speed of five knots. On we steamed, past New London, past Madison, past New Haven. By late afternoon it was evident that our unexpected progress would bring us to the East River in the darkness, an unsafe thing. We dared not attempt to anchor, or even to stop, for the long string of ships making up the tow would drift together in a tangle; even slowing up as much as possible would still bring us in too soon. To avoid this, the tow began to steam in a wide circle, perhaps two miles in diameter, and for the rest of the afternoon and part of the evening, we circled in the Sound to lose time.

Late in the evening, we straightened out and resumed our course towards Execution Rocks. Meanwhile, a radio was sent to the Navy Yard, asking Admiral Plunkett there to have "the best East River pilot" join us to take us through the East River, and in addition to send a navy pilot to take us into the Navy Yard itself after the civilian pilot had brought us to the entrance of the yard basin.

At midnight off Hempstead, two Navy Yard tugs joined us, bringing both pilots.

The *S-51* as she hung between the pontoons drew thirty-three feet of water; the shallowest spot on our trip, with only thirty-five feet of water over it, was just below Execution Rocks. In the early morning of July 7, we steamed over this spot without even stirring up the mud, and entered the approaches to the East River. To make steering easier, Captain King shortened up the tow by having the *Iuka* drop back abreast the *Sagamore* and secure to her; the two tugs thereafter towed side by side. The *Vestal*, as before, led the procession.

The civilian pilot took station on the *Sagamore* at the head of the tow; the salvage officers stayed on the *Falcon*'s bridge.

We reached Hell Gate at high water slack and went safely through when its dreaded currents and swirls were temporarily quiescent.

The last danger point was passed, our last obstacle overcome. We steamed in down the smooth waters of the East River on the top of the morning tide. Our troubles were over.

I went below a few minutes. For the first time in months, I took off my tarnished blouse, my blue woolen shirt, replaced them with a decent uniform, put on a white shirt and collar, prepared to return to civilization. All over the *Falcon*, sailors and divers who had long since grown beards were shaving them off, preparing to greet their wives or their sweethearts. Confusion reigned in the crew's quarters, in the wardroom. It was no longer possible to recognize in the neatly dressed men the rough-looking shipmates who had shared my struggles on deck or at the bottom.

I examined myself in the glass,—with a weather-beaten face and lips puffed and cracked from facing the biting winds and the sharp sun on the *Falcon*'s rail, I doubted whether anyone ashore would know me.

I climbed back on the bridge; Hartley, also dressed up, was there, conning his ship, carefully watching his position astern the submarine. Both sides of the East River were lined with huge crowds as we passed; no cheers, but half-masted flags and bare-headed throngs greeted the *S-51* as the silent procession steamed slowly along.

XXXVII

MAN OF WAR ROCK

We passed under Queensborough Bridge, passed Blackwell's Island on the Manhattan side, could see the entrance to the Navy Yard about a mile below. The *Vestal* cleared the tip of the island, stood on down the river in the deep channel near the Manhattan shore. The *Sagamore* and the *Iuka* followed her.

Just below Blackwell's Island, the two tugs left the *Vestal,* swerved off to port. Trailing on the towlines, the submarine followed.

Before the meaning of this unlooked-for maneuver on the part of the pilot could be learned, the submarine suddenly stopped, the pontoons bobbed violently and lost their alignment, two pontoons broke loose and drifted away! The *Falcon,* only one hundred and fifty feet behind the *S-51,* began rapidly to close on the stern of the submarine.

With only six seconds in which to act before ramming the *S-51,* Lieutenant Hartley swung his rudder "Hard Left" and got his engines going "Full Speed Astern." The *Falcon* closed in spite of everything, but Hartley's lightning action reduced the impact to a slight collision with the amidships port pontoon; he missed altogether the stern of the boat containing the precious buoyancy that the divers had risked their lives so many times to secure!

I was stunned. What could have happened? Wild as the idea seemed, I could only surmise that after holding through one hundred and fifty miles of towing, the *S-51* had finally broken in half abreast the hole made by the *City of Rome;* that the pontoons opposite that spot, their chains pulling through the gap, had broken free.

Meanwhile the *Iuka* and *Sagamore* with the towlines all broken were continuing down the river, while the *Falcon,* her progress checked, lay alongside the submarine. We had been heading downstream also; in a moment we were no longer, for both submarine and *Falcon* were pivoting about the *S-51*'s bow and swinging sharply around till we were heading nearly upstream in a strong ebb tide.

Once more the six remaining pontoons lined up straight; evidently the submarine was still intact. What then had happened? A sunken wreck in our path? Overboard went the surfboat to take soundings along the bow.

There was a terrific tide running. The ordinary sounding lead streamed far out. It took a fifty-pound weight to sound in a reasonably vertical line. We hit bottom,—four fathoms, only twenty-four feet. And the *S-51* had been drawing thirty-three feet!

We reported the depth to the bridge; Captain King had taken some hasty bearings and plotted them on the chart. Over the megaphone I heard him shout:

"We're way off the channel, aground on Man of War Rock!"

We had hit at high water. The tide was rapidly falling. As it did so, the water swirled in violent eddies around the pontoons at the bow which showed higher and higher above the surface. Meantime, the submarine, whose periscopes had been nearly erect before, now began to heel gradually to starboard as the tide fell and she received less and less support from the bow pontoons.

Back on the *Falcon*, I hastily figured up the situation with Niedermair. One pair of pontoons was gone. The tugs had finally stopped, recovered the drifting pontoons, found the chains broken in half. The submarine had been dragged up on a rocky shelf on Man of War Reef; the chains on the second pair of pontoons had been ground in half as they struck, releasing that pair of pontoons. The towlines to the *Sagamore* had torn the bow right out of the *S-51*; the *Sagamore* hauled in the broken stem and part of the submarine's bow plating when she dragged in the useless towlines.

Hurriedly we backed the *Falcon* clear just abaft the submarine and ran an anchor out over our stern to keep her from swinging further.

Several officers from the Army Engineer's office came aboard and offered the services of their tugs and equipment; meanwhile they cut our position in accurately in order to show the wreck of the *S-51* on their charts as a permanent menace to navigation.

The shock of having the pilot shipwreck our submarine, practically at the end of her long tow, was disheartening. A moment before we could see our task over; now once more we had a submerged wreck to deal with, and as we looked over at the tide racing by, our hopes sank. Diving was impossible in that current except at the turns of the tide, perhaps for thirty minutes each six hours. Two of our pontoons were gone. The water over the reef was shallower by eight feet than the draft of the *S-51*, and to make it worse, we had stranded at high tide. We could not look forward to a rise in tide to float us free. Instead we could expect to have our ship try to capsize as the tide dropped.

In this difficulty, Niedermair and I figured feverishly. As in all good engineering practice, we had provided a reserve of buoyancy in our pontoons, over what was needed barely to lift the submarine. Part of this reserve was lost when the control room failed us on the lifting day; practically all the rest was unavailable during the lifting operation when the slope as the submarine lay stern up, bow on the bottom, prevented us from expelling all the water from the pontoons; but when the bow finally rose and the *S-51* floated level, we were able to force the remaining water out of all pontoons. In that position, with nearly a quarter of each of the eight pontoons out of water during the tow, our reserve buoyancy had been nearly one hundred and sixty tons. Now we were shy one pair of pontoons which had been carrying perhaps one hundred and fifty tons. If only we could sink our remaining pontoons till they were again fully submerged, we could just make up for the lost buoyancy required to float the boat; in addition, if we could resecure the pontoons low enough, we might lift the submarine high enough to float her off the reef. It would be nip and tuck on both scores. Considering the poor conditions under which we would have to work, I estimated it might take two weeks for the job, and meanwhile we would have to keep the after compartments on the submarine dry and undamaged or the stern of the vessel would also sink, ruining our prospects.

The river, unlike the sea, had a calm surface, and we could use derricks. A radio was sent to the Navy Yard, asking for two derricks and additional tugs to handle them. While we waited, the sailors cleared away the tangled mass of hoses and towlines, carefully keeping the hoses to the engine and motor rooms unharmed.

Tremendous crowds gathered on the docks along both sides of the East River, while numerous small boats circled round to watch the wreck.

In an hour the first derrick arrived, with a tug on either side to handle it. The derrick was run against the starboard bow pontoon, heading upstream, with the tugs pushing constantly to hold it in position against the outgoing tide. Lowering the boom of the derrick as far over its bow as possible, riggers hooked both pontoon chains with wire slings and heaved in till the strain on the wires took the whole load of the lift off the pontoon. The tide had partly fallen; the pontoons were more than half out of water.

When the derrick had the strain, we opened the flood valves on the pontoon and allowed it to fill slowly and bury itself deeper and deeper. With the pontoon practically all awash, just showing a few inches above water, while the chains stretched taut to the derrick overhead, I burned out the studs in the links just above the top of the pontoon; the riggers pulled the toggle bars out of their old links and resecured them in the newly cleared links nearly seven feet lower. This done, Niedermair, on signal to the *Falcon*, blew air into the pontoon till it became a little more buoyant and took up hard against the toggles, taking the strain back on the pontoon, as the derrick slacked away on the slings.

Quickly the riggers shifted the wires to the mate pontoon on the port bow of the submarine; there in a similar manner we flooded down and resecured in an awash position the other pontoon. It was ticklish work on top of the pontoon as the swift water rushed by; the two tugs had to keep steaming ahead full power to prevent the derrick from being swept downstream.

A little after noon, the two bow pontoons were done. The derrick let go and attempted to back clear, but the tide swept derrick, tugs, and all pell mell down the starboard side of the submarine straight for the hawser holding the *Falcon* in position. Someone on the *Falcon* swung an ax,—the line parted and allowed the hurtling group of vessels to shoot past without becoming entangled in the wreck; some distance down the stream the tugs finally brought the derrick to rest in quieter water close inshore, where they anchored it.

Shortly afterward was low tide; the current slacked off somewhat and we attempted to send a diver down to investigate. Eadie was dressed, and went down from the Navy Yard diving launch abreast the spot where the second pair of pontoons had broken free. We dropped a fair-sized anchor on a line alongside the submarine for him to go down on and prepared to lower Eadie overboard, but just before he started, the tide changed and the submarine, pivoting once more round her bow, swung her stern rapidly upstream nearly one hundred and eighty degrees from its former position, and in a moment was pointing down the river just as she was before she first struck.

We thanked our luck Eadie was not down when the movement started, shifted the diving launch and anchor over to the new position, and Eadie went overboard. He grasped the anchor line, started to descend, and immediately disappeared in the thick water. He was down only ten minutes when he signaled to be hauled up. We brought him up and, while the tenders undressed him, he reported.

"She's resting on a shelf of rock from her bow back about fifty feet. The rest of her is all clear aft and floating in deep water. There's a huge boulder against her port side now that keeps her from swinging to port any further; there's another one just about as big a little ways off on her starboard side that she probably leaned against just before her swing started. Looks to me as if she sort of ran right into a pocket in the reef." He paused a moment while his suit was pulled off. "The current here is fierce. I had to haul myself down that anchor line in order to get down at all, and the sweep of the tide when I reached bottom was so bad that I had to crawl on my hands and knees to keep from being washed away. At that, I couldn't stay down any longer because the current was increasing and I couldn't hold against it another minute."

The prospects did not look bright for diving. That was at slack water as the tide turned; now it was running flood stronger and stronger. I gave up any hope of working with divers to replace the lost pontoons.

A larger derrick from the Navy Yard was nearby with two powerful tugs to handle it. This I brought down against the port midship pontoon with the tugs as before to hold it against the current. Once more the riggers took the strain of the chains off the pontoon, heaving the chains upward with slings made of plow steel wire one and one-half inches thick, till the full strain was off the pontoon.

Then with Badders and Schissel to help, I opened the flood valves on the pontoon and started to flood it down. To let the air out while the water came in, we first opened the air vents on top of the pontoon, but as these vents were only small three-quarter-inch valves, the air could escape through them only gradually and the pontoon accordingly filled very slowly.

The afternoon was getting on and I now hoped to finish before the next turn of the tide; consequently, to accelerate matters, the men on the bow of the derrick over our heads dropped a Stillson wrench down to Badders and he unscrewed both the vent and blow valves in each compartment of the pontoon. That left four clear holes, each one inch in diameter, in the top of the pontoon,—one at each end and two near the middle. Through these clear holes, the air whistled out and the pontoon filled and sank somewhat more rapidly. Badders laid the unscrewed valves carefully on top the pontoon, so that when it was nearly awash we could quickly screw back the valves.

Half an hour went slowly by. Just beyond the pontoon, I could see the periscopes and the top of the conning tower of the *S-51* leaning over about fifteen degrees to starboard against the midship pontoon on that side, which fortunately prevented it from rolling over any farther. The port pontoon that we were standing on had sunk four feet and had perhaps still three more feet to go before it was awash. The heavy nickel steel toggle bars, left behind as the pontoon sank, still dangled through the chain links about four feet above the pontoon, while the wire slings holding the chains up ran far above our heads to the top of the derrick boom. The overhanging bow of the derrick was just over us.

On the far side of the river, a large steamer passed swiftly northward and disappeared behind Blackwell's Island.

A minute later, a heavy swell from the steamer's wake rolled under us. The derrick pitched in the trough of the waves, brought up with a jerk on the slings. The wires parted. The bow of the derrick, freed of the load, flew upwards while the chains, no longer supported, brought the toggles down with the crash of eighty tons weight on top of the pontoon. The pontoon promptly disappeared, taking its three passengers with it. Just before I submerged, I saw the starboard side pontoon suddenly bob up and the periscopes roll heavily to starboard.

"The submarine's capsized now," I thought, "it's all over!"

On the derrick, the crew, looking down over their wildly heaving bow, saw nothing. Hastily they ran aft, seizing life preservers, waiting to throw them to Badders, Schissel, or me, when the tide, carrying us up the river, washed us clear of the bottom of the derrick.

Fortunately for us, the forward toggle bar had snapped under the shock; no longer held down, that end of the pontoon, after a brief submergence, floated up again, just barely showing above water, with the three of us still clinging to it. We came up, soaked, sputtering, still in water over our waists, but all with one mind. The pontoon under our feet was submerged with open flood valves and open vents; soon it would fill and sink to the bottom of the river, and in that tide getting it up again would be a desperate job. It must not sink! With one accord, we plugged the three submerged vents with our thumbs. Schissel, at the deep end, went completely underwater; Badders and I, amidships, could just keep our heads above the surface; the fourth vent hole at the high end was out of water and safe. About once a minute, just Schissel had to pull his thumb out of his hole, come up a second for air, and dive down again to plug the opening.

On the stern of the derrick, the crew waited anxiously, lifebuoys poised, wondering what had become of us. Our shouts finally brought them back to the bow, where, seeing two of us in water up to our necks, apparently standing on nothing, they threw us lines.

"Never mind the lines," I yelled, "cut us some one-inch wood plugs quick!" Schissel popped up, gasped for breath, disappeared again. On deck, the riggers scurried round, smashed a box, whittled out a plug, dropped it down to me. Schissel came up again. I left my hole a second, swam to him, gave him the plug, and went back to my job.

Schissel found his hole, pushed the plug in, hammered it down with his fist, and then, standing erect, stamped it in hard with his heel. Meanwhile, more plugs came down, Badders and I withdrew our thumbs, sealed up the holes amidships. I crawled up the slope to the high end of the pontoon, drove a fourth plug into the opening there, then sat down in water on the pontoon to survey the situation. It was bad.

The starboard midships pontoon was floating high, carrying practically no load. The two pontoons at the stern, which fortunately had before been riding quite high, were now nearly awash, carrying the load lost by the midships pontoons. Another foot down, and the stern pontoons would have sunk, letting the stern go to the bottom of the river.

The periscopes had vanished. Had the boat turned completely over? I looked across, could just barely make out the sides of the periscopes about a foot under the surface. The submarine was only lying on her side!

I breathed a sigh of relief. There was still hope if we could only resecure the midships pontoons. I looked at the remains of the pontoon I was sitting on. Only a few inches of it was visible.

I could cure that. In the surfboat, I ran around to the mate pontoon, clambered aboard with a wrench, opened the flood valves, opened the vents. As this pontoon sank on the starboard side, its mate rose on the port side till the whole top of the submerged pontoon was a foot above water. Then with all valves closed on the starboard pontoon, I went back to the other one.

One chain with its toggle bar still showed above the after hawsepipe. The forward toggle bar had vanished and so had the chain. Looking down the forward hawsepipe, we could just see the remains of the broken wire sling, and that only because a manila line we had secured to the sling shackle as a preventer was still intact and held the broken wire from dropping down the hawsepipe. The manila line was not very strong; gingerly we took it up till we were able to get a firm grip on the wire, when we breathed more freely. We heaved on the wire till the end of the chain came in sight and immediately slipped a spare steel toggle bar through the chain. We were safe. If that chain had got away from us, getting another under the submarine in that tide would have been difficult.

With both chains in sight, things moved rapidly. The port pontoon being already awash, it was only necessary to remove the wood plugs and screw back the vent and blowing valves. Then with a new pair of wire slings, we took hold of the chains on the starboard pontoon, held them up with the derrick while we sank that pontoon till it went awash. To prevent further accident, the toggle bars there were shifted down, link by link, as the pontoon sank, while the harbor police stopped all further traffic in the river.

It was late evening and we were working in the darkness when the second pair of pontoons was finally secured in the awash position. The tide was rising steadily. The bow pontoons, awash when we secured them at low tide, were now four feet below the surface. The middle pontoons disappeared also in the rising water a few minutes after the toggles went in.

At 9 P.M., I boarded the *Falcon* again. Our airhoses were connected to all pontoons. Captain King had rearranged his ships. The *Iuka* and the *Sagamore*, anchored near the Manhattan shore, had lines to the *Falcon*'s stern, ready to heave on her. The derricks were gone; two Navy Yard tugs were lashed alongside the *Falcon*, their bows to her stern, while from the bow of the *Falcon* a solitary wire line ran to the submerged stern of the *S-51*. Michels and Eiben had secured that line around the submarine as she lay at the bottom of the sea off Block Island. Now it was the only hold we had left to the *S-51*, and with it we must drag the submarine off the reef.

High tide came at 9:30 P.M. Just after 9 o'clock, Niedermair turned air on all the pontoons, once more the *Falcon*'s compressors throbbed as they pumped away. But no longer did we have the heavy pressure at the bottom of the sea to buck; here the pontoons were submerged less than twenty feet, and against such a head of water the air went quickly through.

Once again our searchlights gleamed over the spot where lay the

S-51; but instead of the blackness of the ocean night for a background, the fairyland of lights which makes up the New York skyline glittered over Manhattan as we worked; on the riverfront, a vast crowd could still be seen watching.

As the tide rose, our bow pontoons and midships pontoons had vanished completely underwater. Soon bubbles started to rise over the midships pair,—they were dry. All air now went forward. Anxiously I watched, still in my soaked uniform, the spot where the light played over the bow. The air went in steadily. Some bubbles rose, then more bubbles, then a slight disturbance, and in the searchlight's glow we could see a few links of anchor chain rise through the surface,—nothing more. But something must have lifted to bring those chains up. Blinker lights flashed, the *Falcon*'s siren shrieked. The *Iuka* and *Sagamore* heaved on their lines, the *Falcon* and tugs alongside churned up the water violently with their propellers. The line to the *S-51* tautened under the pull.

Eagerly I sighted across our deck to the lights on the Queensborough Bridge. The lights shifted towards our bow, we were moving! The *S-51* pulled smoothly astern off Man of War Rock; she was afloat again! The sailors on the *Falcon* yelled wildly; on the shore, the movement of the pontoons under the searchlights was caught, and a loud cheer roared across the water from the crowd there, answering ours.

The *Falcon* cast off the lines to the *Iuka* and the *Sagamore*; going astern herself but with the tugs lashed to her going ahead, the *Falcon* moved across towards Manhattan till Captain King was certain we were back in the channel, then swung down the river.

Once more we headed for the Navy Yard. For the first time since morning the pilot who had kept out of sight since stranding us came up on the bridge and offered to take charge again. In vigorous terms, his offer was refused and Captain King piloted the rest of the way.

As the crestfallen pilot disappeared from the bridge and we caught the last glimpse of the cause of our troubles on the rocks, Niedermair remarked:

"Well, if a pilot has got to run a ship up on a reef, it's just as well to have him pick out a ship that has a wrecking crew aboard!" A long laugh all around, breaking the tension of our overwrought nerves, greeted his sally.

The makeup of the tow was peculiar. The *Falcon*, running backward, moved down the East River, dragging the *S-51,* which was also going stern first. There was no longer anything secured to the submarine's bow, which now brought up the rear of the procession. On each side, the *Falcon* had a tug, headed opposite to herself, lashed to her, helping her to tow, while the *Iuka* and the *Sagamore* quickly took position again as leaders of the tow and flung new lines to the *Falcon*'s stern to assist in dragging the wreck. And so in the night, we resumed our way towards the Navy Yard.

The tide was again running a strong ebb, and rapidly falling. We covered the mile and a half of river, passed under the Williamsburgh Bridge, and started to make a turn to port to enter the basin of the yard. Immediately trouble started. As we headed across the river, the swift current caught the submarine broadside, and with nothing to restrain it swung the bow of the *S-51* rapidly downstream, dragging the *Falcon* with it. Almost before we knew it, the *Falcon*, the tugs alongside her, and the submarine had rotated one hundred and eighty degrees. To avoid tangling his propeller in the lines leading to the *Iuka* and the *Sagamore* during this unlooked-for maneuver, Hartley had to cut the hawsers with an ax and let those tugs go free.

The tide had us in its grip; in a moment we were swept down the river past the Navy Yard, and well down towards the Brooklyn Bridge. The *Falcon* and the two tugs still tied to her sides struggled desperately; the *Falcon*'s engine, running reversed under a full head of steam, pounded violently, the tugs churned the water to a froth; in spite of all three engines, the tide carried us steadily farther away from our haven.

Whistles shrieked for assistance, the *Falcon* trembled as her engine raced. At the *Falcon*'s bow I looked out over the hoses leading to the submarine below us. The stern pontoons were nearly awash, the bow pontoons were practically out of sight. The reserve buoyancy was negligible, the *S-51* was floating only on a shoestring. Niedermair was blowing constantly through all the hoses; if a few tons of water were to enter, the *S-51* would sink both fore and aft.

While Hartley on the bridge battled the tide and kept his propeller from fouling in the towlines, I watched the single wire line leading over our bow to the submarine's stern. With the tide beating against the flat ends of the pontoons, pulling on the submarine, that wire, taut as a bowstring, was under a terrific strain. Michels and Eiben, working in the mud at the bottom of the sea, had shackled that line round the tail of the *S-51*; now it was taking a heavier pull than had ever been expected of it.

If the wire parted or slipped free, the submarine would go shooting downstream, snapping all the airhoses like threads. Soon she would fill and sink, perhaps at Governors Island, perhaps off Staten Island, and once more we would have the job of salvaging the *S-51* from the bottom. We were worn, we were tired, we were overwrought. Surrounded by divers, I looked out in the blackness where the searchlights played over the bubbles rising through the water from the pontoons. We saw how, inch by inch, the *Falcon* was losing ground against the tide; for nearly an hour we watched the taut towline to the *S-51*. Would it hold?

We had been through much of danger, much of heartbreaking disappointment, but as we stood there, practically at the entrance to the Navy Yard which we had always looked forward to as the goal of our struggles, waiting every second to see the submarine tear free and sink, it seemed like the darkest hour of all.

At last the *Sagamore* freed her propeller from the tangled hawser we had cut loose and was able again to maneuver. Cregan brought his boat to our assistance, threw Hartley another hawser, added his power to the tug of war against the tide. We stopped losing; we held our own; then inch by inch the four straining vessels made headway against the current towards the Navy Yard. The tension in the *S-51*'s solitary towline increased, but it held; amid a din of puffing tugs, hoarse voices shouting orders across the water, and the swirl of the tide as the river raced by, the *S-51* was slowly dragged back up the river and pulled into the quiet water of the Navy Yard basin.

It was 11 P.M.,—two hours past high water. The tide had dropped too much for the wreck to be hauled over the sill into the waiting drydock; besides, the docking crew, never expecting that we would refloat the wreck, had gone home hours before.

The *Falcon* drew the submarine alongside a pier near the drydock; heaving lines flew through the air and shortly we were secured to the dock. All night long we kept watch over our waterlogged wreck, incessantly pumping air to keep her afloat.

In the early dawn, we prepared her for docking, ran new airhoses from the yard mains to the drydock. The submarine, bow first, was dragged to the entrance of the dock, a hauling line tied to the bow pontoons, centering lines secured on both sides. When high tide came at 10 A.M., the *Falcon* hurriedly let go her hoses, cast loose the stern line, and we dragged the submarine across the sill into the largest drydock in New York. Slowly she floated through the gate, the caisson was swung into place behind her, the *S-51* could no longer get away from us!

The pontoons were already sinking forward. Riggers scrambled aboard, connected the new airhoses, and blew out the water which had leaked in.

An all-day struggle followed to land the submarine on the keel blocks in the dock and straighten her up. As a result of her stranding, she was lying far over on her starboard side as she finished her journey. Heavy tackles were secured by the divers to her gun and to the mast; with these we attempted to pull her upright, after lowering the water in the dock enough to let her just rest on the blocks. Three times we heaved and had the *S-51* practically vertical; three times the lines or blocks broke under the strain and let her roll back.

Under the broiling July sun, I directed the work from the top of the starboard midship pontoon; riggers, divers, and shipwrights heaving on the blocks, setting up shores, wrestled with the *S-51*. Late in the day, on our fourth attempt, after ransacking the Navy Yard for the heaviest lines and blocks on hand, we finally held the submarine practically erect while the divers rammed shores under her bilge keels to keep her that way. And so that night the *S-51* rested, still submerged, in the dock.

Next morning we returned. Quickly the water was pumped from the dock. As it fell, the *S-51* was at last exposed to the light of day. Covered with fine seaweed, draped in a tangled net of manila lines that had gradually gathered over her hull as we worked, she lay in the dock,—a huge hole in her port side where the *City of Rome* had cut through.

We opened the hatches. Clad in gas masks, the medical party entered to remove the bodies of eighteen officers and men still inside the hull.

XXXVIII

THE BELL

The expedition was over.

During the following days, hundreds of thousands of people passed slowly round the drydock, gazing at the submarine. And lost in the crowd, gazing with them, might have been seen the various members of the salvage crew, looking for the hundredth time at the *S-51*, trying to convince themselves that it was actually so, that the *S-51* was really there, that it was not merely a dream.

On board the *Falcon*, the divers were packing up, preparing to take the leave they had so well deserved.

I went back to the *Vestal*, dragged out from under my berth the bell of the *S-51*. A coveted trophy. I had hoped to give it to the Naval Academy, but I must forgo that honor.

I wrapped up the bell, strolled down the pier to where the *Falcon* lay, just outside the drydock in which rested the *S-51*. On the *Falcon*'s quarterdeck, a group of divers lazily sunned themselves. Yes, there he was.

"Oh, Smith, come out here a minute. I've got something for you!"

Smith jumped from the low rail of the ship to the dock, walked over. I unwrapped the bell, gave it to him.

"Here's the bell, Smith. It's yours. You earned it!"

A happy smile lighted his face. Without a word he took it, ran back aboard the *Falcon*, exhibited his trophy proudly to the other divers. I looked at him, looked at the *Falcon*, in memory saw myself once more in the middle of the heaving ocean, leaning over that rail, looking into the sea, clutching feverishly a diver's telephone, while far below in the blackness and the mud, Francis Smith struggled for his life, buried in

221

the tunnel beneath the *S-51*. Beyond all human aid, Smith had almost by a miracle wrought his own escape; with a courage undreamed of, he had crawled back into the tunnel to help raise the *S-51*. It was the faith of men like Smith, not the pontoons, which had lifted the submarine.

That vision passed. I found myself once more on the sun-baked pier looking across at the group of sailors gathered round the bell. The group broke up, Smith leaped the rail, came to where I stood. He shook my hand.

"Good-bye. I'm going back to Pittsburgh and in a few months I'll be out of the Navy for keeps. I don't suppose I'll ever see you again, but," he added, pointing to the group of men on the *Falcon*'s quarterdeck, "there isn't one of that bunch of divers, Mr. Ellsberg, who wouldn't go to hell for you!" A squeeze of the hand, Francis Smith was gone. My eyes grew indistinct as I looked after him. Not the acclaim of the press, not the receipt of the Distinguished Service Medal at the hands of the Navy, not even the feeling of having achieved the impossible, could ever mean so much to me as those heartfelt words spoken by Francis Smith.

XXXIX

THE END

It is over. The task is done, the divers have dispersed, the *S-51* is a memory. But to the families of the men who formed her crew, we have brought back the bodies of their loved ones, heroically dead at their posts on the *S-51*. To the Navy, we brought back its ship. And to the Nation, we brought back a story of victory over the sea, wrought by the quiet courage of men who could face death in solitude, disregard failure, and still fight on till they had wrested from the ocean the tomb of their shipmates.

GLOSSARY

BITTS: A pair of steel horns around which a hawser can be belayed or secured.

CHAIN FALL: A mechanism comprising a number of steel gears which is capable of lifting heavy weights when a much smaller pull is exerted on the operating chain.

CLAPPER VALVE: A valve with a hinged disk operated by a lever outside, which swings the valve disk against its seat somewhat like a hinged door.

DOGS: The steel clamps which are swung down over wedges on a watertight door to jam it tightly closed. TO DOG: To jam down the dogs.

KINGSTON VALVE: On a submarine, a valve in the skin of the ship through which water is admitted for submerging the vessel.

MANIFOLD: A casting comprising a number of interconnected valves for distributing oil, water, air, etc., through any combination of the pipes connected to the manifold.

MARLINE: A small line about one-eighth inch in diameter, made of dark colored hemp; much used for wrapping the ends of larger lines.

MOUSE A HOOK: To wrap a number of turns of marline between the point of the hook and the shank of the hook, to prevent the slipping out of the object in the bow of the hook.

PELICAN HOOK: A hook with a hinged bill held in place by a locking link slipped down over its point. When the link is knocked up, the bill flies open on its hinge, releasing the hook.

ROLLING CHOCKS: Bilge keels or flat steel plates secured longitudinally to the underwater shell of the ship. These plates project perpendicularly from the ship's side a distance of several feet; as the ship rolls they are forced to swing flatwise through the water and the resistance thus created tends to reduce the rolling very markedly.

SHANK (Anchor): The steel shaft to which the flukes of the anchor are secured.

SPILLPIPE: A pipe with its lower open end hung in the lowest part of a compartment; the water is forced overboard through the opening in the spillpipe while the compressed air in the compartment is prevented from escaping till the water level inside falls to the bottom of the spillpipe. A dapper valve, or non-return valve, on the bottom of the spillpipe prevents the water outside from flowing back through the spillpipe.

SQUILGEE HANDLE: A long wood handle on a rubber-edged implement much used aboard ship for drying down the decks.

STRONGBACK: A bar (usually of steel). On the salvage hatches, a bar which straddled the inside of the hatch opening. To this strongback was attached a heavy bolt projecting upward through a hole in the center of the salvage hatch cover. When the outside nut was screwed down the bolt, it jammed the coverplate down tightly, sealing the hatch opening.

TOGGLE PIN: A split pin, similar in design to the locking pins used on automobile bolts. On a pelican hook, a split pin about one-half inch in diameter pushed through a hole in the point of the bill to prevent the locking link from slipping up and allowing the hook to open.

TURNBUCKLE HOOK: A hook with a turnbuckle screwed to its shank. Revolving the turnbuckle tightens up the hook.

WINCH: A windlass; a mechanically rotated drum on which a line can be wound and heaved in.

Publisher's
Afterword

While *On the Bottom* proved to be a bestseller and brought the story of deep-sea salvage to public attention, it was almost not published at all. The manuscript had been rejected by a number of publishers as too technical.

In typical Edward Ellsberg fashion, however, he, along with his wife Lucy, reworked the text and persisted. A chance reading at a cocktail party brought the book to the attention of Frank C. Dodd of the venerable New York publishing house Dodd, Mead & Company. After a late-night read he knew it was a good story and the very next morning sent Ellsberg a telegram with a contract offer.

On the Bottom launched a relationship which would span more than thirty years as Dodd, Mead & Company would publish all seventeen of Ellsberg's books, the last, *The Far Shore*, in 1960. The story of the salvage of *S-51* remained in print until 1981—a remarkable fifty-two years—nearly eclipsing the life span of the publisher, which shuttered operations in 1990.

Throughout its long run, *On the Bottom* was read by thousands. Special editions were released in Great Britain, Germany, France, Denmark, Spain, and Argentina, even in Braille. As much as Ellsberg's account thrilled and inspired, it also left readers wondering a bit more about the collision, the vessels, and the men.

The primary purpose of this Afterword, and the Appendixes which follow, is to answer as many of these questions and provide context to the author, the incident, and the aftermath.

S-51

The submarine USS *S-51* (hull number SS-162) was launched at Bridgeport, Connecticut, by the Lake Torpedo Boat Company on 20 August 1921, and was commissioned 22 June 1922. She was among the early submarines which carried an unglamorous alphanumeric "name."

Her class represented the largest and latest type of sub in the U.S. Navy at the time. *S-51* was 240 feet, 6 inches, in length; her beam was 25 feet; and her surface displacement measured upwards of 1,000 tons.

Attached to Submarine Base New London, *S-51* spent most of its short career in the routine of torpedo practice and diving exercises. *S-51* was operating out of her home port when she was sunk at 2224, on the night of 25 September 1925, in collision with the steamship *City of Rome*.

The *S-51* was raised on 5 July 1926, struck from the Navy list on 27 January 1930, and sold for scrapping on 23 June 1930.

City of Rome

The cargo-passenger steamer *City of Rome* was hull number 108 from New York Shipbuilding in Camden, New Jersey. The 331-foot ship was launched 25 February 1911 as the *Suwanee* for the Merchant & Miners Transportation Company and ran between Philadelphia, Baltimore, Savannah, and Jacksonville. Sold to the Ocean Steamship Company of Savannah, commonly called the Savannah Line, in 1917, she was renamed *City of Rome* and operated between Boston and Savannah.

Making six knots, the *City of Rome* was Boston bound, via the Cape Cod canal, with freight and more than 200 passengers en route from Savannah when she struck the *S-51*.

City of Rome was sold back to Merchant and Miners in 1928 and renamed *Somerset*. She was broken up in Baltimore in 1938.

The Collision

At the time of collision, *S-51* was acting as a surface vessel, steering a steady course, of about northwest, at a speed of 11.5 knots. The seas were moderately rough, and all hatches were secured, except the conning tower hatch. But for the officers and men on watch, the crew had turned in.

S-51 had her running lights on, and her white masthead light was first picked up by the lookout on the *City of Rome* about twenty-two minutes prior to the collision, when the steamer was some five miles away. The light was observed by the *City of Rome* for approximately twenty minutes without other lights being seen or any action taken. The watch officer on board the *City of Rome* misjudged the lights bearing drift and, seeing no sidelights, concluded that he must be overtaking a small tug or fishing vessel or that he had encountered a rumrunner.

Shortly after 2200 the crew of the *S-51* observed the masthead light and green sidelight of the steamer *City of Rome* off their port quarter. The submarine held her course and speed, as she was required to do under the International Rules of the Road at Sea.

When the red sidelight of the *S-51* came into view, the mate of the *City of Rome* ordered a course change to port and sounded the ship's whistle. Meanwhile, the *S-51* took action and altered course to starboard when it seemed the steamer was not taking sufficient action to avoid collision. Captain John H. Diehl, realizing that the submarine was crossing in front of them from right to left, then ordered the rudder shifted in an attempt to come right and pass astern of the submarine—action he should have taken earlier. He then ordered engines full astern. The last-minute maneuvering proved too late to prevent the collision, and in fact, may have worsened the impact.

The *S-51* was struck at an angle of about 40 degrees abaft the port beam, and a hole about thirty inches wide, extending from the port bilge keel to the superstructure deck, opened up. As an immediate result of the collision, a large volume of water poured into the battery room. Under the increasing pressure, water flooded the boat so rapidly that the crew was unable, against the rush of water, to close any of the interior doors. The steamer then ran over the submarine, forcing it underwater.

Three men, asleep in the battery room, escaped through the conning tower hatch and were picked up alive about an hour later. Seven sailors, two officers and two men forming the bridge watch, and three others who were inside the boat, managed to get through the conning tower hatch and were washed overboard. These seven were seen swimming, after the *S-51* sank, by the men who were later rescued, but not one of these seven was found when the *City of Rome* finally managed to get a boat overboard. The body of one man in this group was later found alongside the hull; the bodies of the other six were never recovered.

The *City of Rome* spent approximately two hours on scene searching for survivors, employing what lights it could since its main searchlight was inoperable. It had never occurred to anyone on board the *City of Rome* that there might be men still alive in airtight compartments on board the sunken sub. The first word of the collision was sent to the steamer's owners shortly after midnight.

The U.S. Navy submarine base was notified of the collision at 0120 and all available vessels were rushed to the scene. The wreck was located at about 1045 the following day by a search plane.

The position of the *S-51*, as reported by the *City of Rome*, proved to be several miles in error, but no special difficulty occurred in locating the wreck, as a considerable oil slick was soon discovered by the vessels searching, and a moderate stream of air bubbles in this slick gave the exact location. The *S-51* was found in the open sea, about fifteen miles south of Brenton Reef Lightship, and about fourteen miles east of Block Island, the depth of water being 132 feet (22 fathoms).

The first divers reached the sunken *S-51* fifteen hours after the crash. They were disheartened when they got no response as they tapped along the hull. All hope for survivors was gone.

Findings

The 1926 Court of Inquiry held that Captain John H. Diehl was directly responsible for the loss of *S-51* and the lives of thirty-three sailors. The captain of the *City of Rome* was held at fault for not reducing speed when in doubt as to the movement of the *S-51*, and was also faulted for not signaling his change of course.

However, at subsequent civil action, it was determined that the Navy and the *S-51* was also at fault for having improper masthead and sidelights. The submarine's masthead light was only eleven feet, six inches, above the deck (not the twenty feet required by law) and the sidelights were fixed in a recess, and, at seven feet, six inches, above the hull, were too close to the masthead light, which reduced their visibility.

Despite the Navy's arguments that the class of submarines could not comply with literal provisions of the law, the court held that her status as a warship did not grant the *S-51* any special privileges. In the end the court found that the failure on the part of the *S-51* to show proper sidelights not only contributed to but was the principal cause of the disaster.

The incident was used in classrooms to teach the prevention of collisions at sea and was the subject of a 1942 U.S. Navy training film to teach the Rules of the Road.

Innovations and Inventions

As is so often the case with accidents, the tragedy and salvage operations of *S-51* produced both awareness and advances in technology, all of which were useful to the U.S. Navy, particularly the young submarine service, in future operations.

The raising of *S-51* revealed that as a result of World War I cutbacks, the Navy only had twenty divers qualified to dive deeper than ninety feet. Among Edward Ellsberg's most vehement recommendations in his 1927 *Report on Salvage Operations Submarine S-51* was that the Navy have more experienced divers. He summarized his findings saying, "For the next operation of a similar nature, the most important feature is to provide the men in adequate numbers; the material can always be quickly fabricated."

The salvage of *S-51* led to the development of better underwater lighting. The divers made recommendations to the Westinghouse laboratory as to how the lights could be modified to better withstand water pressure. The solution, a lamp with a watertight rubber sleeve from the glass base to the electric cable, was adopted by Westinghouse as their standard design.

During the fall operations, the need for some method of cutting metal underwater was made all too clear. The torch then available for use by the Navy failed to operate on every occasion it was tried.

One of Ellsberg's primary objectives during the winter period, in addition to qualifying as a diver, was to develop a practicable underwater cutting torch. His experiments led to the "Ellsberg cutting torch" which proved to work remarkably well. Ellsberg later patented the design and it became the standard for underwater work.

Yet another breakthrough was the burrowing nozzle which greatly facilitated underwater removal of mud and debris. Referred to by Ellsberg as "Waldren's special balanced nozzle," it was developed by Machinist's Mate Lomie Waldren, who at the time was attached to the *Falcon*. It also became known as the "*Falcon* nozzle" and today it is most often referred to as the "Ellsberg jetting nozzle" due to the popularity of *On the Bottom*.

Although the nozzle was found to have been patented a few years earlier for other uses, the salvage of *S-51* was the nozzle's first diving application. In this particular nozzle there were six jets, one large one ahead and five smaller ones radially astern. It was found that the jet arrangement abolished the reaction which previously had made it impossible for the diver to hold a two-and-a-half-inch hose with any special pressure; further, the radial jets enlarged the the hole cut by the forward jet and shot the material cut loose astern at considerable speed. Like the Ellsberg cutting torch, it is still used by the Navy and commercial divers.

The raising of the *S-51* also pioneered the use of stabilized pontoons in deep-sea salvage operations. Once it was decided that the maximum lift of derricks was insufficient to raise the submarine, in addition to their being unsuitable for open sea work, it was decided to raise the submarine through a combination of restored internal buoyancy, and of external buoyancy to be furnished by pontoons. During the operation the salvage pontoons were altered to overcome the difficulties encountered in handling them. Some bulkheads were removed, others added, and in the end the pontoons could be lowered and raised horizontally.

Awards, Advancements, and Life After *S-51*

There were many honors for those who raised *S-51*, including medals and recommendations for promotion. Captain Ernest King, the officer in charge of the salvage efforts, and who rarely handed out praise, recommended that forty men receive special commendations. The Navy Cross was awarded to many of the sailors, including William Wickwire, Thomas Eadie, James Frazer, Raymond "Tugboat" Wilson, Francis Smith, William Badders, Solomon Schissel, Richard Hawes, and J.R. Kelley.

Three men walked away from the salvage of *S-51* having earned the Navy's Distinguished Service Medal. Joining Edward Ellsberg as the first recipients ever during a time of peace were Captain Ernest J. King and Lieutenant Henry Hartley.

Many of the individuals highlighted in *On the Bottom* went on to great achievements and brilliant naval careers.

Diver Tom Eadie received the Congressional Medal of Honor for rescuing fellow *S-51* diver Fred Michels, who had become caught in the wreckage of submarine *S-4* (SS-109) in 1927. William Badders was awarded the Medal of Honor for heroism during the rescue of survivors of USS *Squalus* (SS-192) and subsequent salvage of that submarine in 1939.

A special act of Congress elevated Richard Hawes to officer rank in 1929 in recognition of his salvage feats on submarines *S-51* and *S-4*. Hawes commanded the salvage ship *Falcon* from 1935 to 1938, and distinguished himself in World War II.

John C. Niedermair, who served as a technical aide to Ellsberg on the raising of *S-51*, went on to be the top civilian engineer at the U.S. Navy's Bureau of Ships. In addition to his pioneering work on combat vessels, he became widely known for a simple sketch which marked the real beginning of the LST. His basic design became the pattern for all of the 1,051 LSTs built during World War II, and the concept is considered the true ancestor of other oceangoing amphibious ships of later design.

Ernest J. King would be called on to oversee the recovery of the submarine *S-4*. He was selected for flag rank in 1932, and in World War II served as both commander-in-chief, U.S. Fleet, and chief of naval operations. He was the first and only officer to hold such an assignment, and in December 1944 he was advanced to the newly created rank of fleet admiral. In December 1945 he was relieved by Fleet Admiral Chester Nimitz.

A specialist in salvage work, Lieutenant Henry Hartley was instrumental in salvaging the *S-4*. After establishing the Navy's Deep Sea Diving School at Washington, D.C., in 1928, he served as its commander while continuing his research in techniques of marine salvage. He helped supervise the dramatic rescue and salvage work on the sunken submarine *Squalus* in 1939. Hartley served with great distinction in World War II and retired from the Navy in 1947 with the rank of rear admiral.

Edward Ellsberg left active duty in December 1926 due to the slow promotion process for Navy constructors and became chief engineer of the Tide Water Oil Company (Tydol). He was recommissioned briefly in 1927 to aid in the rescue of trapped sailors on the submarine *S-4*. While a civilian he turned to writing and during this time wrote eleven books. As an engineer Ellsberg patented several inventions, including a method of increasing the yield of high-octane gasoline and a process for removing water from lubricating oil. He resigned from Tide Water in 1935 and continued to write and lecture.

Ellsberg volunteered for active duty service on 8 December 1941 at age fifty-one. As Pearl Harbor had made the Navy desperate for salvage expertise, Ellsberg received a commission, but only as a lieutenant commander. By March 1942 Ellsberg was in Massawa, Ethiopia, where he was responsible for clearing the port and returning the drydock and ship repair facilities to service. The previous year, the Italians had scuttled some forty vessels and two invaluable drydocks. Under extreme heat, and with very little experienced personnel and equipment, Ellsberg again accomplished seemingly impossible feats. The British hailed his work as "the Miracle of Massawa." His book *Under the Red Sea Sun* (1946) is an account of his experience.

Ellsberg moved on to North Africa where newly captured port facilities required clearance and ship repair work. Out of this period came his book *No Banners, No Bugles* (1949). He was sent to England in April 1944 and played an instrumental role in the establishment of the artificial harbors for the Normandy invasion. His book *The Far Shore* (1960) resulted. Ellsberg retired from the Navy in 1951 with the rank of rear admiral.

Two of the vessels used in the salvage of *S-51* went on to play noteworthy roles in U.S. naval history.

After *S-51* was raised to the surface, *Falcon* (ASR-2), a minesweeper specially fitted with air compressors and a recompression chamber for diving and salvage work, followed the wreck and provided air pressure for the pontoons supporting the submarine, as well as her compartments.

Falcon was a key asset in raising the submarines *S-4* in 1927, *Squalus* in the summer of 1939, and in the rescue operations on *O-9* (SS-70) in June 1940. Throughout World War II, the aging but still able *Falcon* sailed out of New London, Connecticut, and Portsmouth, New Hampshire, in salvage, towing, and experimental operations. The 188-foot vessel was decommissioned in 1946 and sold in 1947.

The USS *Vestal* (AR-4), a 466-foot repair ship, furnished repair facilities, boat service, supplies, and berthing for *S-51* salvage personnel. Launched as a collier in 1908 from the New York Navy Yard, *Vestal* was converted to a fleet repair ship in 1913, and relaunched under the command of Commander Edward L. Beach, father of renowned submariner and writer Edward L. Beach—author of the introduction of this edition of *On the Bottom.*

On 6 December 1941, *Vestal* was moored alongside USS *Arizona* (BB-39), off Ford Island, to provide services to the battleship. At 0755 on 7 December 1941, *Vestal* went to general quarters. She was hit by two bombs but her crew managed to cut mooring lines and run the ship aground. Her captain, Commander Cassin Young, was awarded the Medal of Honor for his actions during the attack on Pearl Harbor. *Vestal* was repaired and spent the remainder of the war in the Pacific. She was decommissioned in 1946.

Lessons Learned

Many of the recommendations put forth by Edward Ellsberg following the raising of *S-51* were largely pigeonholed by the Navy. Ellsberg suggested that the S-class submarines be equipped with lifting eyes; that a sufficient number of pontoons, capable of raising a submarine, be assembled at an Atlantic and Pacific port; and, that the Navy train more of its sailors to be divers.

The Navy's shortfalls and neglect of Ellsberg's recommendations came to light following the tragic loss of submarine *S-4* on 17 December 1927, when it was rammed and sunk by the U.S. Coast Guard Cutter *Paulding* off Provincetown at the tip of Cape Cod. The collision ruptured

S-4's ballast tank and ripped a hole in the battery compartment. The submarine went down with her entire forty-man crew, coming to rest in mud 102 feet below.

The Navy assembled all available personnel and sent the USS *Falcon*, under the command of Commander Hartley with a crew of Navy divers, including *S-51* veterans Tom Eadie, Fred Michels, and Bill Carr. Captain Ernest J. King, again, commanded the rescue.

Diver Tom Eadie was first to reach the *S-4*. From tapping he heard on the hull he learned six men were still alive in the torpedo room, where they managed to survive for seventy-two hours.

Ellsberg, then a civilian, had opened up his morning paper on 18 December 1927 only to read the headline "Submarine *S-4* Sunk! Forty Men Trapped!" He was stunned and amazed that the tragedy of the *S-51* would be so soon repeated. He knew something about salvage and diving and knew, if there were men alive, he could help. While Ellsberg wished only to volunteer his services, he was sworn in to active duty so that his wife Lucy would be eligible receive full death benefits. He rushed to the scene, arriving on board the *Falcon*, and dove on *S-4*, narrowly escaping death. The weather worsened and rescue operations were discontinued. When the forces on scene were reorganized for a salvage operation, Ellsberg bid farewell.

In his book *I Like Diving*, published in 1929, Tom Eadie recounted the helplessness and despair of the rescue crews in the face of adverse weather as they realized they could not save the men. In his book *Men Under the Sea*, published in 1939, Ellsberg remained convinced that with the men and means at hand, and the cooperation of the weather, they could have saved the trapped men.

The *S-4* was raised exactly three months after her sinking by the same methods pioneered by Ellsberg and his men on the raising of *S-51*.

The Bell

In *On the Bottom* Edward Ellsberg noted how he hoped the bell of the *S-51* would go to the U.S. Naval Academy. Instead, he awarded the bell to diver Francis Smith, who had brought it up from the wreck. Smith lived out his later years in Key West, Florida, and upon his death, the bell was given to the local lighthouse museum. Eventually the bell made its way to the U.S. Navy Submarine Force Library and Museum, in Groton, Connecticut, home of the USS *Nautilus* (SSN-571) and home port of the *S-51*. Today the bell serves as a memorial to the thirty-three sailors who perished on 25 September 1925 in what was the submarine service's worst accident to date.

APPENDIX A
USS S-51 (SS-162)
FINAL SAILING LIST

25 September 1925

Berk, Paul Daniel, *Engineman*	Lost
Cassidy, Ralph Edward, *Gunner's Mate*	Lost
Crawford, Henry Lee, *Radioman*	Lost
Dobson, Rodney H., *Lieutenant*	Lost
Earle, Allan Clifford, *Engineman*	Lost
Egbert, Edmund Webster, *Ensign*	Lost
Elser, Harry Dick, *Coxswain*	Lost
Firm, Rudy, *Motor Machinist's Mate*	Lost
Foster, Frederic David, *Lieutenant (j.g.)*	Lost
Geier, Alfred, *Electrician's Mate*	Saved
Gibson, John Law, *Engineman*	Lost
Glascock, Turner-Ashby, *Lieutenant (j.g.)*	Lost
Haselton, James Dudley, *Lieutenant (j.g.)*	Lost
Hiltbord, Valentine, *Chief Torpedoman*	Lost
James, Franklin Pierce, *Chief Motor Machinist's Mate*	Lost
Kile, Dewey G., *Engineman*	Saved

Lawton, Walter Edward, *Electrician's Mate*	Lost
Lindsay, Brady Domore, *Engineman*	Lost
Lira, Michael, *Fireman*	Saved
Martin, George Henry, *Officer's Cook*	Lost
McCarthy, John Joseph, *Seaman*	Lost
Milot, Oscar Joseph, *Fireman*	Lost
Mims, Frank Lester, *Seaman*	Lost
Noble, Robert S., *Motor Machinist's Mate*	Lost
Pino, Harlow Milton, *Lieutenant (j.g.)*	Lost
Schofield, James Marland, *Radioman*	Lost
Shea, Frank Archibald, *Electrician's Mate*	Lost
Sheehan, John Joseph, *Motor Machinist's Mate*	Lost
Smith, Augustus Alexander, *Torpedoman*	Lost
Snyder, Herbert Eadleman, *Chief Signalman*	Lost
Teschemacher, Frederick Peter, *Seaman*	Lost
Teschemacher, William Charles, *Seaman*	Lost
Thomas, Charles Carrol, *Fireman*	Lost
Triffit, Stephen Hartley, *Torpedoman*	Lost
Wills, Robert Holland, *Torpedoman*	Lost
Wiseman, Frank Collins, *Torpedoman*	Lost

APPENDIX B
ADDITIONAL SOURCES

Additional information on Edward Ellsberg is available from his seventeen books (listed in front of this book) and:

• *Salvage Man: Edward Ellsberg and the U.S. Navy,* by John D. Alden. A biography of this less than conventional Navy officer, published in 1997 by the Naval Institute Press, Annapolis, Maryland.

• www.EdwardEllsberg.com (with links), a website run by Ted Pollard, Edward Ellsberg's grandson and curator of the Ellsberg Historical Archives.

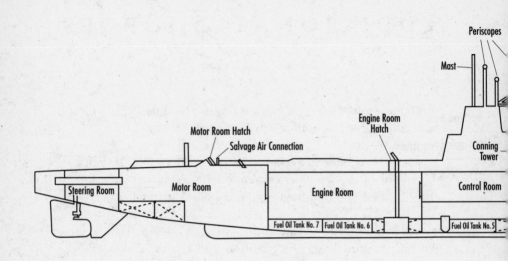

SUBMARINE S-51
PLAN & ELEVATION
COMPARTMENTS, SALVAGE HOSES, ETC.

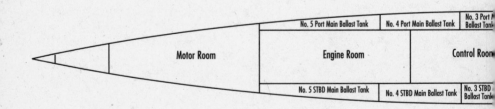

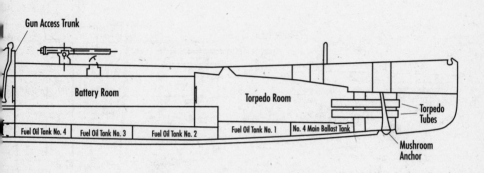

Gun Access Trunk

Battery Room

Torpedo Room

Torpedo Tubes

Fuel Oil Tank No. 4

Fuel Oil Tank No. 3

Fuel Oil Tank No. 2

Fuel Oil Tank No. 1

No. 4 Main Ballast Tank

Mushroom Anchor

No. 2 Port Main Ballast Tank

No. 1 Port Main Ballast Tank

Battery Room

Torpedo Room

No. 2 STBD Main Ballast Tank

No. 1 STBD Main Ballast Tank

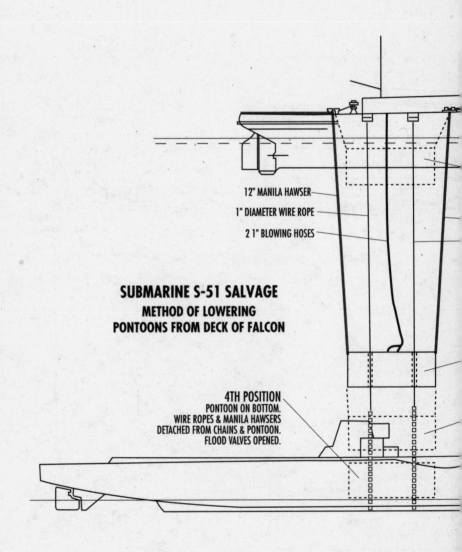

12" MANILA HAWSER
1" DIAMETER WIRE ROPE
2 1" BLOWING HOSES

SUBMARINE S-51 SALVAGE
METHOD OF LOWERING
PONTOONS FROM DECK OF FALCON

4TH POSITION
PONTOON ON BOTTOM.
WIRE ROPES & MANILA HAWSERS
DETACHED FROM CHAINS & PONTOON.
FLOOD VALVES OPENED.

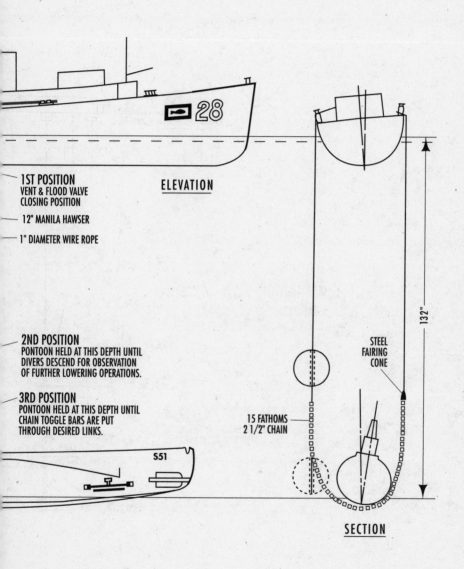

ELEVATION

◨ 28

1ST POSITION
VENT & FLOOD VALVE
CLOSING POSITION

12" MANILA HAWSER

1" DIAMETER WIRE ROPE

2ND POSITION
PONTOON HELD AT THIS DEPTH UNTIL
DIVERS DESCEND FOR OBSERVATION
OF FURTHER LOWERING OPERATIONS.

3RD POSITION
PONTOON HELD AT THIS DEPTH UNTIL
CHAIN TOGGLE BARS ARE PUT
THROUGH DESIRED LINKS.

S51

STEEL
FAIRING
CONE

132"

15 FATHOMS
2 1/2" CHAIN

SECTION

243

INDEX

report of accident, 4, 5, 229

rescue efforts, 5–8, 229

salvage of (*see* Salvage operation of *S-51*)

shipwrecked on Man of War Rock, 209–217

size of, 227

sold for scrapping, 228

survivors of collision, 4, 26, 77, 111, 229

towing to New York Navy Yard, 206–210, 217–219

USS *Squalus,* 232, 233

USS *Vestal* (AR-4), 13, 19, 26, 35, 44–47, 55, 61–62, 68, 80, 81, 83, 88, 90, 94, 127, 132, 134–137, 140, 142, 146, 152, 163, 168, 170, 171, 188, 196, 198, 203, 206, 207, 209, 237

Waldren, Lomie, 160–161, 231

Weather conditions, 44–46, 52,
53, 61–62, 79–81, 83, 93, 94, 118, 145, 147–152, 160, 163, 165, 170–172, 178–181, 186–191, 204

Weaver, 93–95, 152, 158, 165, 190

Westerly, Rhode Island, 206

Westinghouse Company, 43, 231

Wickwire, William, 112–114, 136, 156, 164, 182–184, 190, 197, 198, 201–203, 232

Wills, Robert Holland, 238

Wilson, Raymond "Tugboat," 18, 46–51, 57–58, 64–66, 72, 77, 78, 88, 95–96, 105, 116–118, 123, 127–129, 132–134, 145, 148, 157, 162–165, 175–176, 196, 232

Wiseman, Frank Collins, 238

Young, Cassin, 234

The son of Jewish immigrants, **Edward Ellsberg** was born in 1891 in New Haven, Connecticut, but his family moved to Colorado when he was a boy. He entered the U.S. Naval Academy in 1910 and graduated first in his class in 1914. After varied service on the USS *Texas,* he was ordered to the Massachusetts Institute of Technology for postgraduate work in Naval Architecture and graduated in 1920.

In 1925 he hed the salvage efforts to raise the sunken submarine USS *S-51,* for which he became the first sailor to earn the Navy's Distinguished Service Medal in peacetime and was promoted to Commander by a special act of Congress.

Shortly after the raising of *S-51,* Ellsberg entered civilian service but remained in the naval reserve. He returned to active duty briefly in December 1927, to assist with the rescue of men from the sunken submarine USS *S-4.*

In the late 1920s Ellsberg began his long and prolific career as a writer of naval history and fiction. *On the Bottom,* first published in 1929, is his account of the raising of the USS *S-51.* During this time Ellsberg wrote a novel about World War I submarines called *Pigboats,* which was later made into the movie *Hell Below,* and the important *Hell on Ice,* about the ill-fated U.S. Navy *Jeannette* Expedition to the North Pole.

Ellsberg reentered the active Navy on December 8, 1941, and his World War II accomplishments in Ethiopia, North Africa, and the Invasion of Normandy are considered his most valuable work. He chronicled his war years in the books *Under the Red Sea Sun; No Banners, No Bugles;* and *The Far Shore.*

Edward Ellsberg retired from the Navy in 1951 with the rank of rear admiral. He returned to private life as a consulting engineer and continued to write and lecture. He and Lucy, his wife of sixty years, divided their final years between Maine and Florida. He died in 1983 at ninety-one and was buried in Willimantic, Connecticut.